IMAGES
of America

Cape Ann in Stereo Views

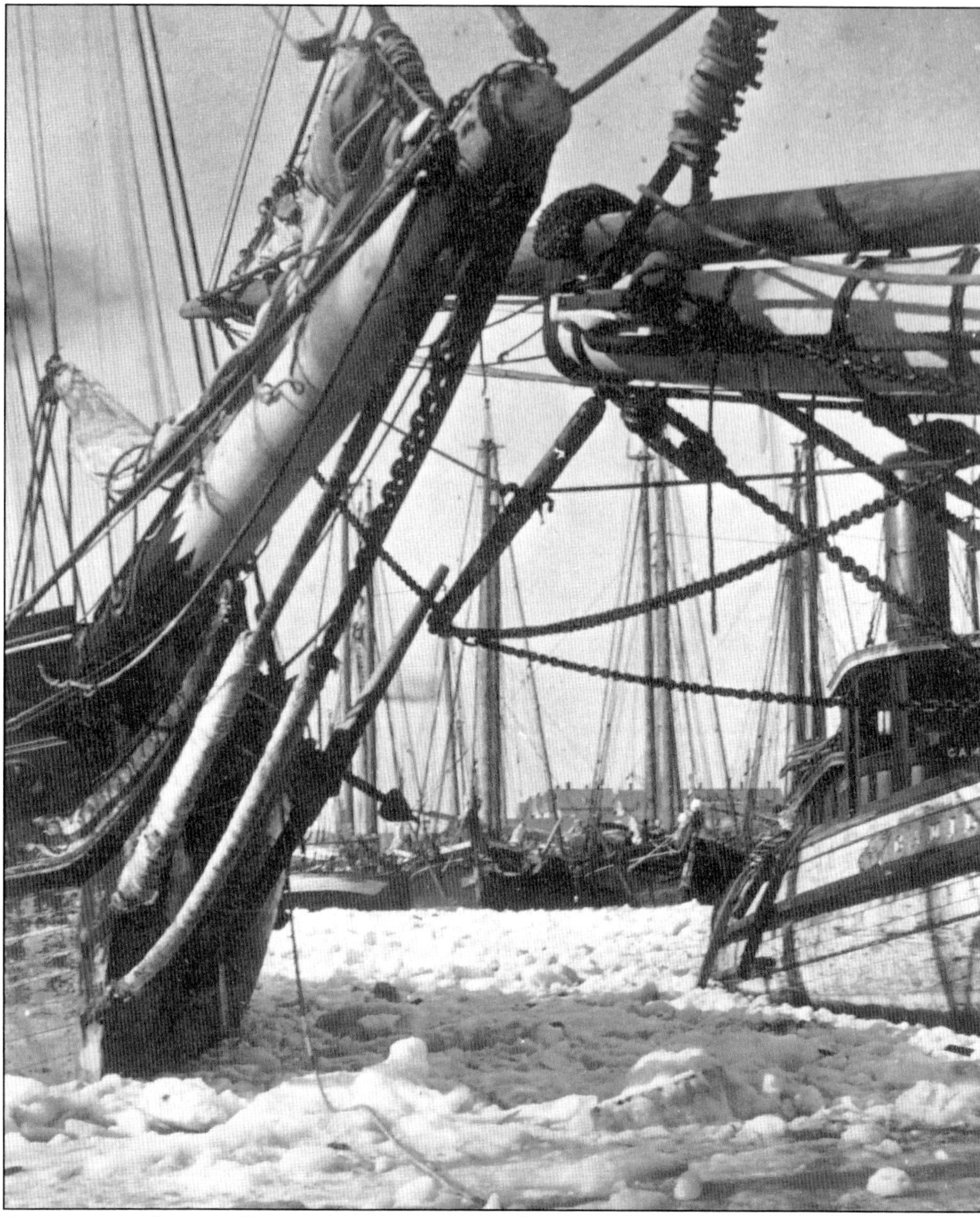

GLOUCESTER HARBOR, WINTER OF 1875. With the steam-powered tug *Camilla* alongside, an ice-bound schooner of the Georges Fleet sits solidly frozen in during a brutal cold spell that winter. Some of its sister ships can be seen to the rear. (Stereoview published by the Procter Brothers of Gloucester.)

Cover Image: **THE PAVILION HOTEL, GLOUCESTER.** (Photographed by J.W. and J.S. Moulton, Salem.)

IMAGES
of America

CAPE ANN IN STEREO VIEWS

Carolyn and Jim Thompson

ARCADIA
PUBLISHING

ISBN 978-0-7385-0491-9

Published by Arcadia Publishing
Charleston, South Carolina

Printed in the United States of America

Library of Congress Catalog Card Number: 00-106518

For all general information contact Arcadia Publishing at:
Telephone 843-853-2070
Fax 843-853-0044
E-mail sales@arcadiapublishing.com
For customer service and orders:
Toll-Free 1-888-313-2665

Visit us on the Internet at www.arcadiapublishing.com

Authors' Note: The majority of photographs are from the authors' stereoview collection, unless otherwise credited. Other photographic formats are duly noted.

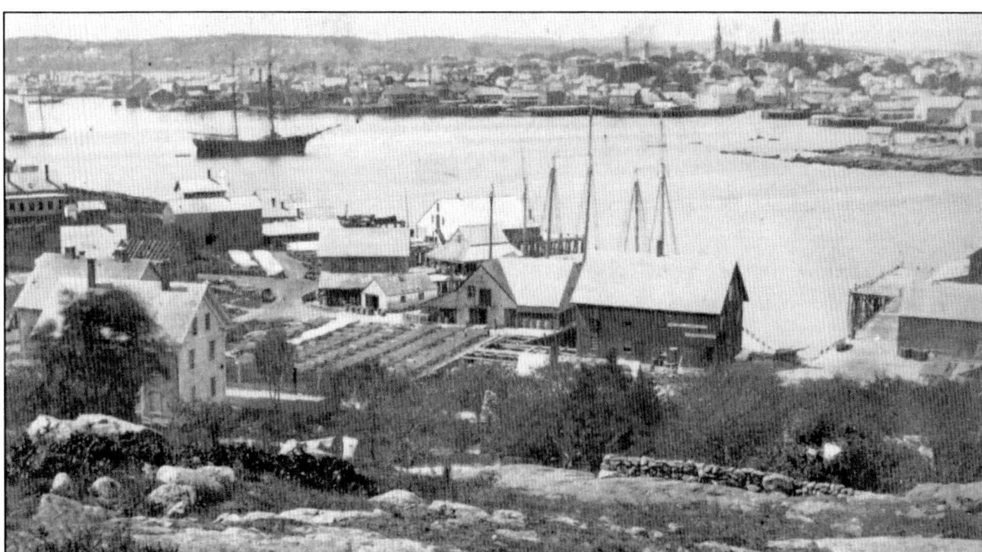

GLOUCESTER FROM EAST GLOUCESTER. This stereoview by E.G. Rollins is from the mid-1870s.

Contents

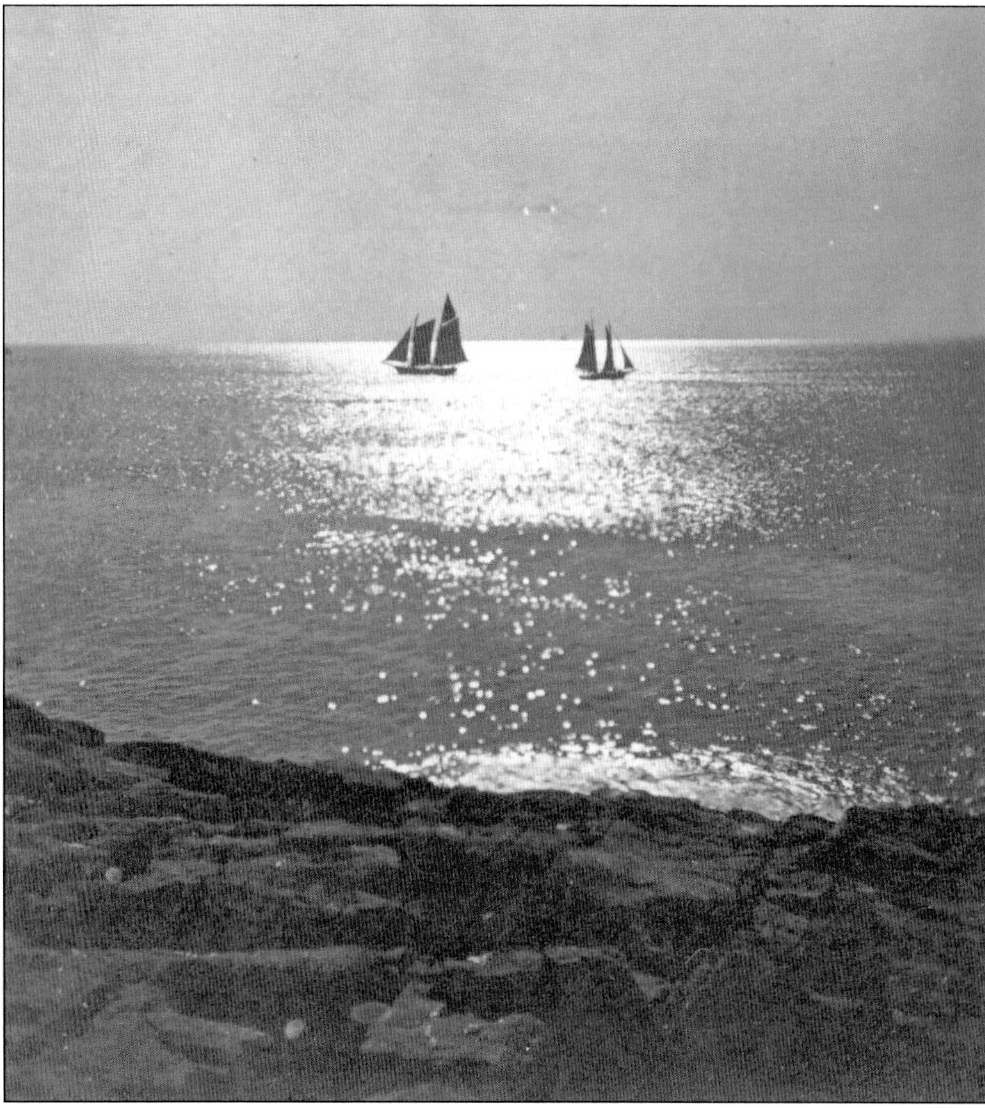

Marine Study by John Heywood. This mid-1860s stereoview is No. 323 from a fine seascape series entitled "Cape Ann Scenery." Heywood, along with the noted western photographer Carleton Watkins, was one of the most sensitive stereo-conscious photographers in terms of aesthetic composition. Heywood views were published either by Hervey Friend of Gloucester or Frank Rowell of Boston.

In loving memory of
Willa Trask Smith Jenks and "Uncle Joe" Joseph Osborne Taylor,
whose hearts are forever in Gloucester.

Introduction

While most people easily recognize the giant "flexed arm" that is Cape Cod in the southern part of Massachusetts Bay, the remarkable promontory jutting eastward and opposing its granite "fingertip" out into the relentless tides of the Atlantic north of Boston is Cape Ann. The "other cape," as some Bay State residents fondly call Cape Ann, comprises the northern end of the bay.

Although overshadowed by its much larger and better-known brother to the south, Cape Ann has an equally rich history and heritage because of its wealth of natural wonders, rocky fastness, hardy and industrious townspeople, and, of course, the immutable sea.

First settled in 1623 by colonists more intent on farming and lumbering than on harvesting the sea, Cape Ann grew and prospered thanks to an abundant fish supply. Gloucester was the young nation's busiest commercial fishing port in the grand days of sail. Fishing was also an early staple in nearby Rockport, first called Sandy Bay, where settlers planted their roots in 1690. Rockport soon became famous for fine granite laboriously cut from its bountiful quarries. The shipbuilding yards of Essex produced many swift-sailing fishing and granite-hauling vessels of all types. Magnolia and Manchester-by-the-Sea were graced with beautiful homes owned by master mariners and wealthy businessmen.

The years following the Civil War—the bloody conflict that divided and nearly ruined the nation—up through the early 20th century were marked by a dramatic surge of growth and prosperity throughout Cape Ann. Population increased sharply, and the fisheries sustained their expansion created by the demands for dried fish during the war. An enormous wave of immigration of hardy fishermen—primarily from Nova Scotia, Cape Breton, and Prince Edward Island—resulted in an even greater consumer demand for fish of all kinds.

Also during this time, tourism became a major industry. Dozens of the famous and grand North Shore hotels and summer haunts catering to the rich and famous from Boston and New York were erected along the coast in Gloucester, Rockport, Magnolia, and Manchester-by-the-Sea.

Millions of tons of granite, mostly harvested from the quarries in Rockport, were shipped to cities throughout the nation to pave streets, to be used in the construction of tunnels and monuments, and to become part of some of the finest and best-known buildings of the era.

The booming granite enterprises of Rockport and the fishing industries of Gloucester helped to spur shipbuilding activity in Essex to far greater heights. The years from 1870 to 1900 have been labeled the great years of Essex, a period during which many developments and improvements in construction enabled the yards in Essex to turn out more and bigger ships.

Coincidentally, the years beginning around 1865 through the turn of the century were also a time when stereo photography and stereoscopic images, especially stereoview cards, enjoyed immense popularity. The variety and volume of stereoview cards produced was remarkable; millions of them were published and marketed. Nearly every home, even those of families of modest means, had a hand-held viewer and assortments of cards for entertainment and amusement.

Cape Ann was fortunate to have several outstanding stereo photographers and publishers during this grand era, including John S.E. Rogers, E.G. Rollins, Hervey Friend, the Procter Brothers, George F. Burnham, and William A. Elwell, to name only a few. Fine photographers from nearby Salem included C.A. Beckford, J.W. and J.S. Moulton, and T.S. Lefavour. Among the great stereo photographers making the 30-mile trip to Cape Ann from Boston were John P. Soule and John Heywood, both of them producing several beautiful and excellent series of the cape's natural wonders, its commercial activities, and the life and times if its townspeople.

Their achievements in documenting and preserving Cape Ann's rugged beauty, heritage, and cultural diversity have provided us with an extraordinary pictorial record of the past. It is to their talents and artistry that *Cape Ann in Stereo Views* is dedicated.

One

Wonders Natural and Man Made

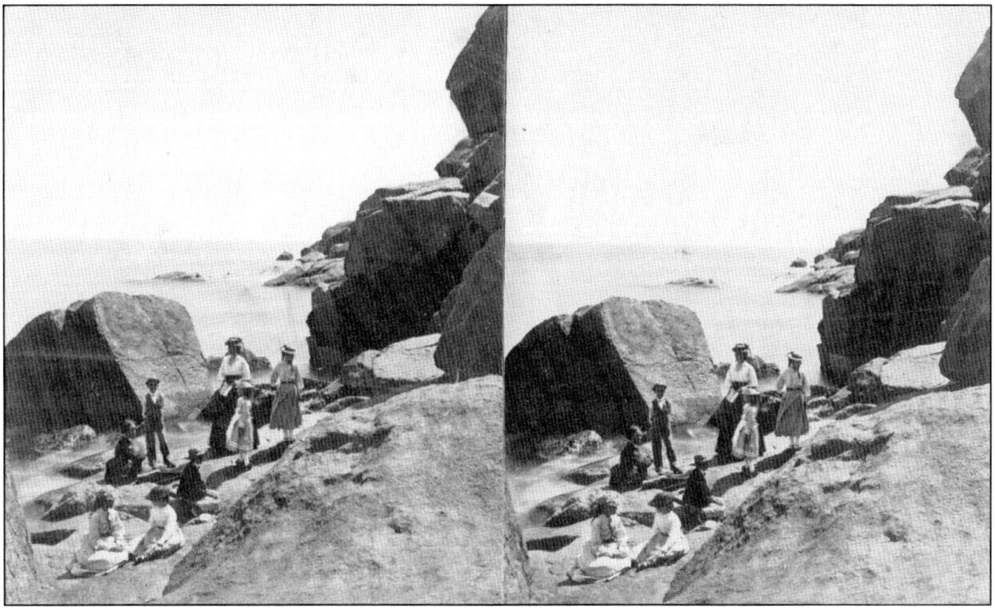

The Old Man's Cavern. Cape Ann's spectacular coastline scenery consists of bold and rocky ledges created by glacial action and other geological upheavals. Interesting and impressive rock formations include Rafe's Chasm, "Old Mother Ann," and Old Man's Cavern, shown in this 1880s stereoview by J.W. and J.S. Moulton of Salem.

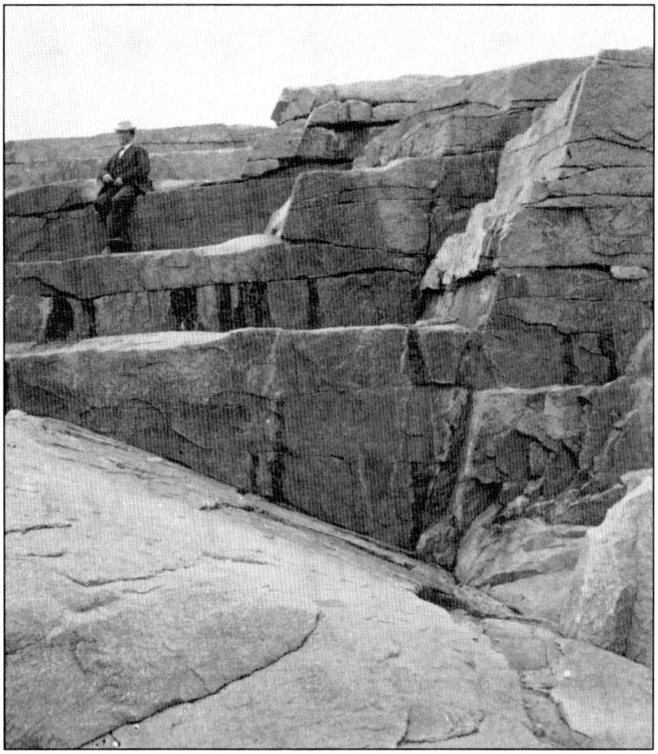

The Giant's Stairway and Bass Rocks. Cape Ann's rocky shores feature magnificent natural outcroppings, massive ledges (some also shaped by wedge and drill), and immense boulders left by the glaciers. The J.W. and J.S. Moulton stereoview (left) shows Giant's Stairway at Pigeon Cove in Rockport. The mid-1870s stereoview by Hervey Friend of Gloucester (below) was taken from the headland of Bass Rocks on Gloucester's Back Shore. A portion of Little Good Harbor Beach can be seen to the rear and north.

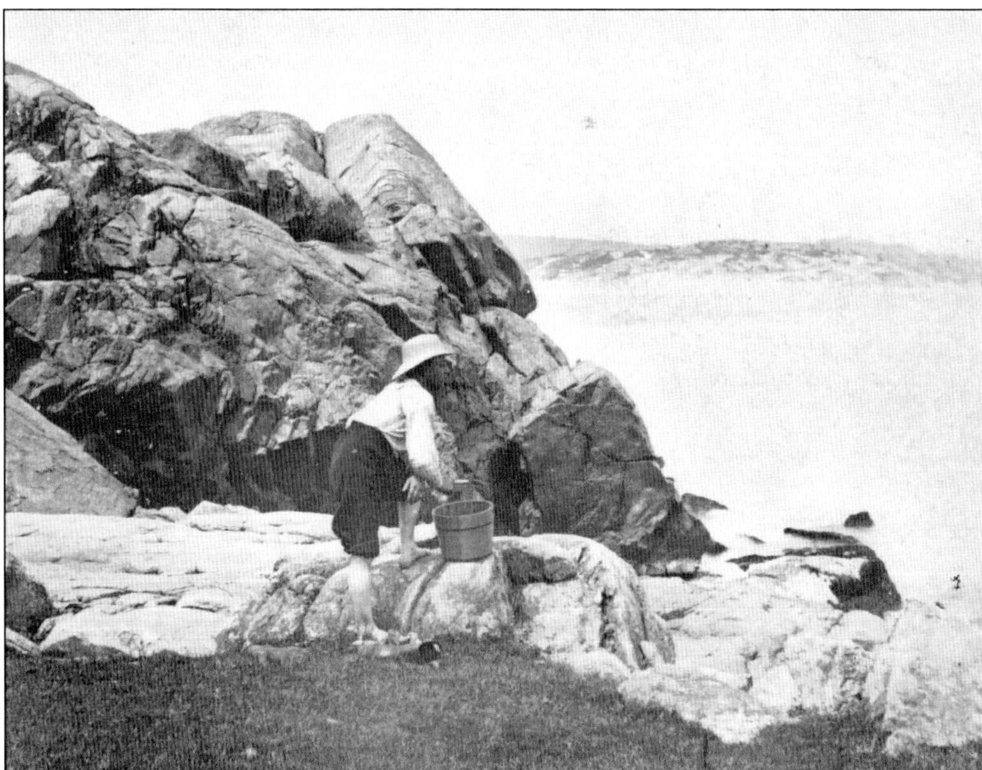

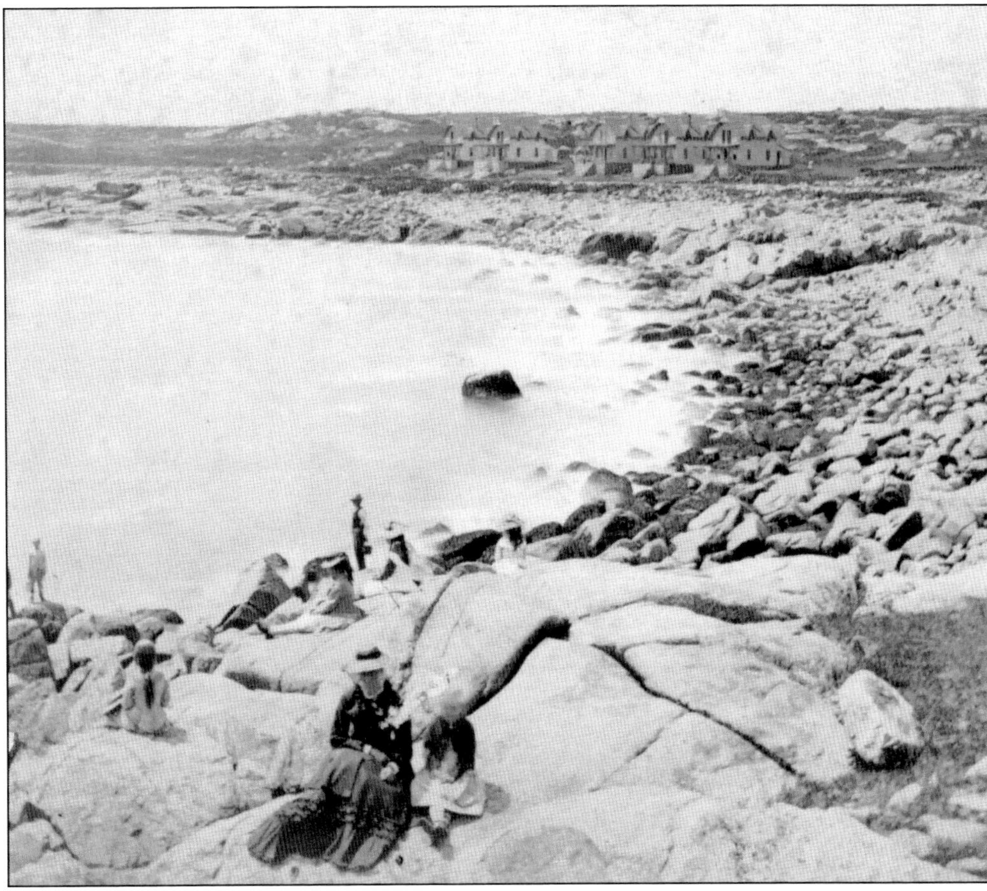

BASS ROCKS AND LITTLE GOOD HARBOR BEACH. This early view from the Procter Brothers (top) is of the coast southwest from Bass Rocks. Breathtaking ocean vistas from this vantage point have awed sightseers and picnickers for countless generations. The J.W. and J.S. Moulton stereoview (right) shows Good Harbor Beach (the name has been shortened over the years), whose smooth sands have attracted many a summer visitor. Salt Island is at the upper right of the image.

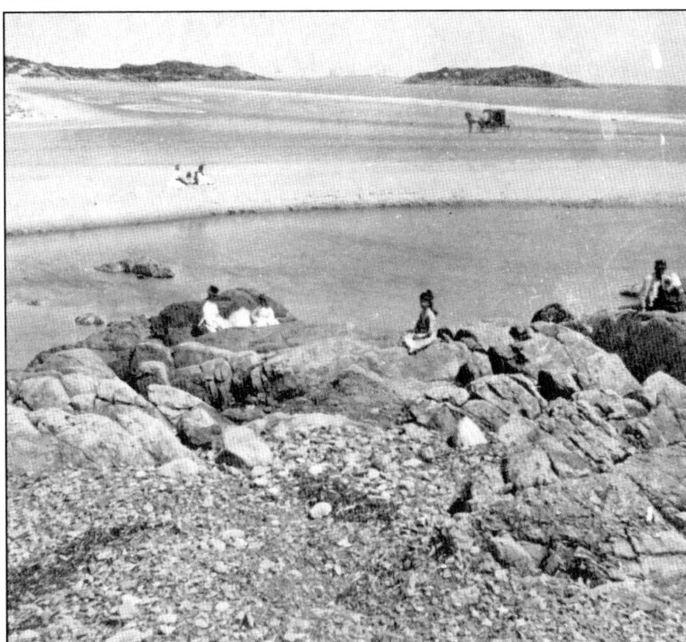

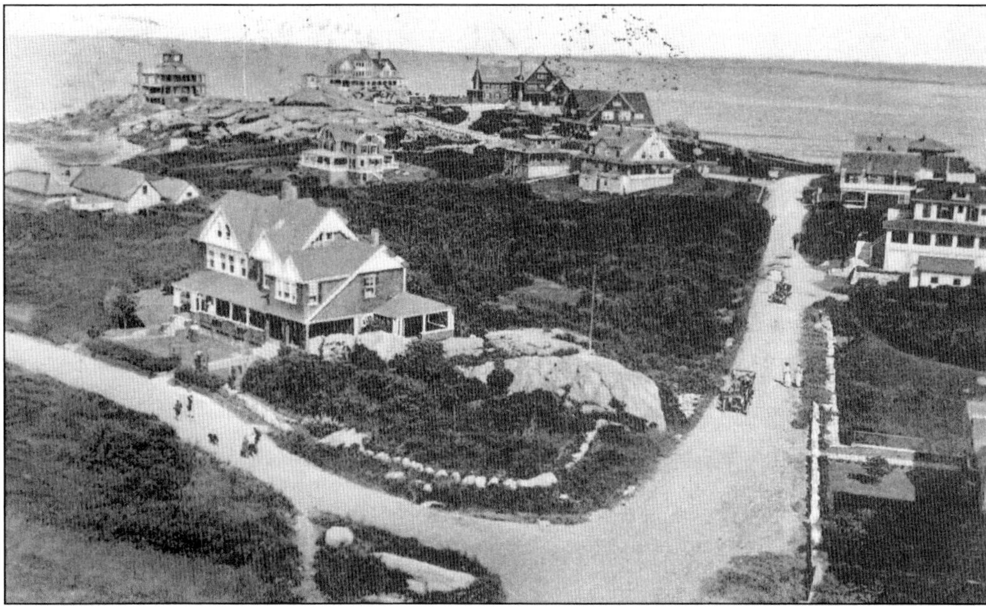

BASS ROCKS COTTAGES AND LONG BEACH. The early-1900s postcard at top shows the buildup of some of the beautiful homes and summer cottages at this particular area of Bass Rocks. The unique-looking structure with the cupola at upper left was the home of Judge Edgar J. Sherman; the building was actually bolted to the rock. Below, Long Beach appears in another early postcard; it was located slightly north of Good Harbor. The twin lighthouses of Thachers Island can be seen in the distance.

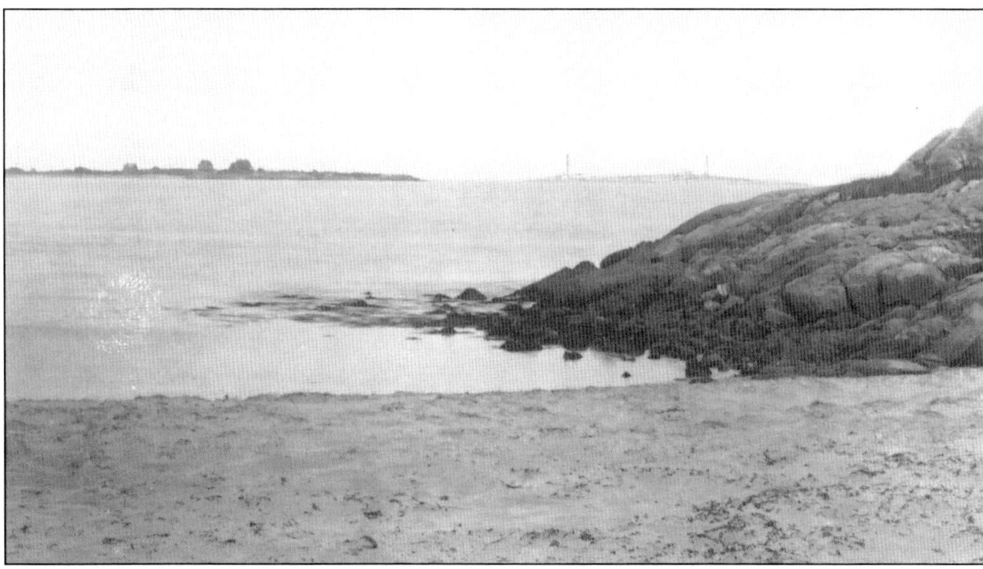

Reef of Norman's Woe and Rafe's Chasm. Two of the most famous natural landmarks on Cape Ann include the reef of Norman's Woe (the small island to the right of the cliff, at right) and Rafe's Chasm. The reef of Norman's Woe was made famous in Longfellow's poem "The Wreck of the Hesperus." Rafe's Chasm (below) is a great fissure cut into the rock and is about 60 feet deep and 12 feet wide at its mouth. When breakers surge into the crevice, the result is a mighty spectacle of spray and foam.

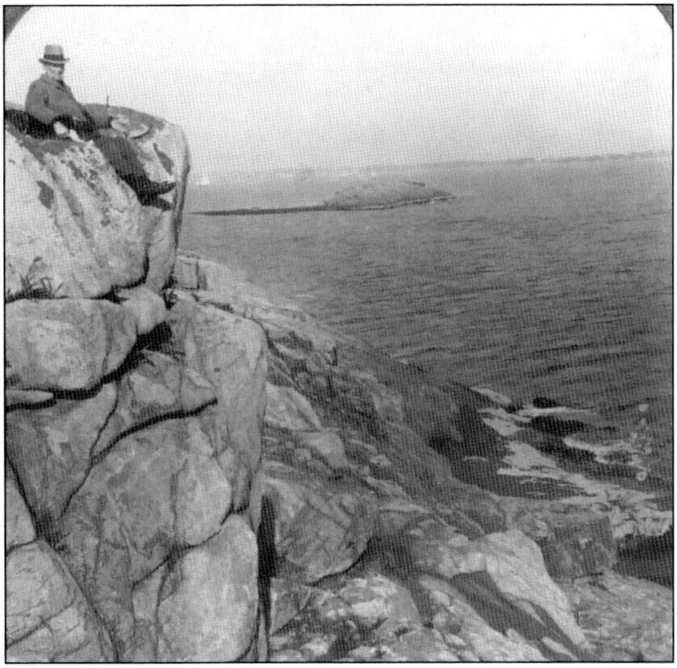

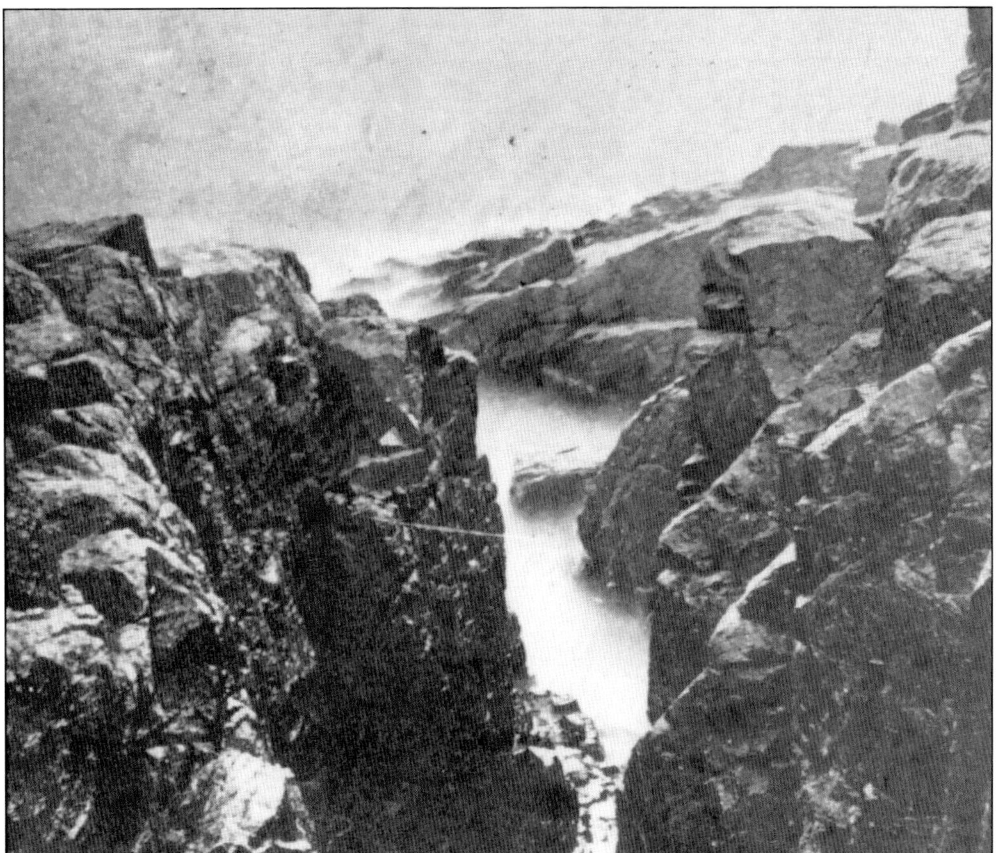

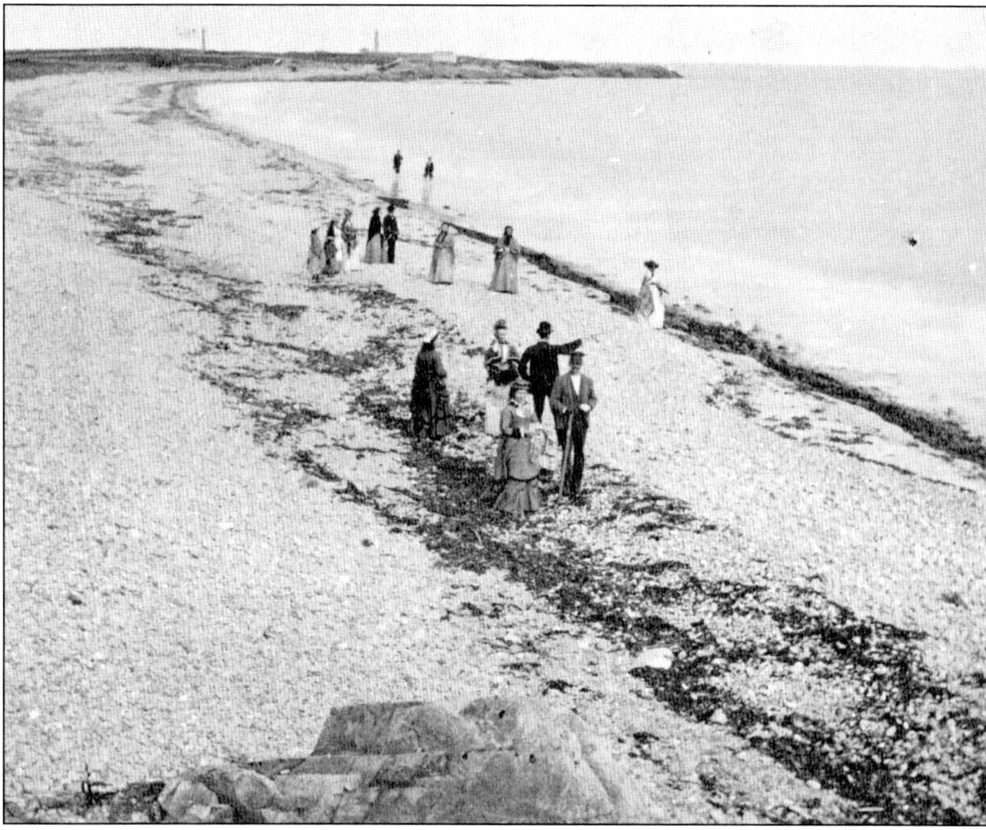

Pebble Stone Beach and Singing Sand Beach. A party of summer visitors is on the shore at Pebble Stone Beach (above, in an 1880s John S.E. Rogers stereoview). Pebbles from the beach, most very smooth and round, were used in Gloucester schooners for ballast. The Best Series stereoview (below) shows a group of people enjoying a day at Singing Sand Beach in Manchester. This beach's pinkish, coarse sand "squeaks" or "sings" when you walk on it.

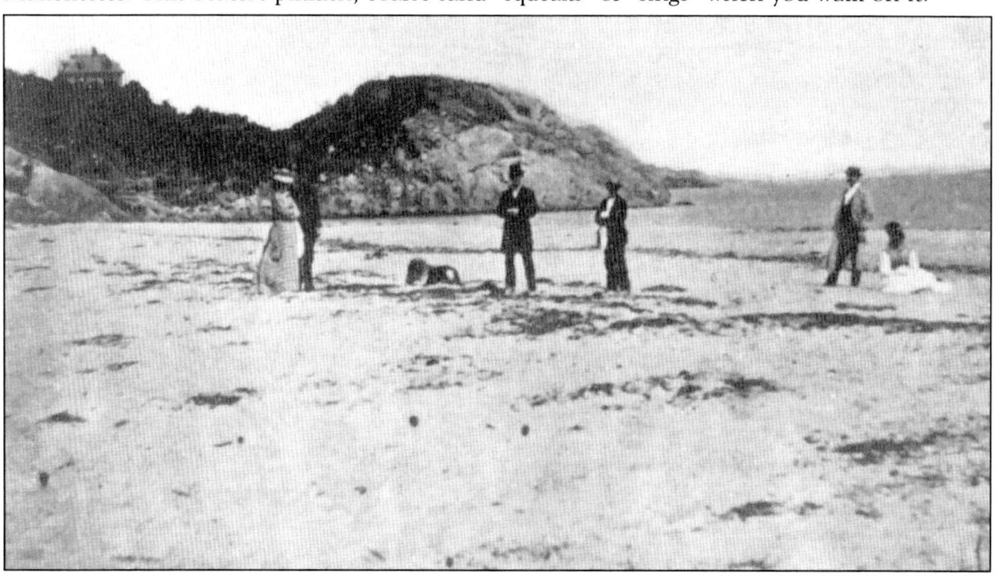

The Old Cedar and Halibut Point. A solitary man gazes eastward out into the Atlantic (right) in this breathtaking 1870s Procter Brothers stereoview entitled "The Old Cedar." Halibut Point, the northernmost tip of Cape Ann, is in the background. Another Procter Brothers view (below) from a different series shows visitors venturing out onto Halibut Point, so named because early sailing vessels would "haul about" (change direction) as they rounded the point.

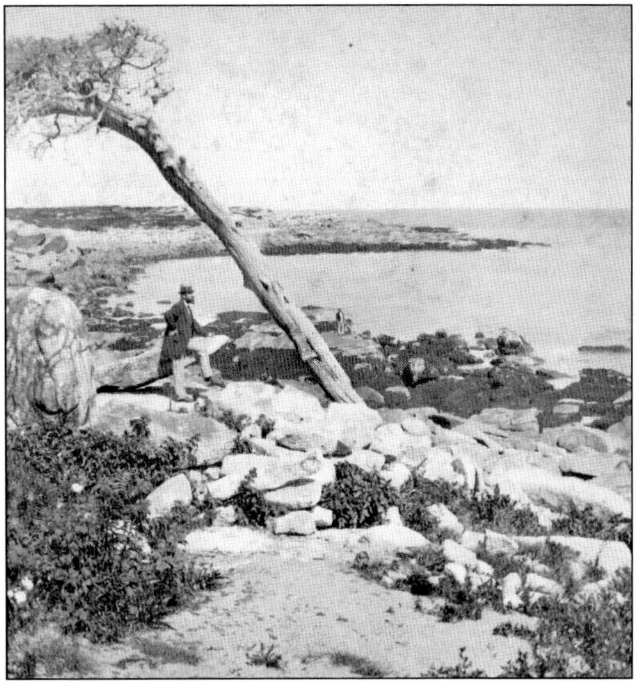

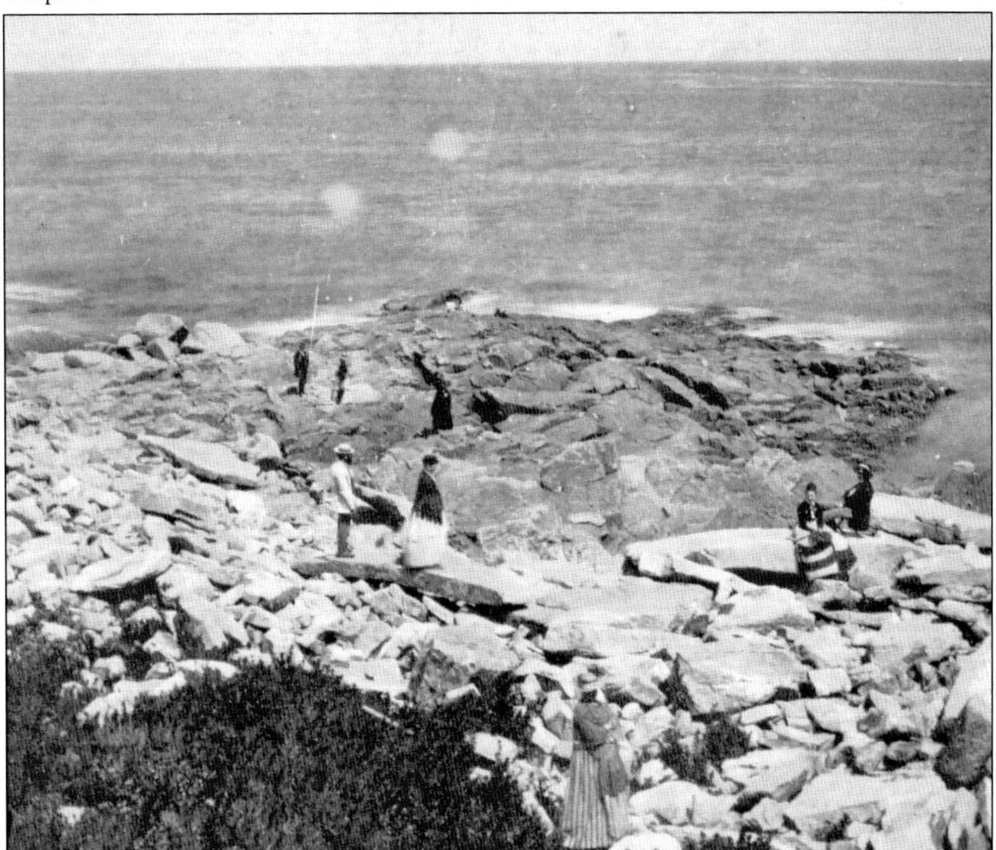

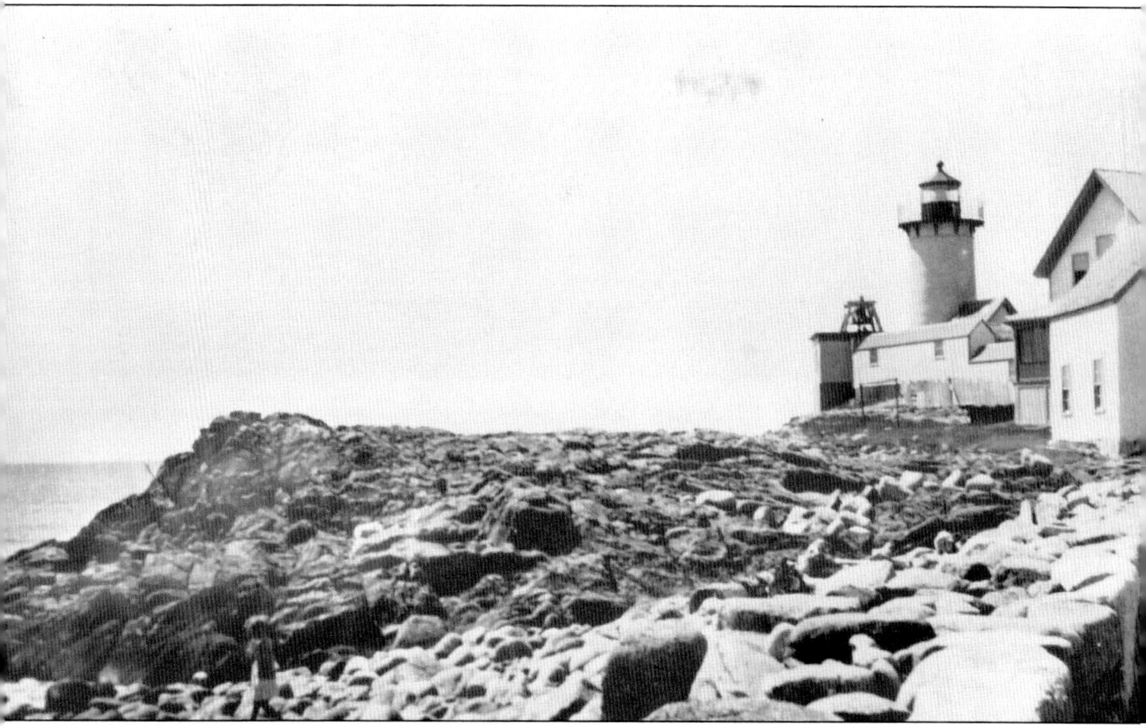

Mother Ann and Eastern Point Light. This early-1900s real photo postcard shows two of Cape Ann's most recognizable shoreline landmarks. At the far left, overlooking the Atlantic Ocean, is a remarkable rock formation resembling the face and figure of a reclining woman. "Mother Ann," as she is known to fishermen and other maritime travelers, has been there for centuries, "keeping watch" over them as they pass by in seas both stormy and smooth. At the far right is a part of the Eastern Point Lighthouse. Land for a lighthouse was purchased in 1829 by the U.S. government. A beacon with a stone base was erected, a more "modern" lighthouse was built in 1831, built anew in 1848, then rebuilt in 1890, looking much as it does today. The revolving lantern and fog bell were first operated by hand-wound devices.

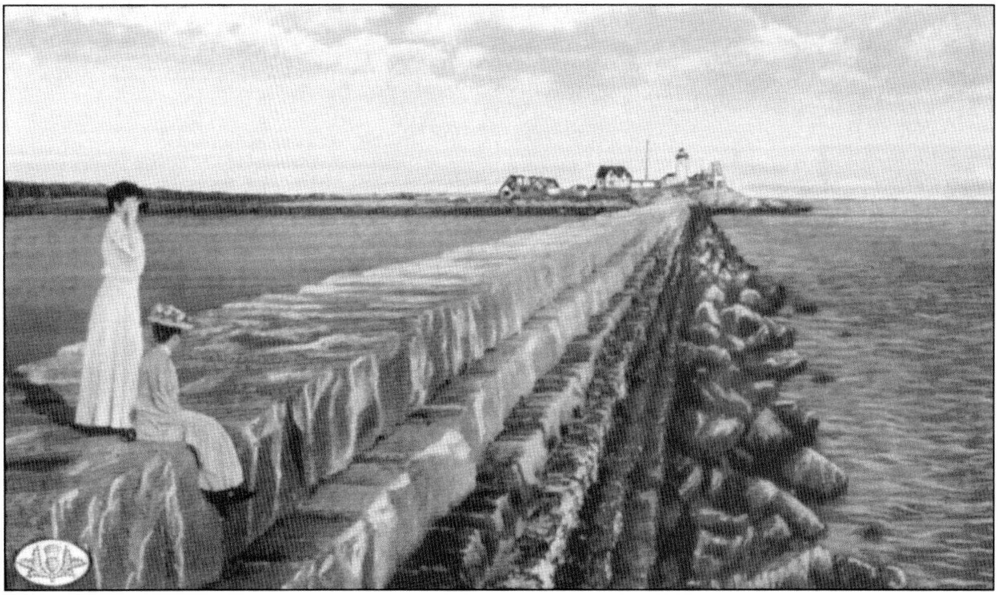

Dog Bar Breakwater and Blynman Bridge. Gloucester's harbor comprises a large basin, called the outer harbor, and a naturally protected inner harbor. The postcard scene above shows Dog Bar Breakwater stretching out for nearly a half-mile from Eastern Point Light. Constructed by the U.S. government, the breakwater protects the outer harbor from violent storms and is made up of a substructure of heavy stone about 30 feet wide and a rubblestone interior, topped off by massive 10-foot-wide granite blocks from the quarries in Rockport. The breakwater took 11 years to build, from 1894 to 1905. Another very recognizable man-made Cape Ann structure is the Blynman Bridge in Gloucester, seen below in an early-1900s postcard. The bridge spans "the Cut," which is a canal (first dug in 1642) that allows the Annisquam River to empty in Gloucester harbor. The drawbridge was previously made of timbers and was swung open sideways by hand. This *c.* 1910 view shows a reconstructed and electrified bridge about the same as it looks today.

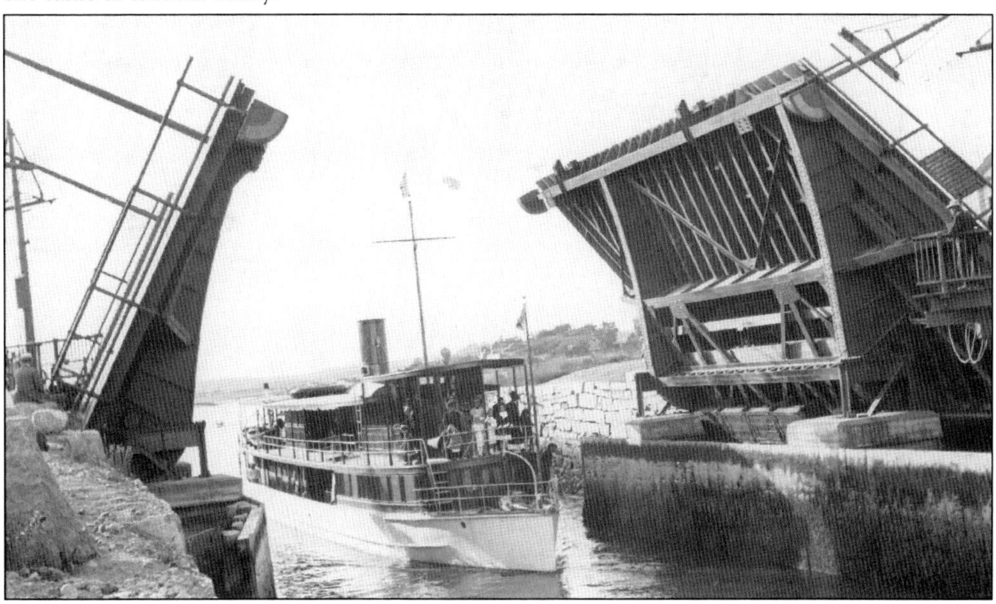

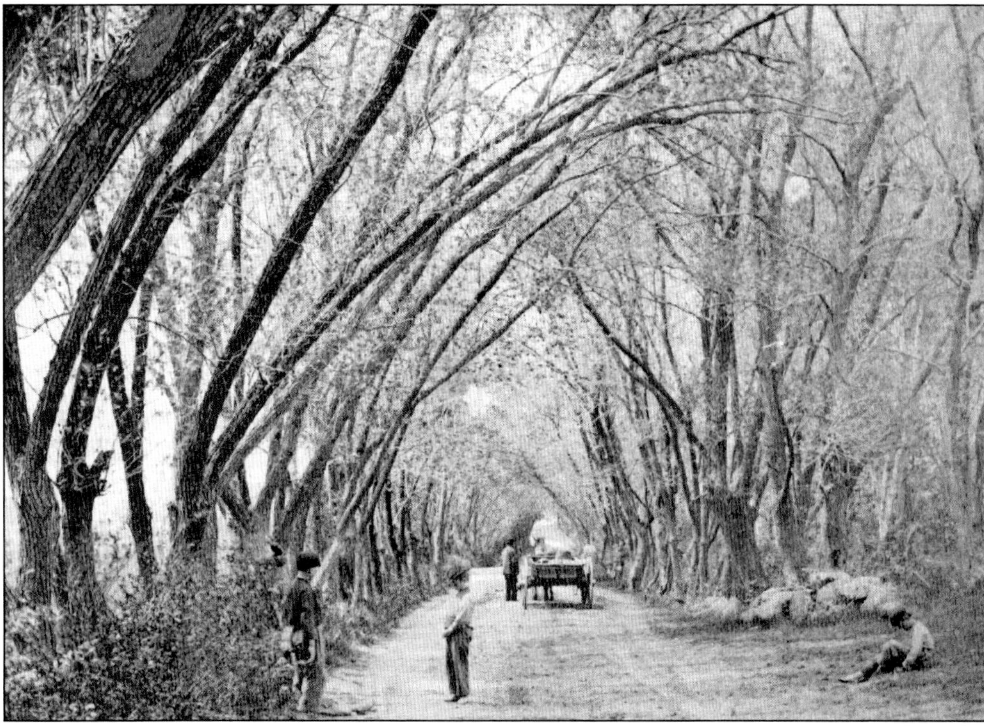

WILLOW ROAD, LANESVILLE. Similar 1870s stereoviews from Cook (Oliver H.) & Friend of Gloucester capture the protective canopy formed by the giant willows bending over the dirt road in the village of Lanesville, which was first called Flatstone Cove. Both images bear the same Cape Ann Scenery series number, but were clearly taken from different negatives.

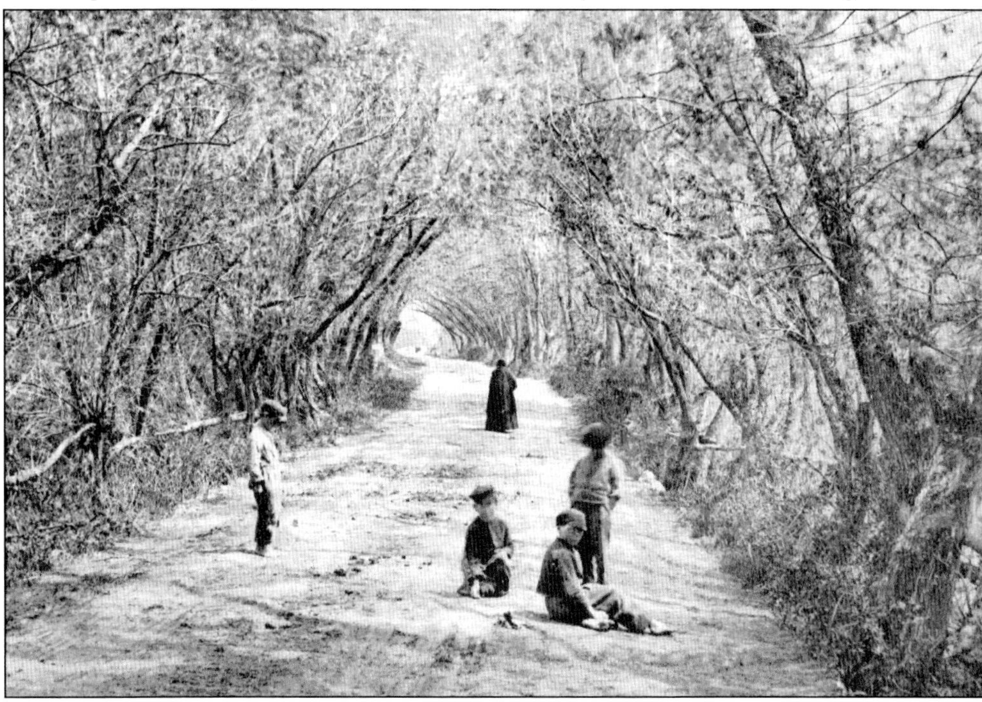

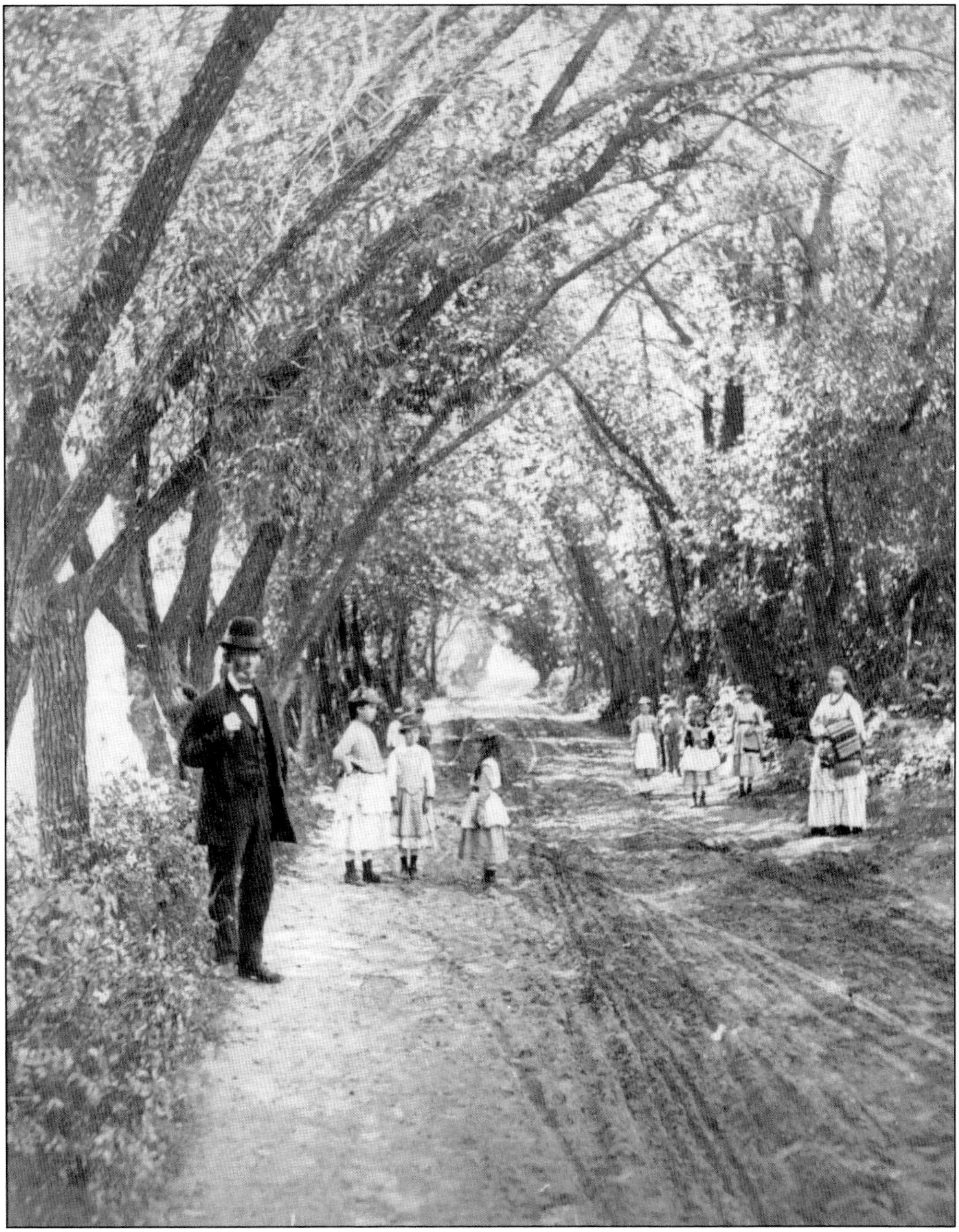

Willow Road, Lanesville. This magnificently composed photograph, taken from a stereoview published by E. (Erastus) G. Rollins of Gloucester, shows a party, presumably schoolchildren, enjoying a hike and picnic along Willow Road. The stern-looking fellow at left is quite likely their teacher. The young woman at right has a blanket folded over her arms.

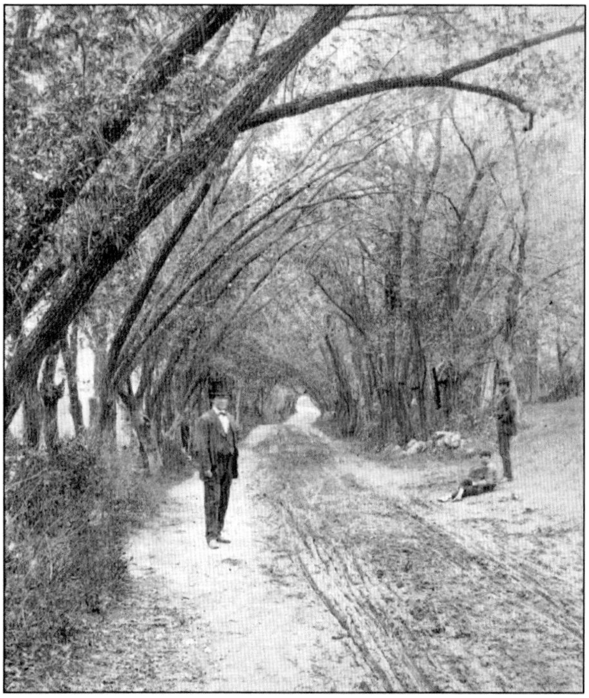

WILLOW ROAD, LANESVILLE. Completing our visit to this scenic spot are two early stereoviews from J.W. and J.S. Moulton (left) and John S. Moulton (below). The left image comes from a late-1870s series. John Moulton published the photograph below independently from a Gems of American Scenery series, *c.* 1872.

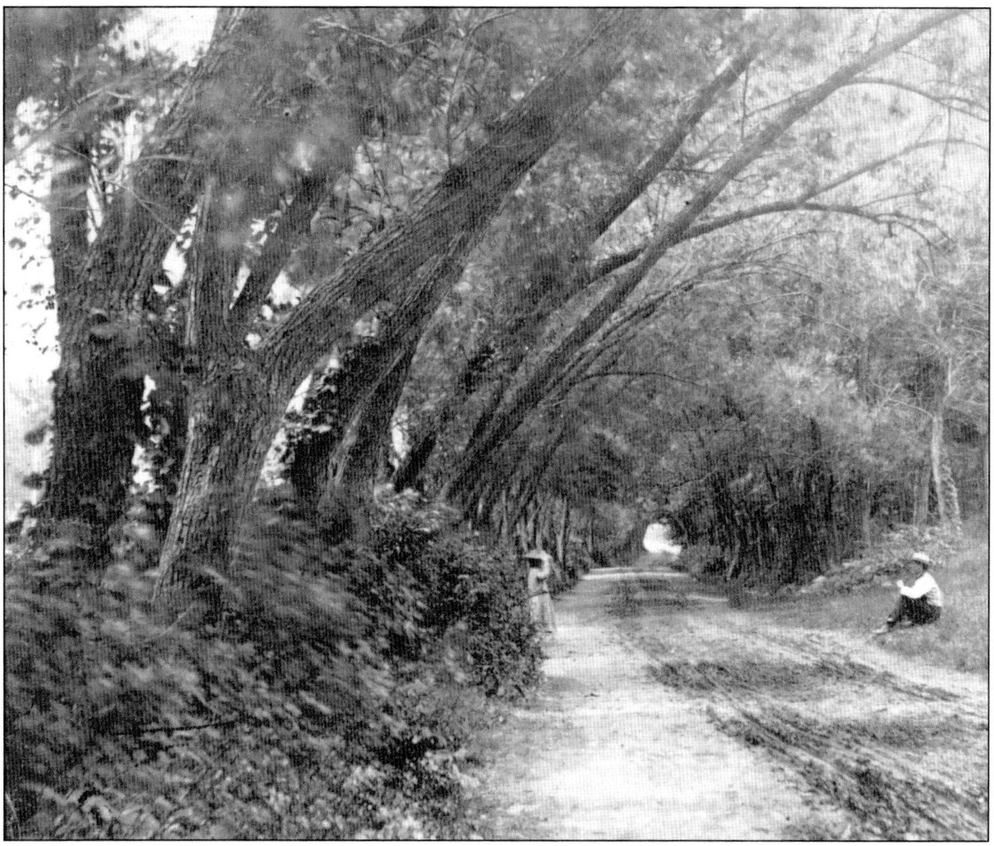

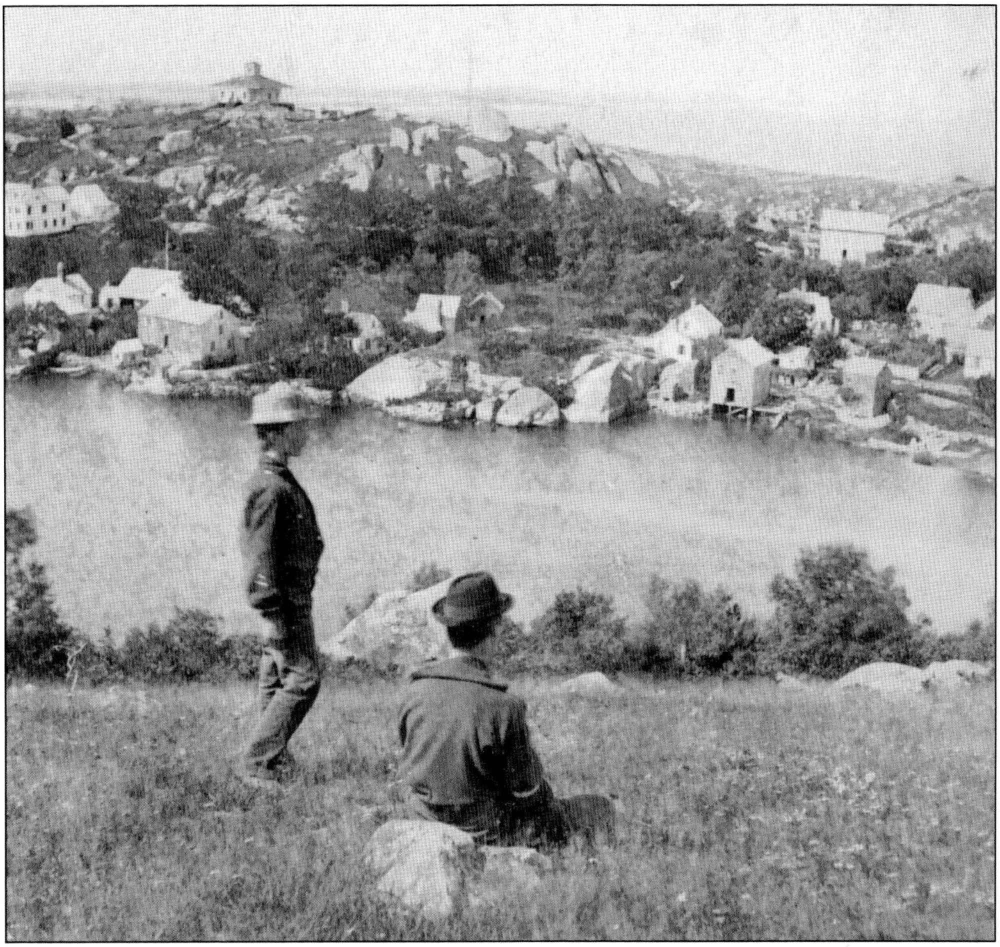

ANNISQUAM AND ANDREWS POINT. This mid-to-late-1870s stereoview (top) from E.G. Rollins, later republished by the Procter Brothers, shows two young lads atop Barberry Hill looking across Lobster Cove toward the village of Annisquam. Called "Squam" by Cape Ann residents, the village has many unique topographical features. The Procter Brothers stereoview at right is No. 107 from the Cape Ann Scenery Unique Series; it was likely taken on the rocks near Rockport's Ocean View House. A bathhouse for guests of the hotel can be seen in the background.

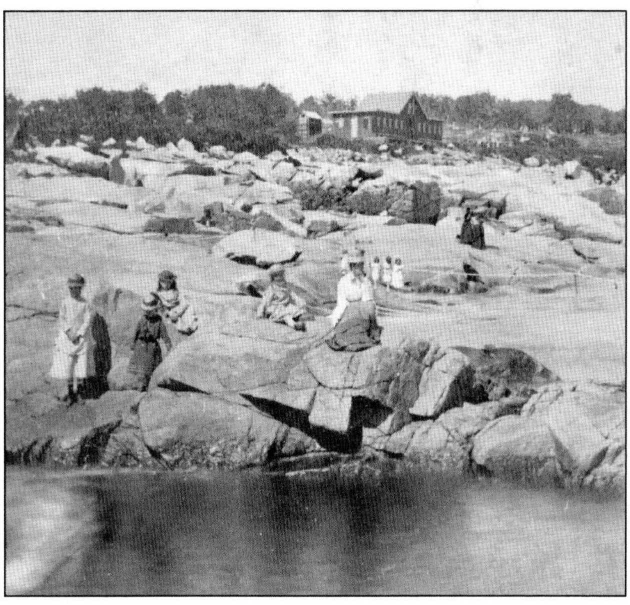

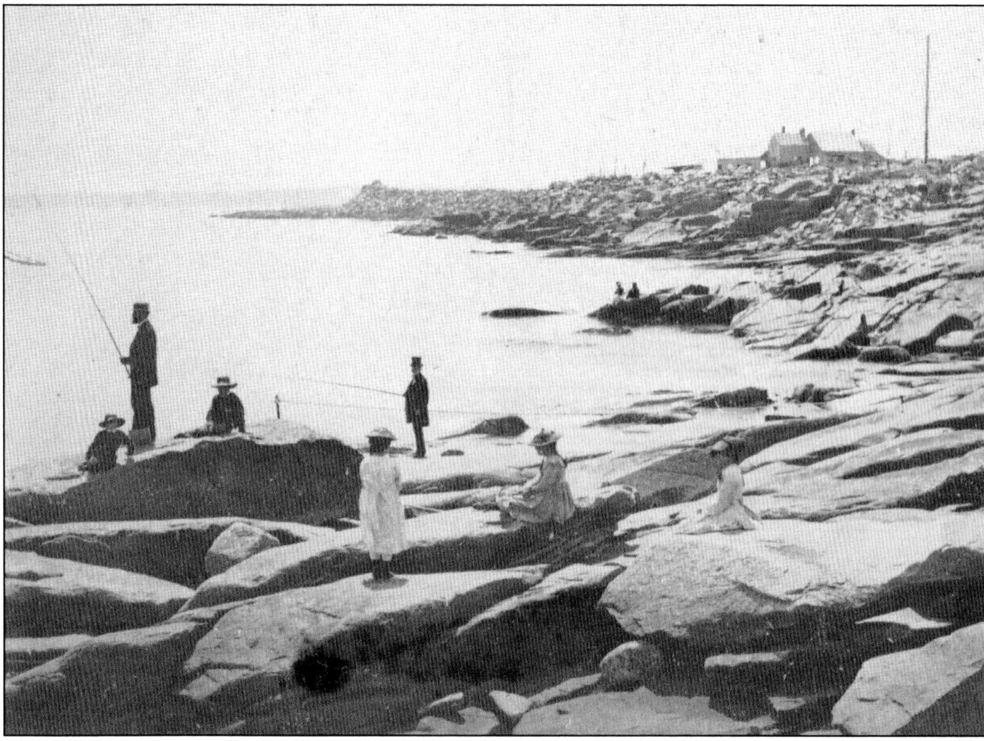

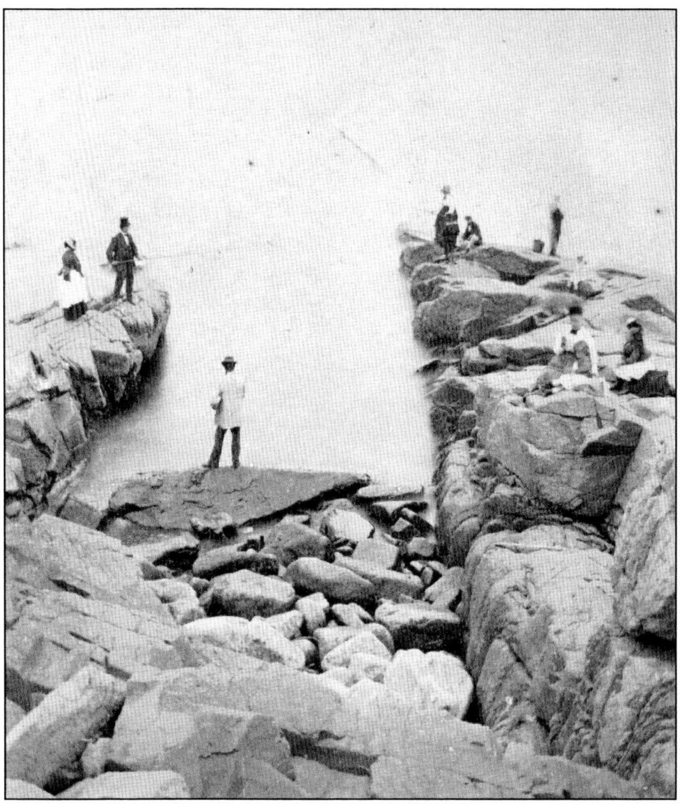

PIGEON COVE AND GREAT GULLY, ROCKPORT. This Cape Ann Scenery view with a Cook & Friend backlabel shows two formally dressed men (above) fishing off the rocks at Pigeon Cove. The cove was named for a huge flock of pigeons that died there in a violent storm many years ago. The stereoview at left, No. 311 from a series published by the Moultons, is titled "Great Gully, Pigeon Cove." Here, too, formal attire was the order of the day for those people on the rocks.

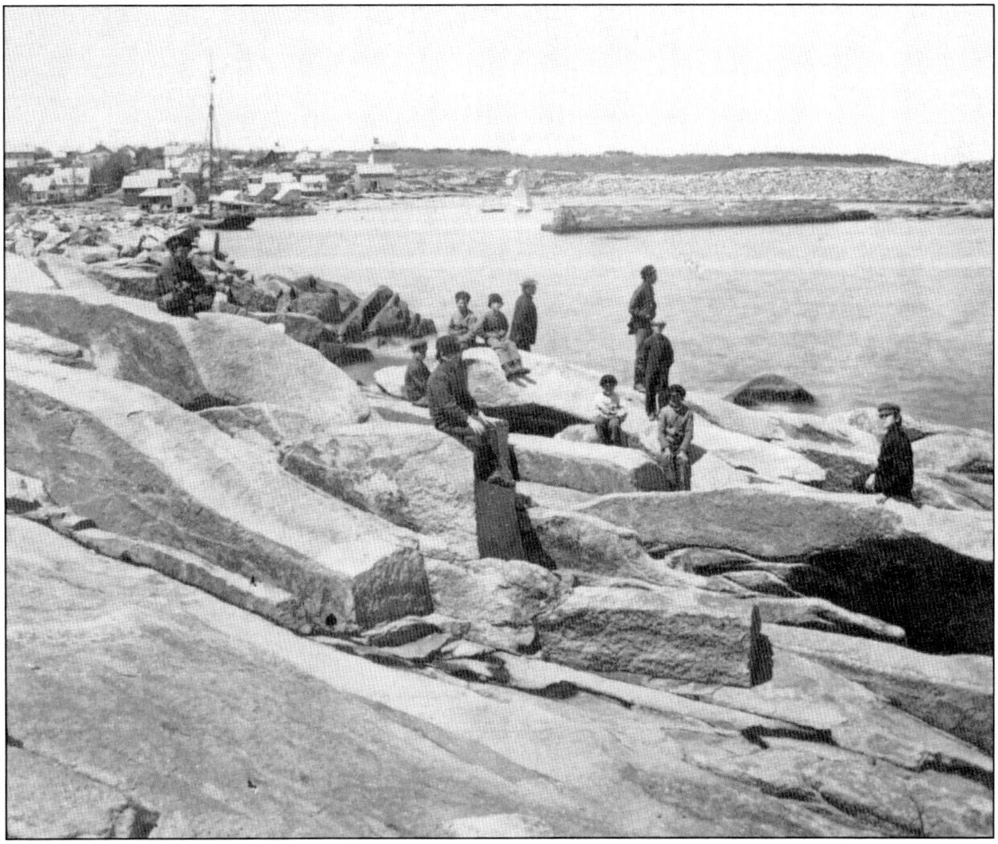

PIGEON COVE HARBOR AND GEORGE WASHINGTON PROFILE. This beautiful 1860s stereoview (above), photographed by John Heywood of Boston and published by Hervey Friend of Gloucester, shows the entrance to Pigeon Cove harbor in the background. A granite-hauling sloop with its prominent high mast used for loading is at the pier in the left background. Not as famous as the stone figure of "Mother Ann" in Gloucester, the rock formation (below, c. early-1900s postcard) at the Rockport shore is known as the George Washington Profile because of its striking resemblance to our nation's first president. (Stereoview courtesy of Larry Gottheim.)

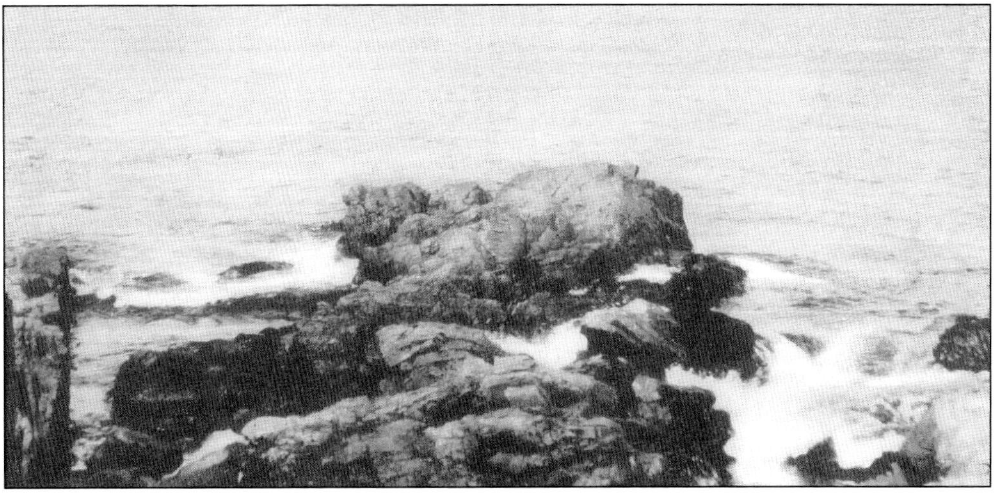

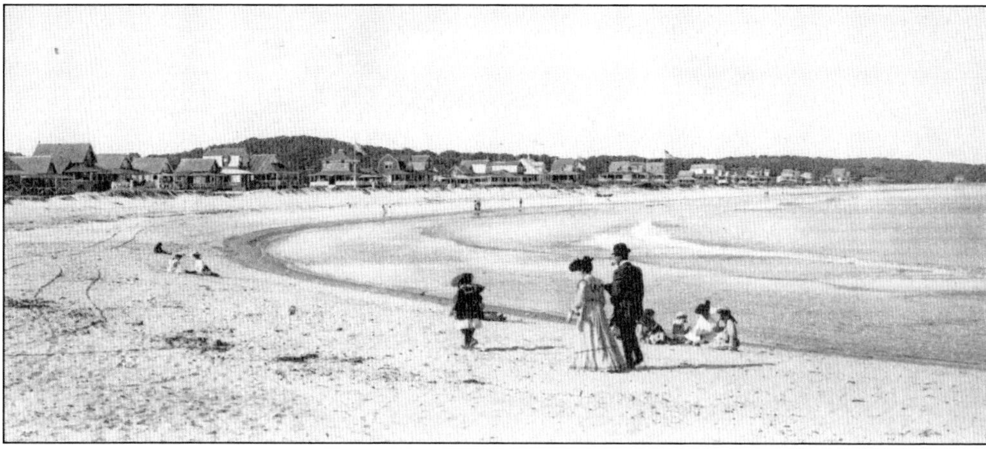

LONG BEACH. These two early-1900s photographic postcards catch the beauty of the cottages, sand, and surf at Long Beach in Rockport. A mecca for bathers, Long Beach extends to the Gloucester town line. Quite a few of the summer-only cottages are now year-round homes. Long Beach was a very popular destination during the trolley car era, with runs from Gloucester that crossed the dunes behind neighboring Good Harbor Beach. The Long Beach Pavilion (see page 120), dance hall, and small theater were quite the attractions for thousands of visitors. Great views of the twin lights on Thachers Island can be afforded from the beach.

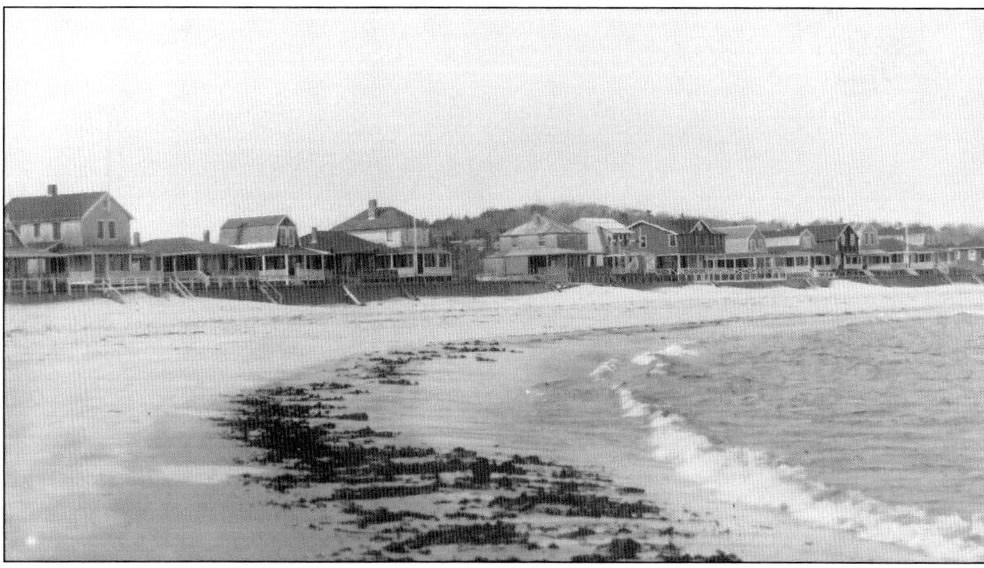

Two

The Working Waterfront

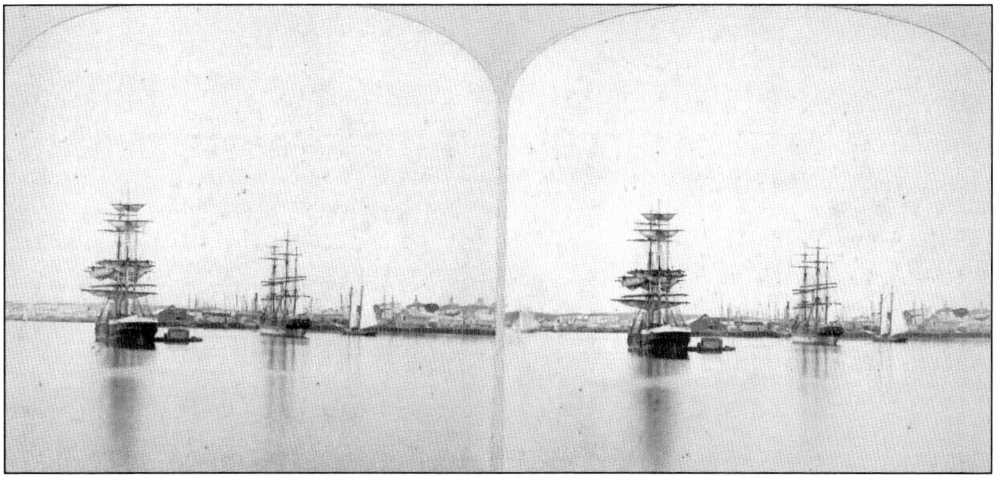

Gloucester Harbor. Two large ships are at anchor at the mouth of Gloucester's inner harbor in this early-1870s stereoview from Cook & Friend.

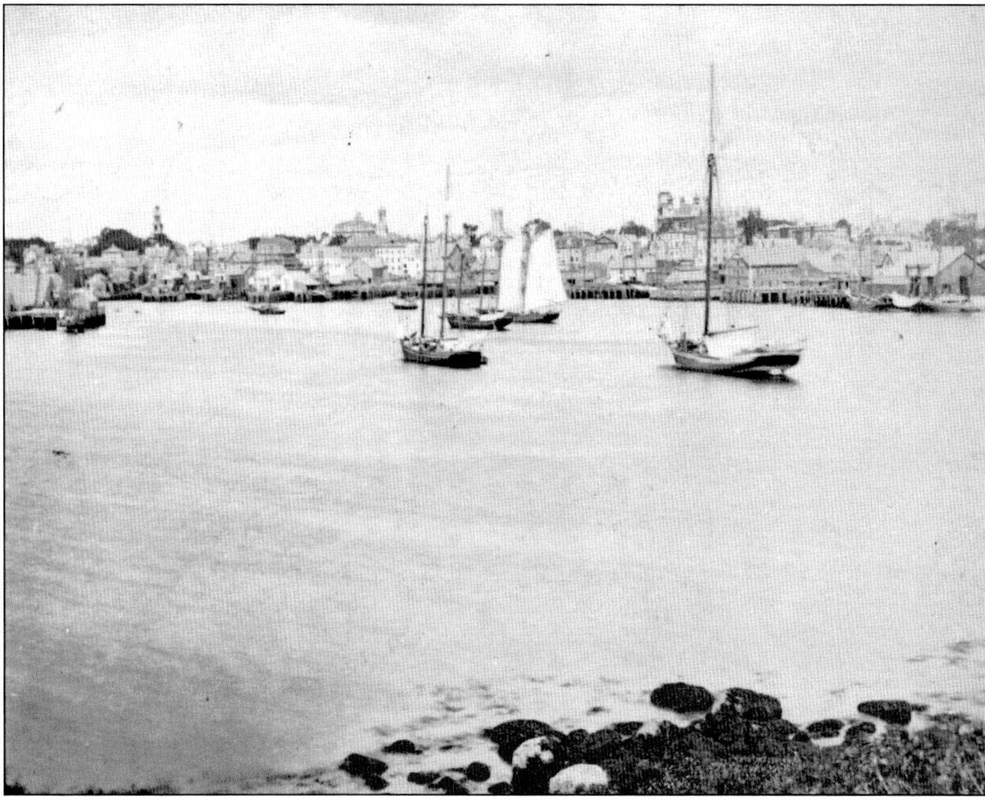

GLOUCESTER FROM THE HARBOR. This early-1870s stereoview (top) from Cook & Friend, No. 45, shows Gloucester from the Neck (presumably Rocky Neck), which, along with Ten Pound Island, gave some protection to ships at anchor in Gloucester's inner harbor. The real photo postcard below captures Gloucester's outer harbor, c. 1910. The white steamer in the center is quite likely a cutter from the U.S. Revenue Service.

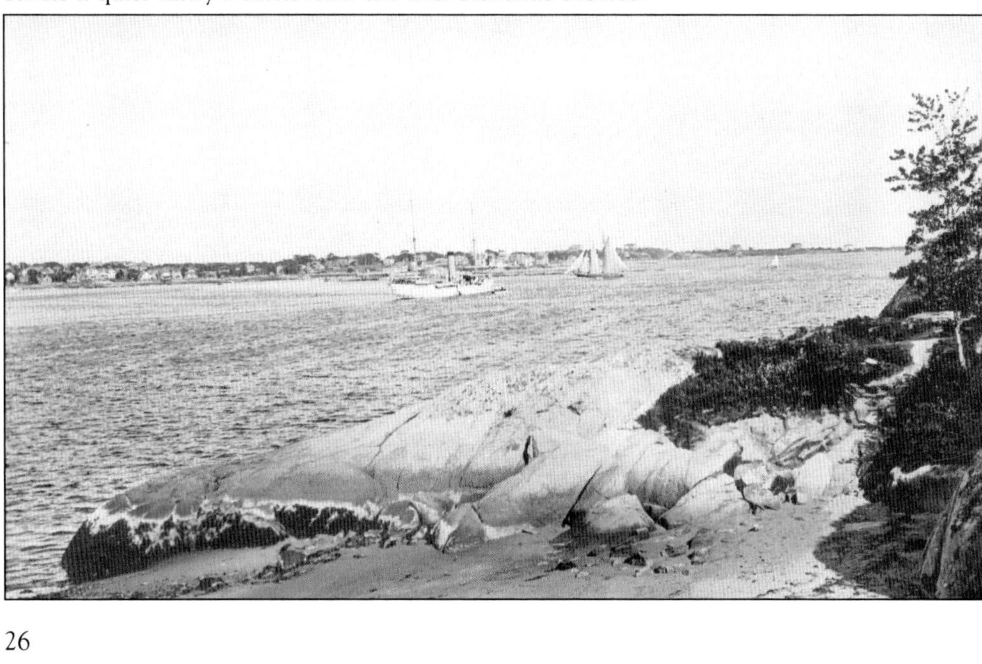

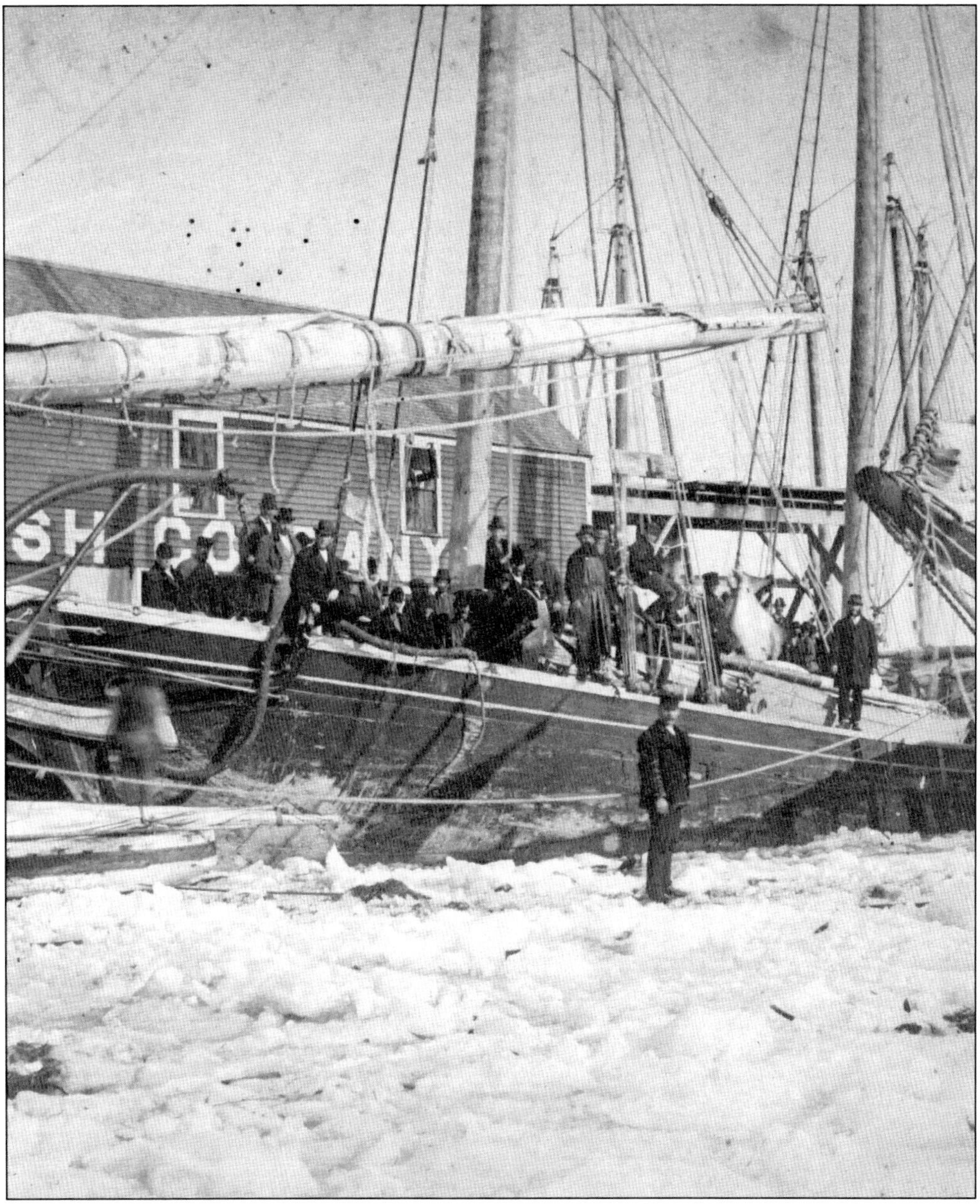

UNLOADING THE CATCH. A stereoview from a series published by the Procter Brothers in 1875 shows a catch of halibut being unloaded at the Union Fish Company's wharf on Duncan Street. Note the man standing on ice in the foreground. At least 50 Georges Bank schooners were frozen solid in Gloucester harbor at one point during the extremely cold winter of 1875.

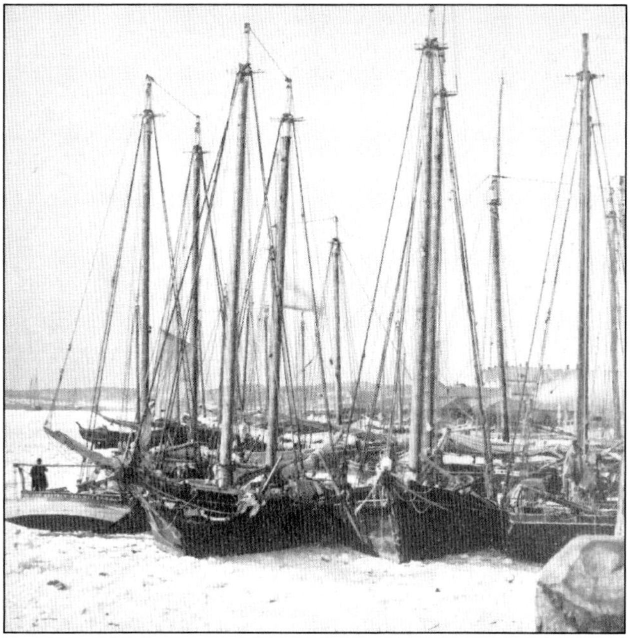

FROZEN IN. Two more extraordinary stereoscopic images from the Procter Brothers series dramatically show the winter of 1875's frigid grip on the Georges Fleet and on the waterfront itself. No. 911 (left) shows a portion of the fleet held fast by the harbor ice, which, in some places, measured 16 inches deep. No. 6 (below) shows two men fearlessly walking on the ice, a schooner, the Gloucester Fish Company at left, and Fears' sail loft at right.

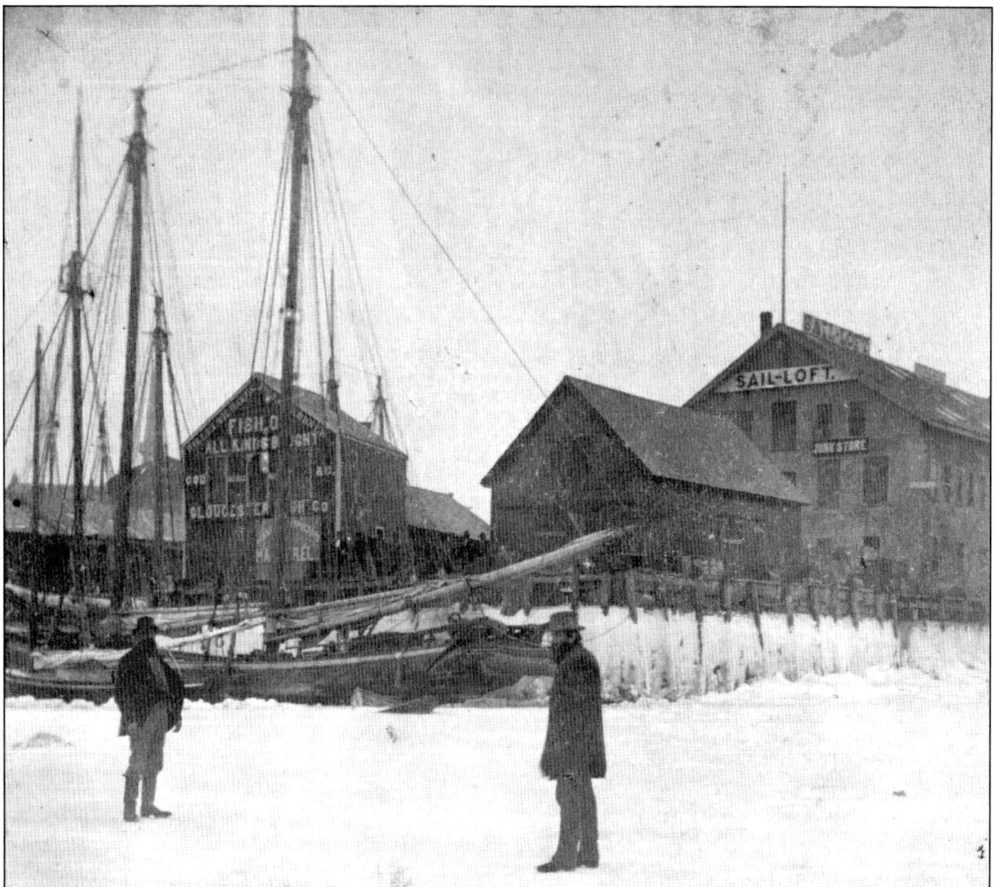

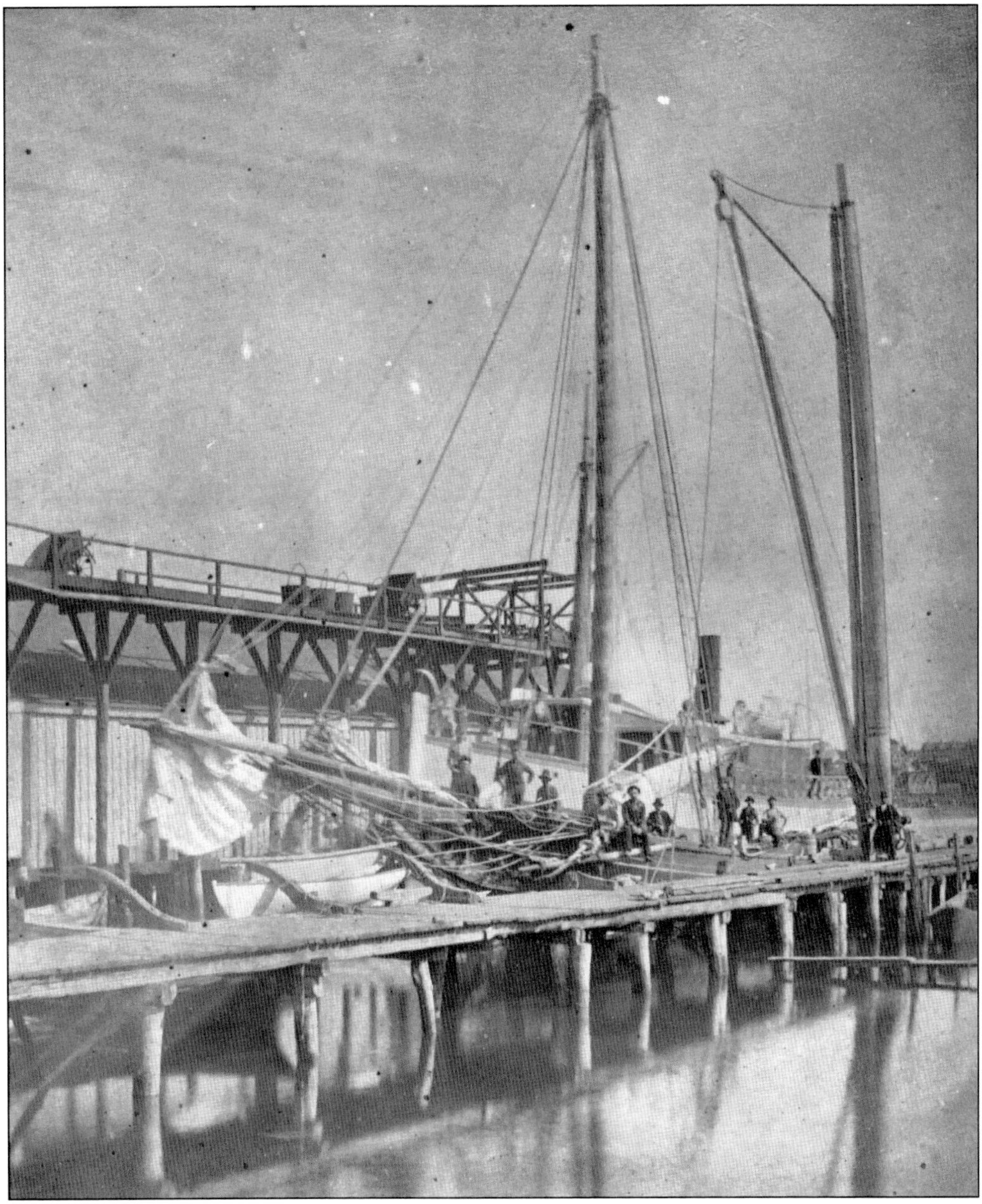

TIED UP. The crew of this ship, identified in pencil on the verso as the *Fleetwood*, pose for the stereo camera at a wharf in Gloucester, *c.* 1885. (Unknown maker.)

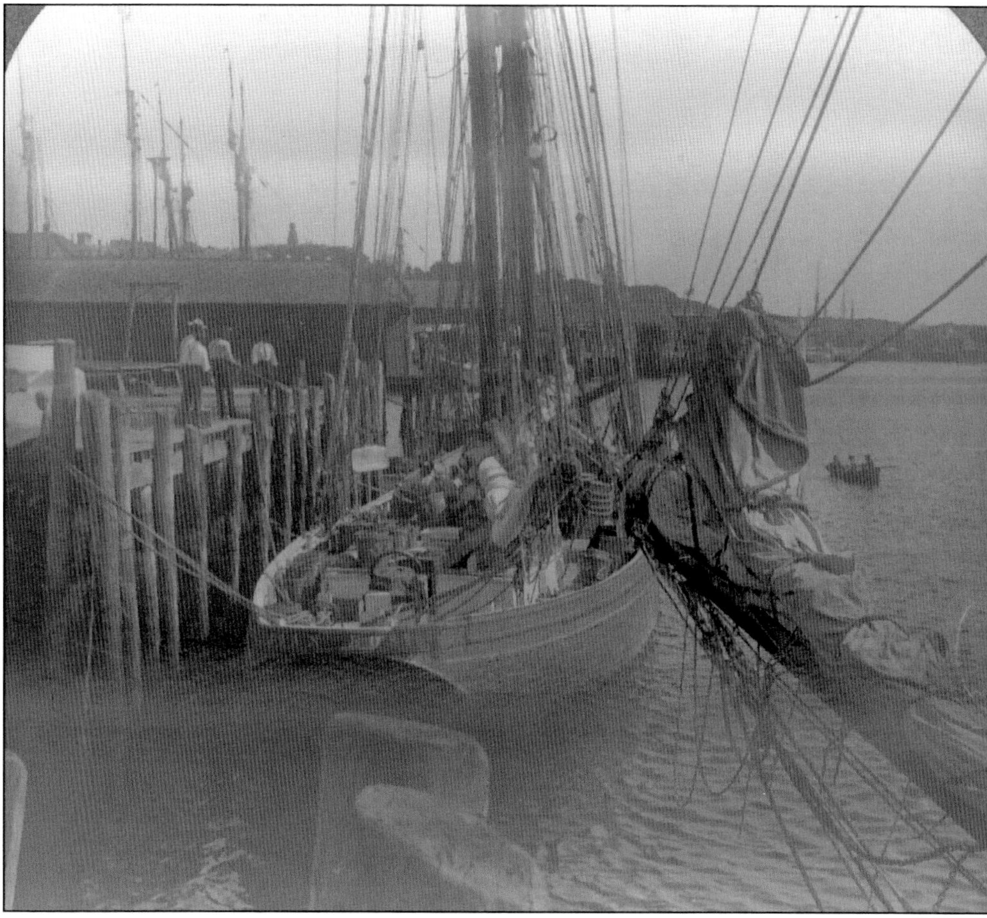

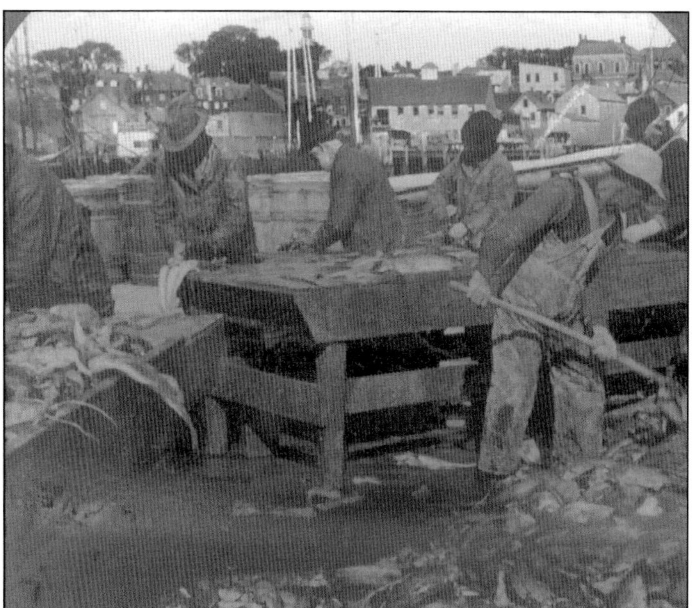

READYING FOR SAIL AND THE CLEANING OF COD. Dock workers (top) lower a block of ice aboard an unidentified Gloucester schooner that is getting ready to set sail from its wharf. Freshly unloaded codfish (left), forked up by the man on the right, are being cleaned and split before being fully cured. Both c. 1915 images were published by the Keystone View Company, although the view at left was taken from an Underwood & Underwood negative that was published earlier.

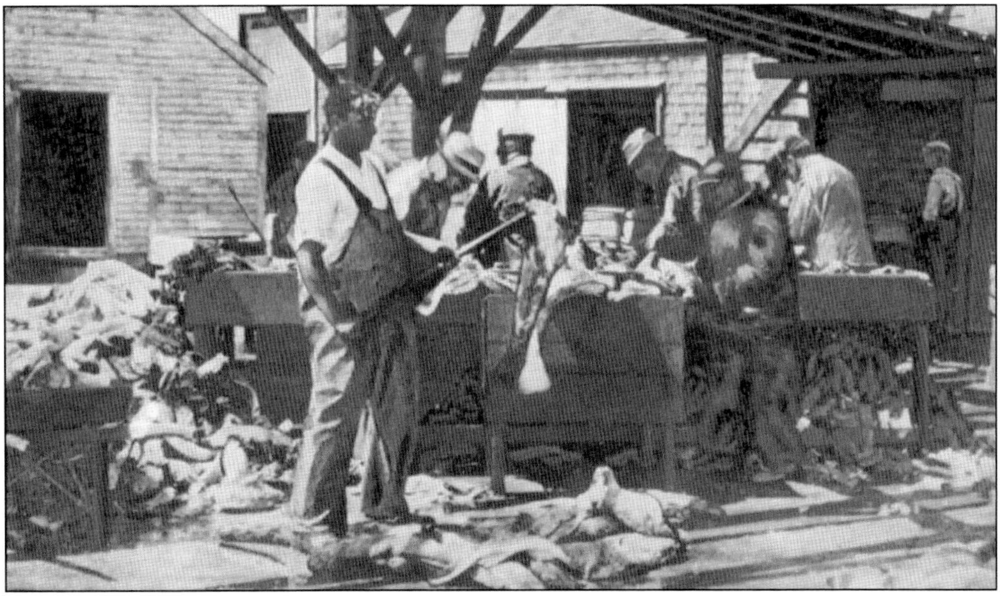

Sorting, Boxing, and Drying. Ten to 15 years later, methods used by the splitting gang (see opposite page) have not changed much. The *c.* 1920s postcard above shows a sorter handing up a fresh load of fish for trimming, or, if directly headed to fresh markets, for boxing and shipment. Freshly washed, trimmed, and resalted cod not shipped directly to market ends up being placed on outdoor wooden racks called flakes for curing, shown in the Underwood & Underwood view below.

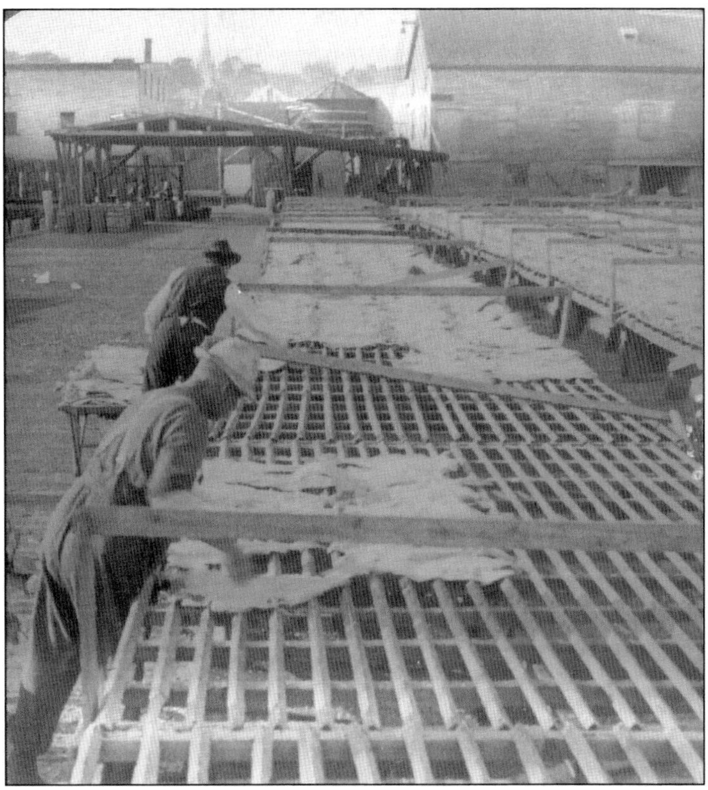

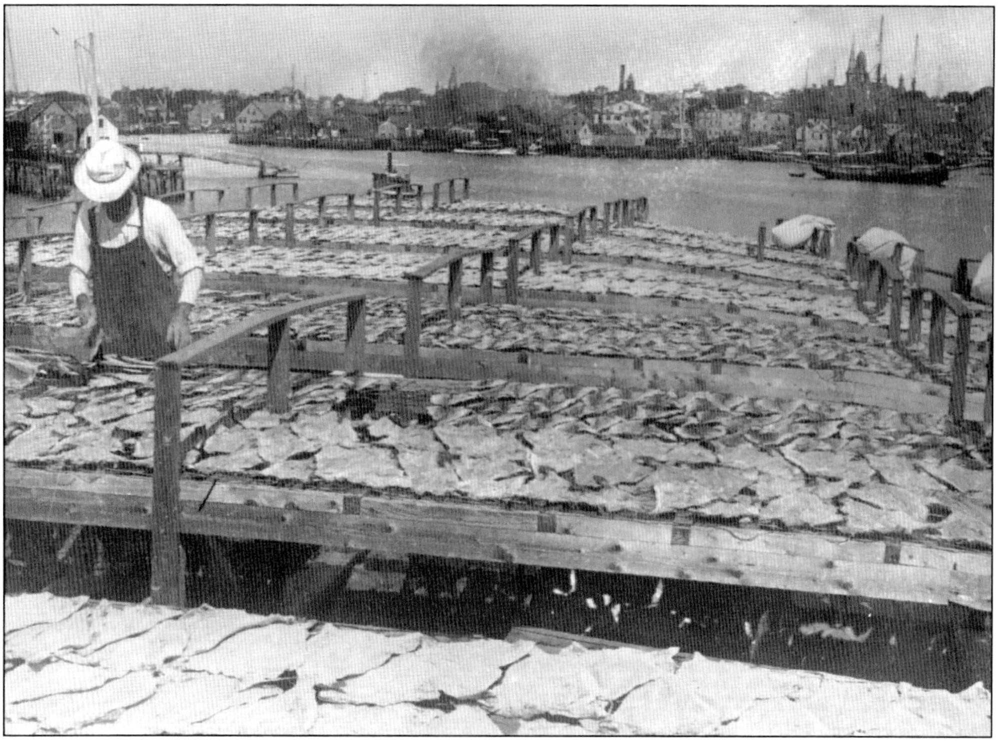

On the Flakes. With Gloucester harbor mid-distant and the city in the background, fish cures in the sun on the rows of flakes (above). The flakes were often covered by cloths to protect the fish from too much of a summer day's heat. The covers were taken off at day's end (below). If rain threatened, the fish would quickly be removed and stacked under the ends of the flakes. (Above, published by the Keystone View Company. Below, published by the H.C. White Company, c. early 1900s.)

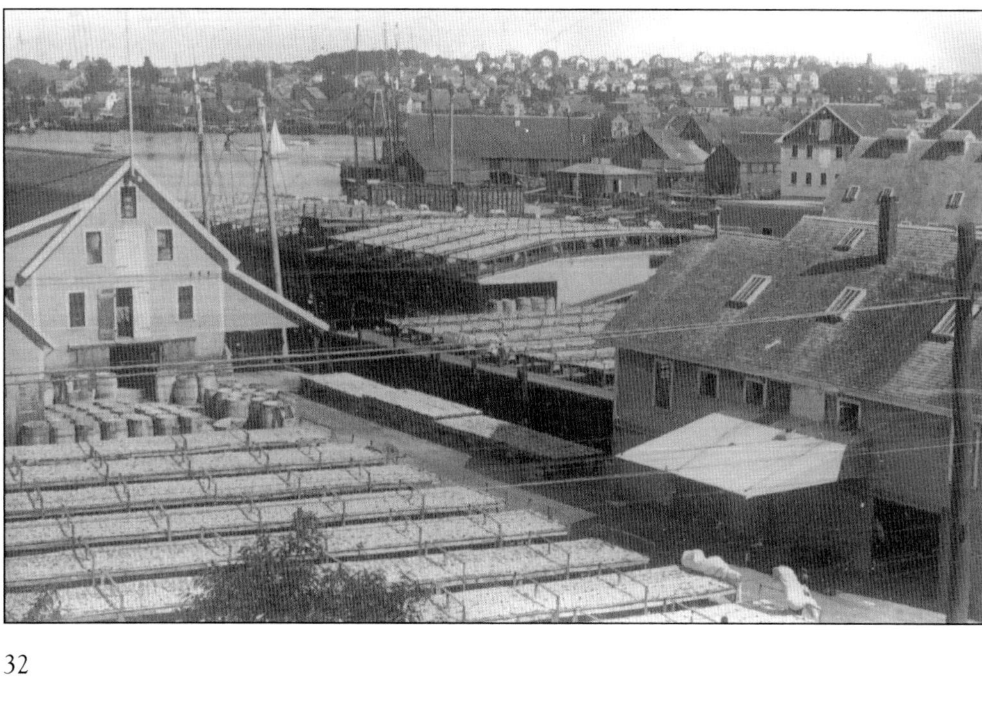

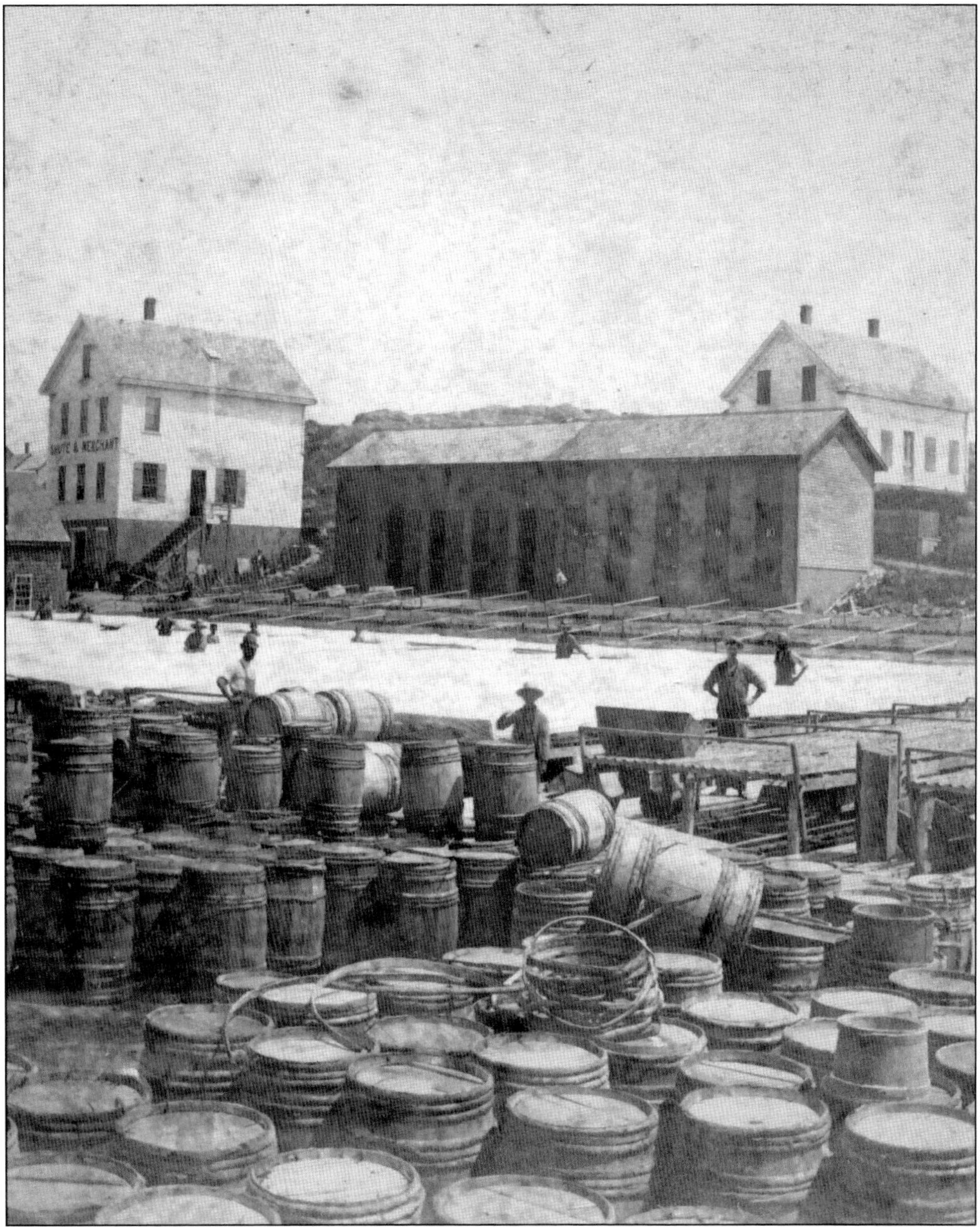

MASS PRODUCTION. Salted codfish and smoked halibut were the specialties of the wholesale firm of Shute (J.L.) and Merchant (W.T.), whose large processing plant on Parker Street can be seen in the background of this J.W. and J.S. Moulton stereoview, *c.* 1880. Barrels in the foreground are called butts, and hundreds of thousands were used every year by the leading Gloucester packers of the day. Flakes in center are covered.

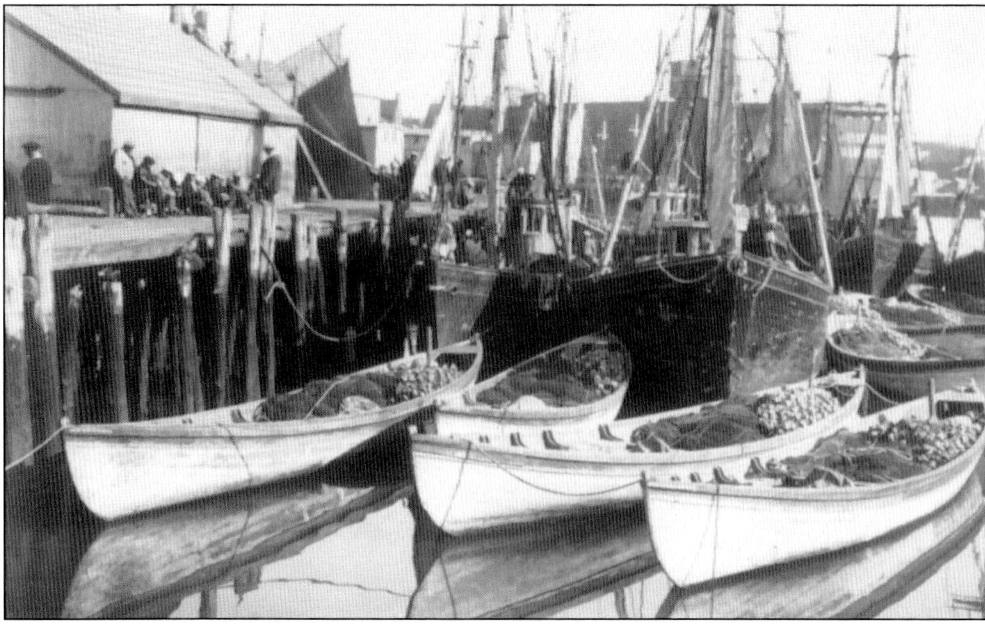

ALONG THE WHARF. With sails taken in and nets properly stored in the dories, a pair of Gloucestermen (above) rub against each other at their pilings. Crewmen, at left, on the pier enjoy the sun's warmth. Drying the fish nets on giant spindles (below) was also a required task after each hard voyage. Netting mends were also done at this time. The top view was taken from an early-1900s real photo postcard. The bottom postcard image of later vintage was published by Frank M. Shurtleff of Gloucester.

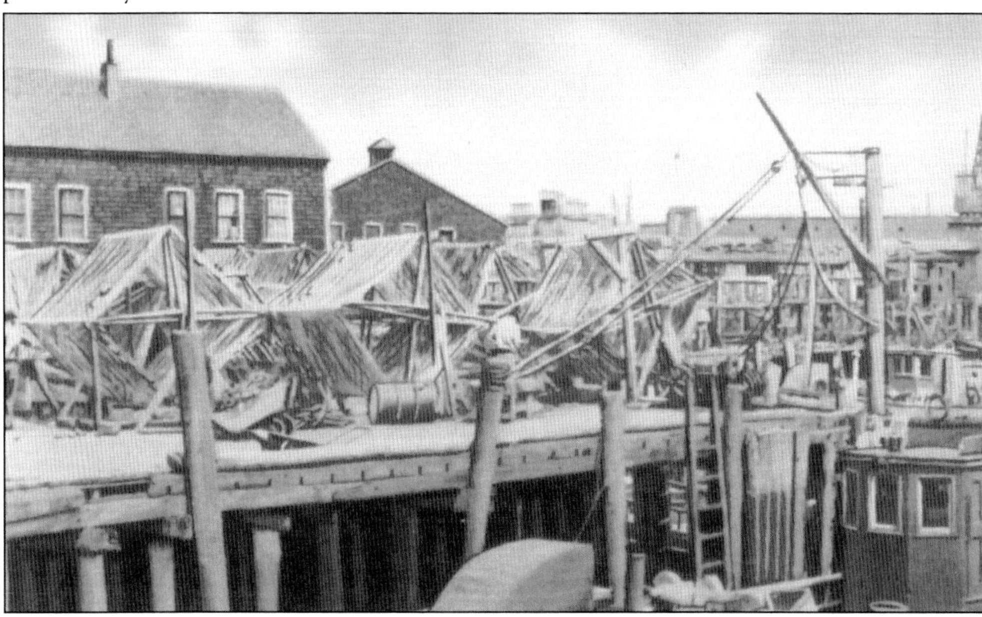

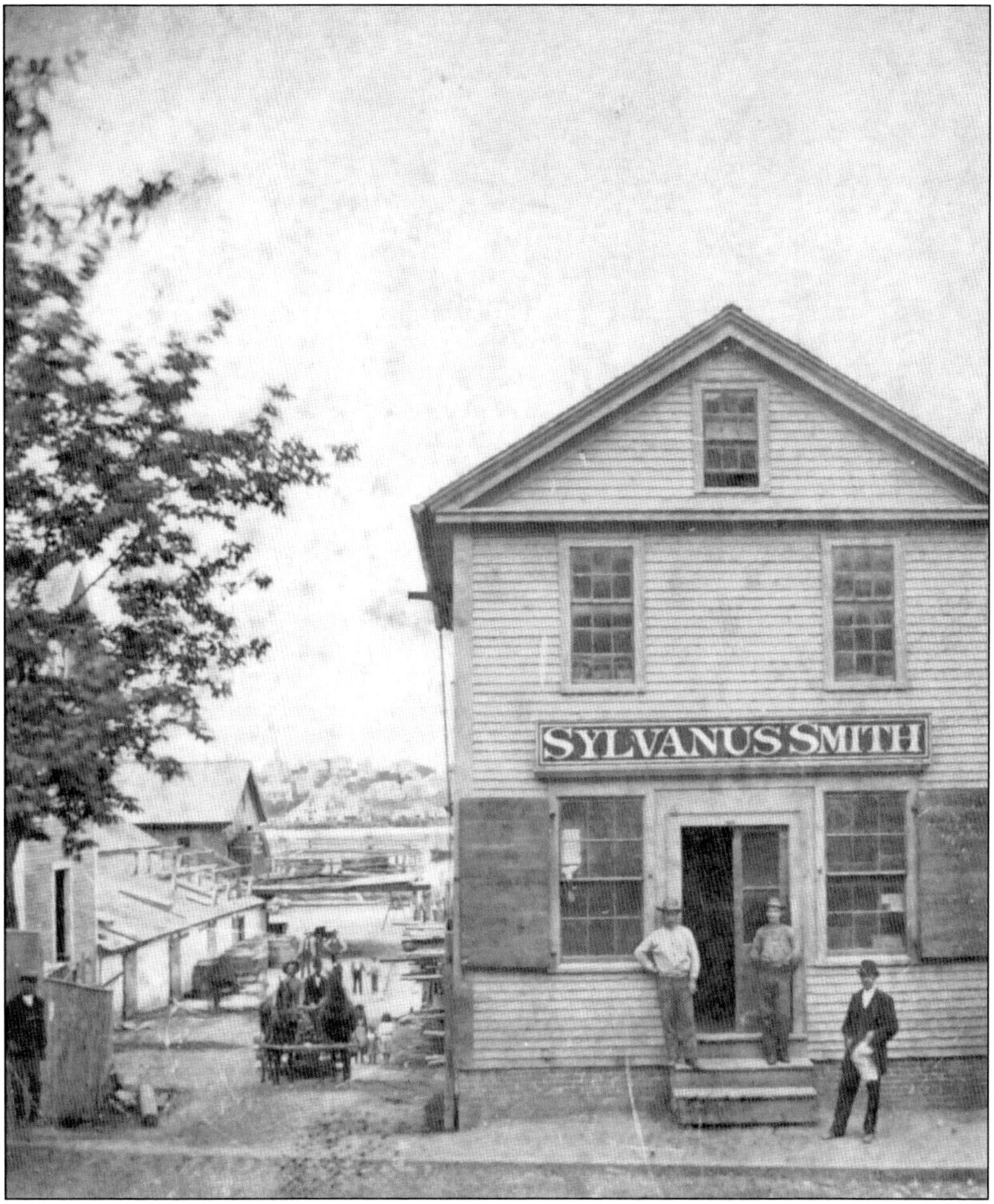

THE STOREFRONT OF SYLVANUS SMITH. Sylvanus Smith & Company, wholesale fish dealers, was established in 1867; the business was listed at 401 Main Street in Gloucester. The firm was among the largest in New England and employed a large fleet of vessels. Smith, a native of Rockport, was active as the first president of the Gloucester Board of Trade, as a director of the First National Bank, and as a state representative. (No photographer or publisher indicated, but presumably E.G. Rollins.)

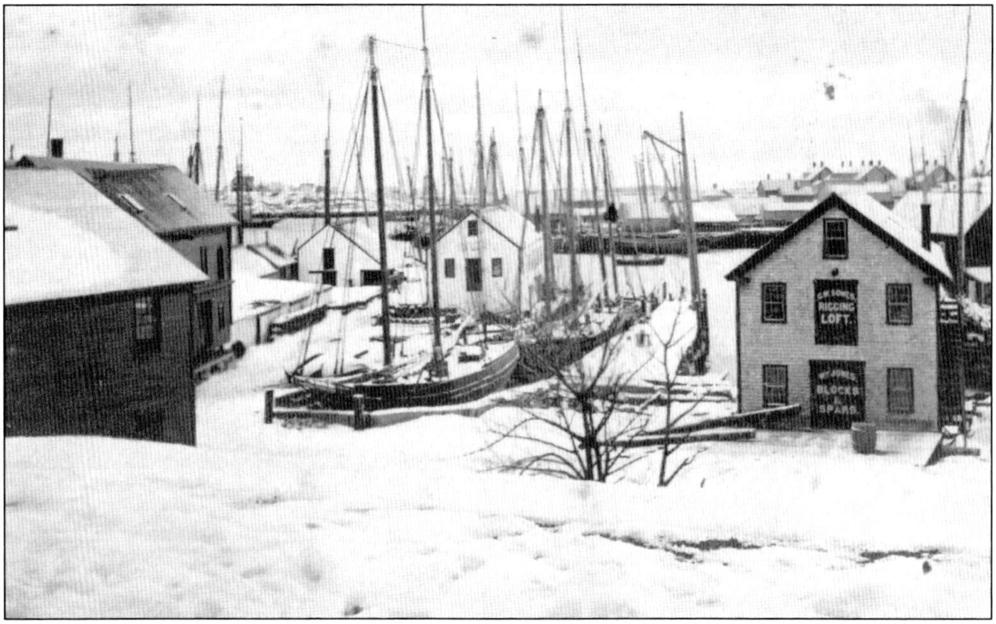

DEAD OF WINTER. All's quiet in Gloucester harbor in these two John Heywood stereoviews taken on a winter's day. The building (above, right) housed the G.W. Somes Rigging Loft and W.T. Jones Blocks & Spars, *c.* 1865. Heywood photographed this harbor view (below) a few years later from about the same spot and issued the image in a differently numbered series. Norman's Woe is barely visible in the background. The harbor would come to life again in early March.

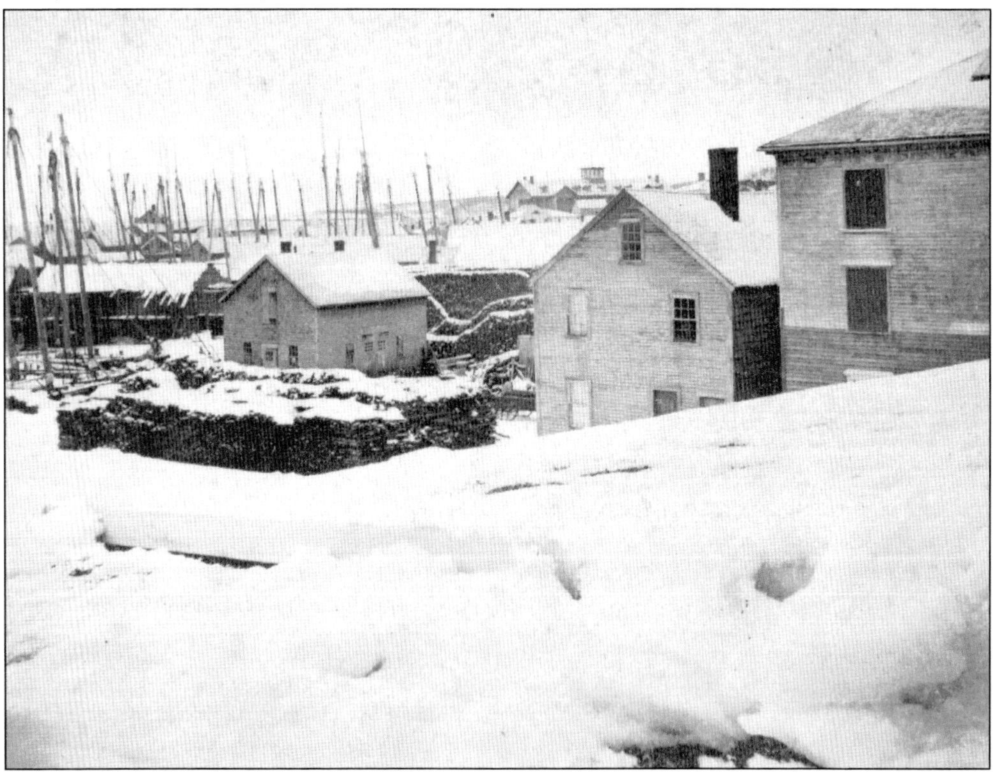

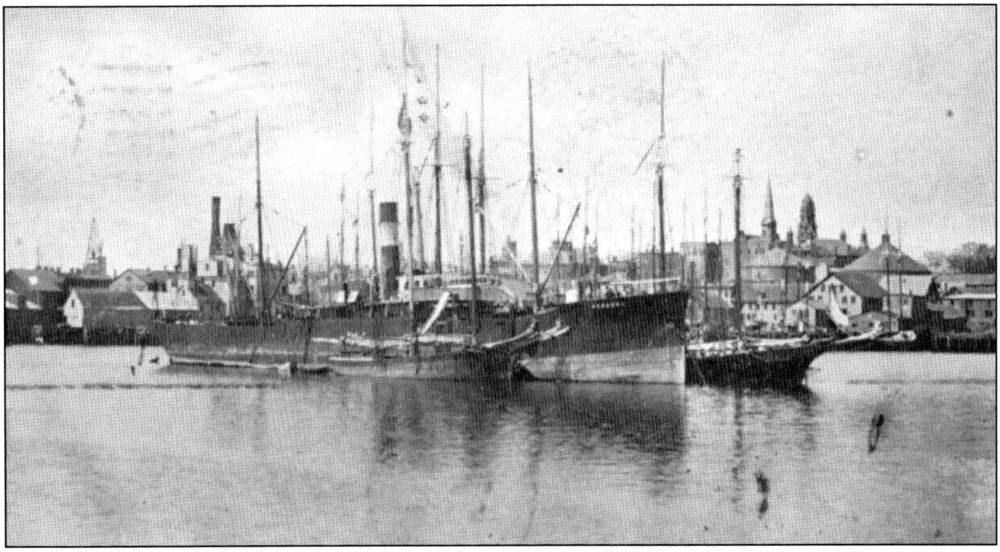

Discharging Salt and In Tow. In the early-1900s photo postcard above, a salt steamer is at anchor in the harbor. At least two schooners, visible alongside, take on the vital preservative, which would be stored below deck. Below, in a photo postcard from the same time, a steam tug helps ease a two-masted schooner toward its pier at right.

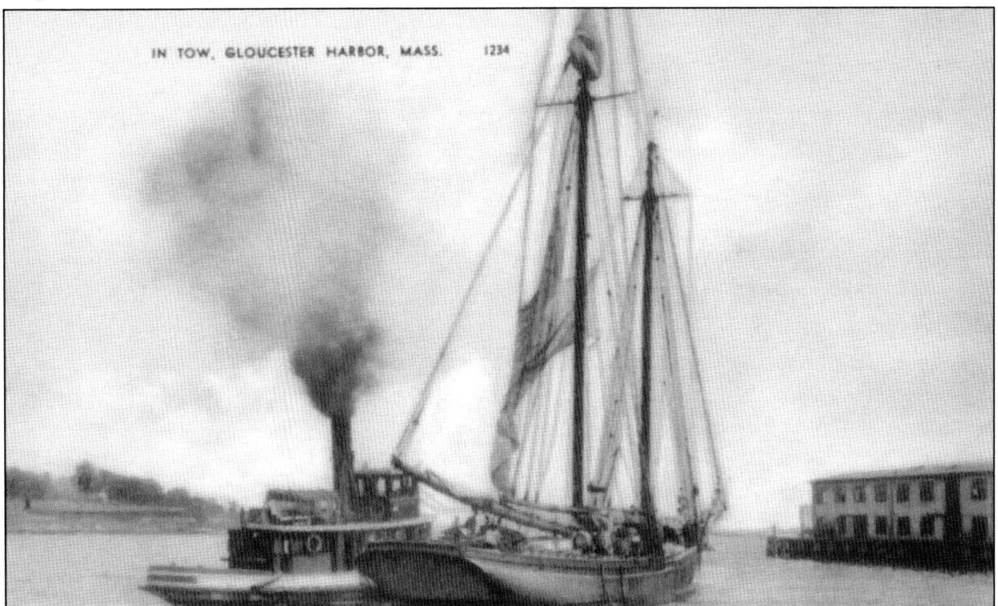

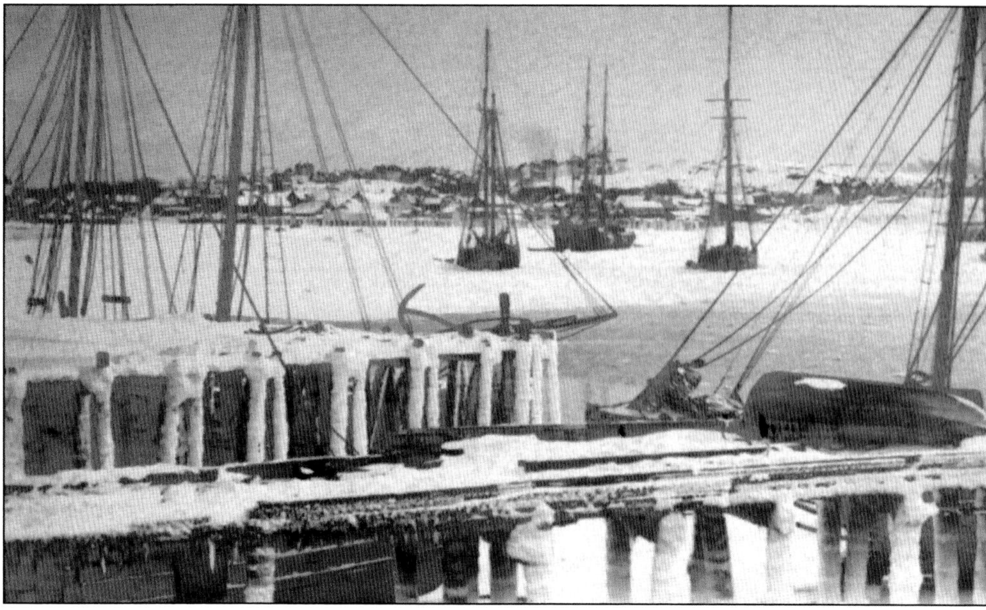

Another Hard Winter and the Fish Hatchery. Three schooners lie at anchor in the harbor ice (above) in this real photo postcard taken during the hard winter of 1905. Two of the vessels ride low, indicating they were caught by the freeze before unloading their cargoes. The early-1900s postcard below shows the U.S. Fish Hatchery Station on Ten Pound Island in Gloucester harbor. Started in 1887 (or 1889 by another account), the station hatched codfish and lobster in an effort to maintain its stocks.

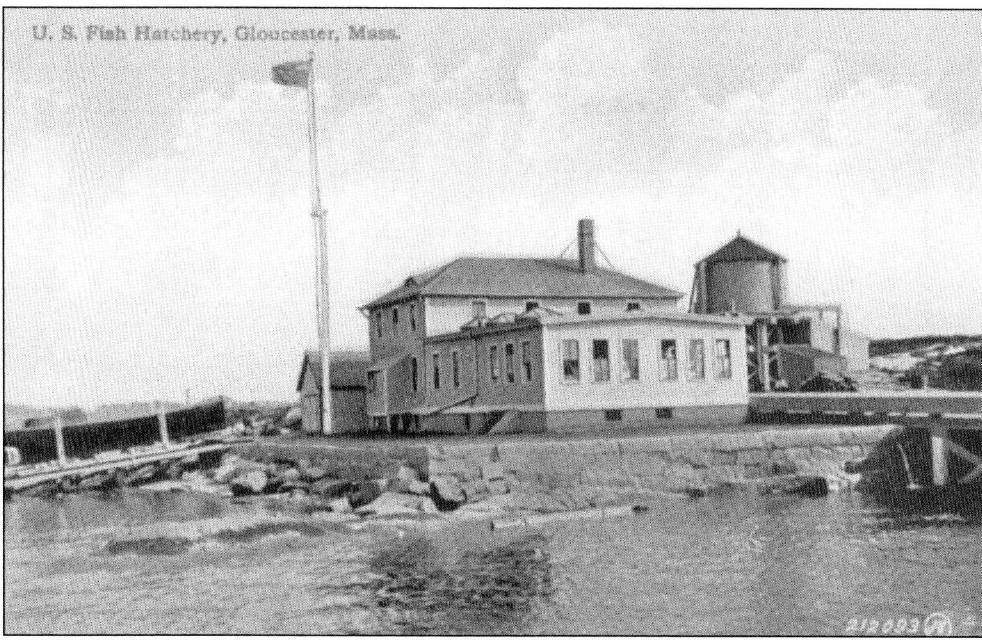

Three

ON SHORE

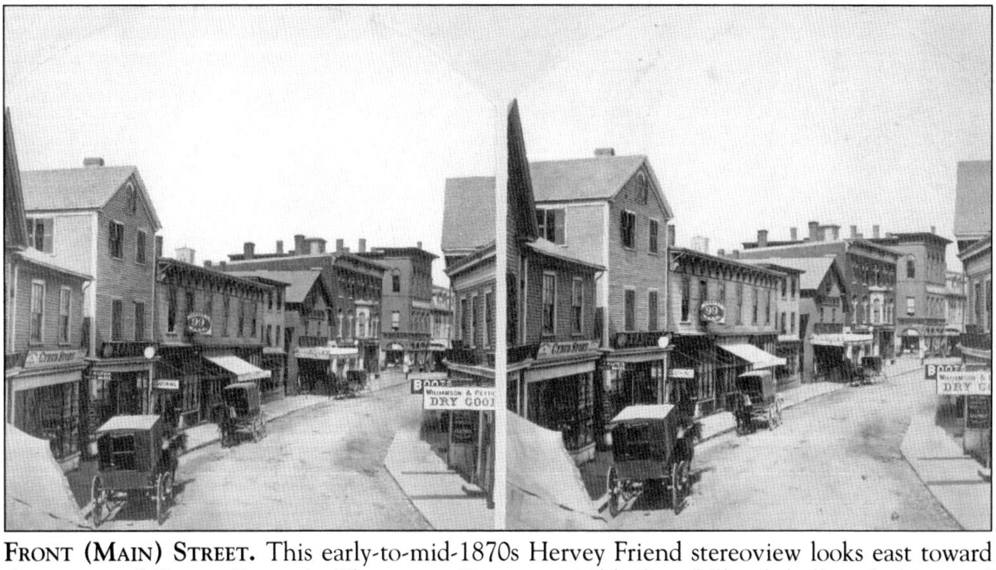

FRONT (MAIN) STREET. This early-to-mid-1870s Hervey Friend stereoview looks east toward the corner of Center Street in Gloucester. Signs are visible for a billiards hall, a clothing and dry goods stores, and a dress maker. Friend may well have taken this photograph himself from the building that housed his studio; he was listed at 77 1/2 Front Street in 1872.

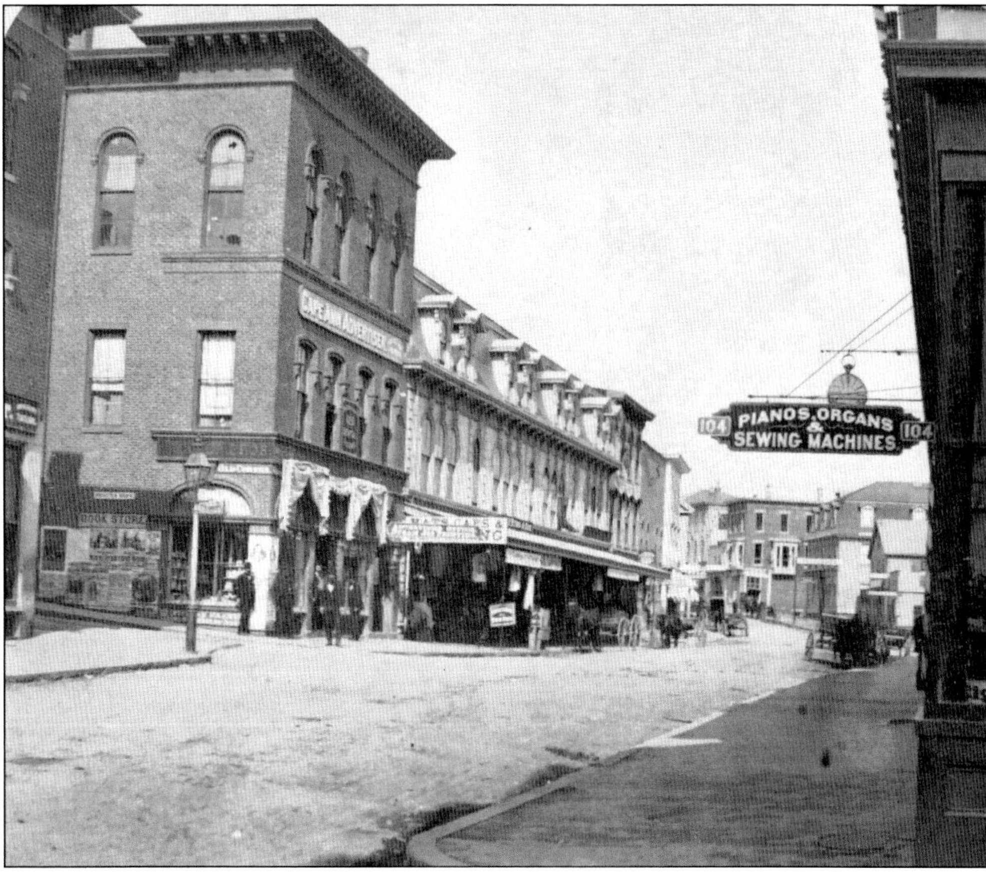

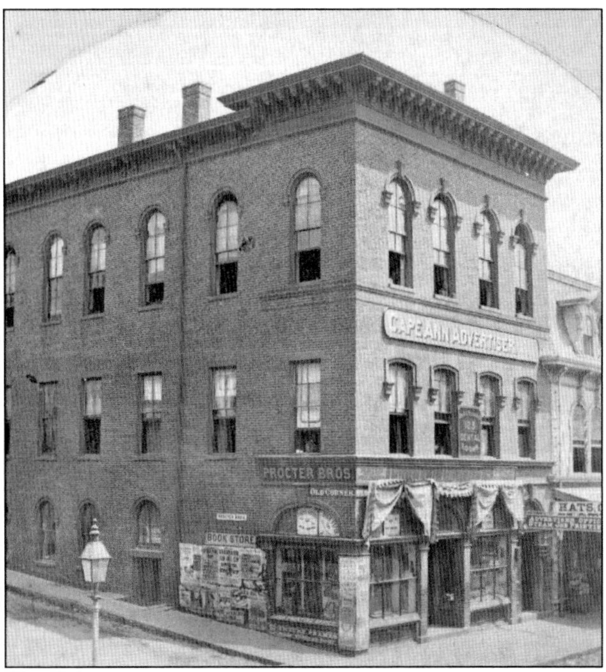

THE OLD CORNER. Procter Brothers published this early-1870s stereoview, No. 17, (above) in a Cape Ann Scenery series. The image looks east on Front Street in Gloucester toward the "Old Corner" at left. The mid-1870s view (left), photographed and published by Cook & Friend, takes a closer look at the bookstore at 123 Front Street, later known as Main Street. Brothers Francis and George H. Procter were proprietors of the firm, which published the *Cape Ann Advertiser* and, later, the *Gloucester Daily Times* newspapers.

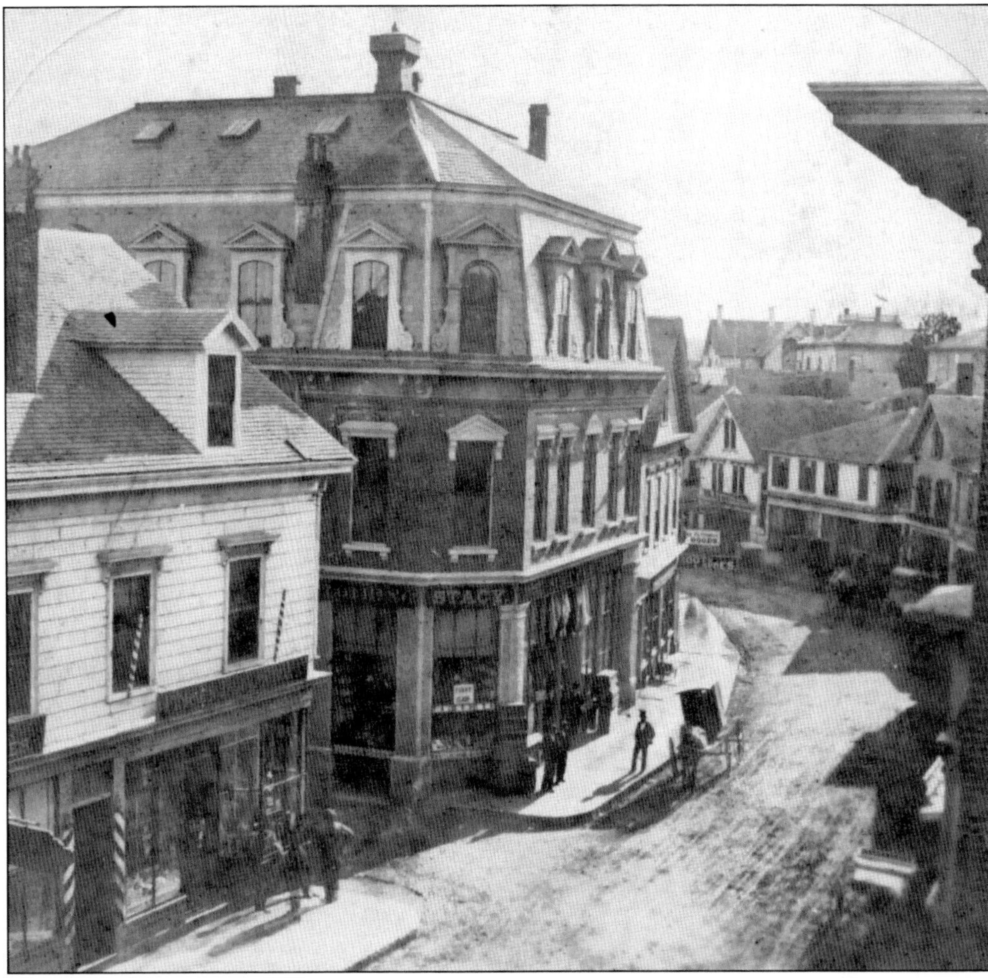

BUSINESS CENTER. Two more fine 1870s stereoscopic images show parts of Front Street in Gloucester, which teemed with commercial activity among the shop owners and traders. The Procter Brothers image (above) looks west from Hough's Block. Stacy's Clothing Store is at center. The buildings to the far right were later torn down, and the area became terraces and gardens for the Sargent-Murray-Gilman House. The E.G. Rollins view (right), looking west, was taken before horse-drawn trolleys appeared. It shows a billiards parlor, sellers of boots and shoes, stoves, clothes, and six gents posing for the photographer on Front Street.

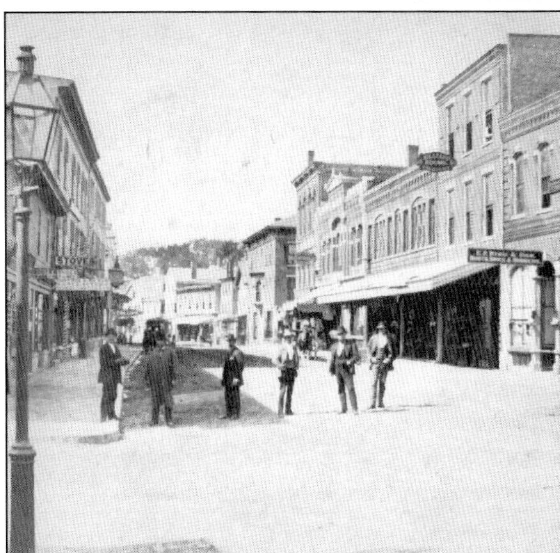

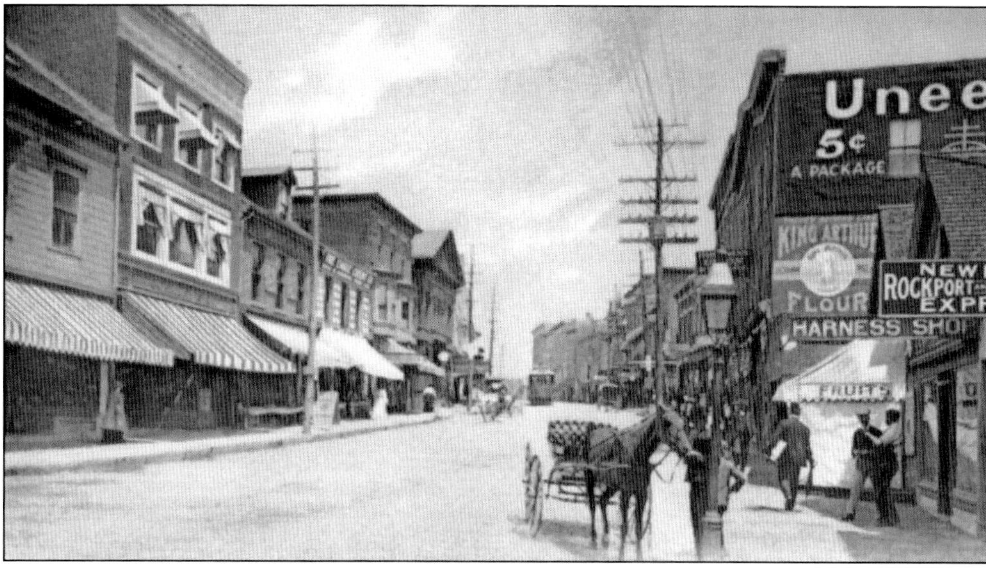

Main Street. In 1864, a wind-whipped fire destroyed a great many of Front Street's businesses and residences. During the reconstruction that followed, Front Street, along with Spring, Union Hill, and Jackson Streets, became one and were renamed Main Street in 1878. Trolleys pulled by horses arrived *c.* 1885; they became electrified in 1890. Here, in two postcards published in the early 1900s (but taken from earlier images), Main Street is alive with horse-drawn carriages, trolleys, and people strolling and shopping.

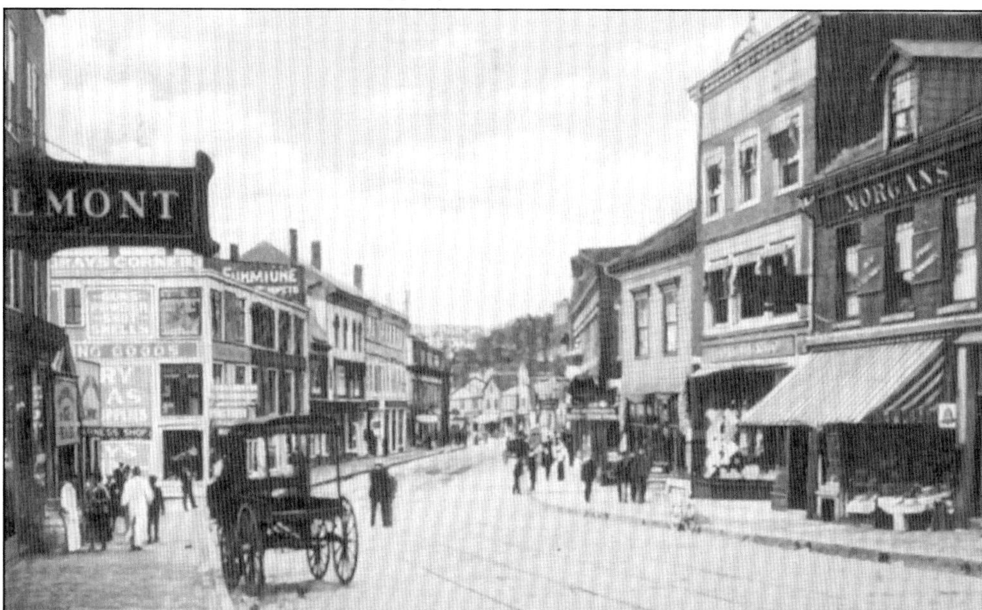

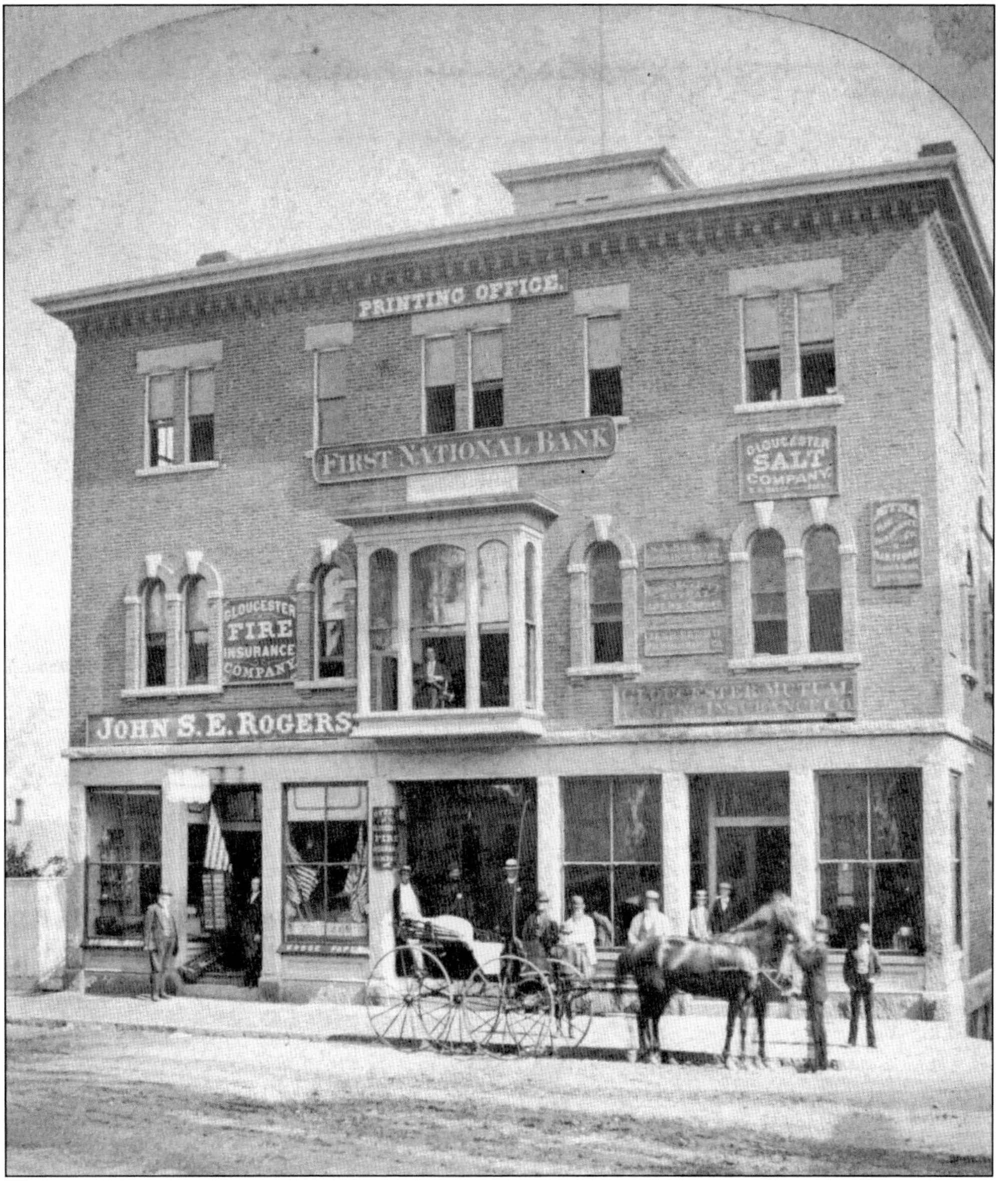

A GLOUCESTER PHOTOGRAPHER'S STUDIO. This *c.* 1870 stereoview with a John S.E. Rogers backlabel shows the First National Bank building at Low's Block. The building, on the corner of Spring and Duncan Streets, was erected in 1864 by Capt. Frederick G. Low and was later purchased by First National Bank. Rogers's studio and rooms appear at the lower left. Other signs are for the Gloucester Salt Company, the Gloucester Fire Insurance Company, the Gloucester Mutual Fishing Insurance Company, and a printing office upstairs.

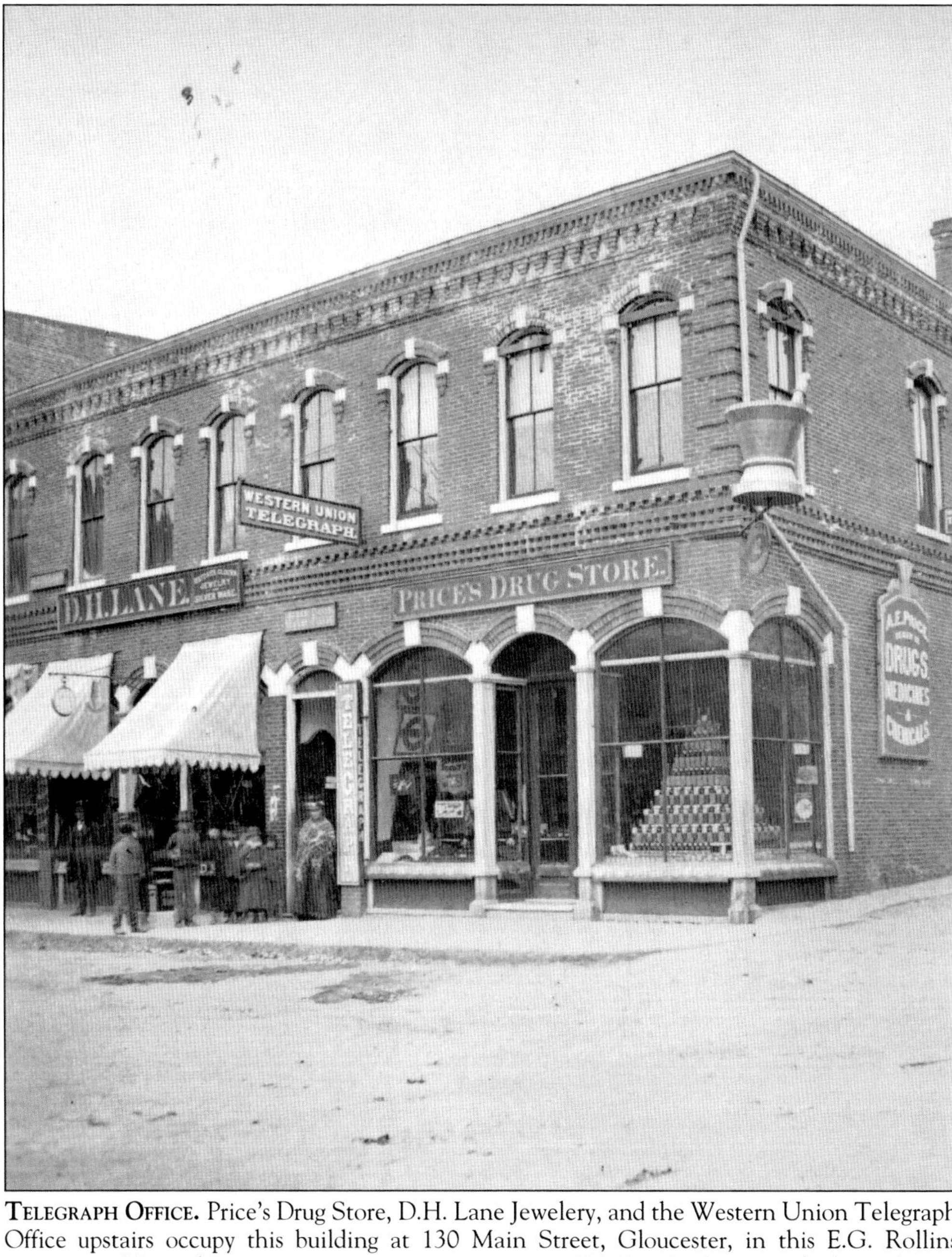

TELEGRAPH OFFICE. Price's Drug Store, D.H. Lane Jewelery, and the Western Union Telegraph Office upstairs occupy this building at 130 Main Street, Gloucester, in this E.G. Rollins stereoview. Howard Lane was a state representative in 1892. Lane's also carried a line of Cape Ann Scenery photographs.

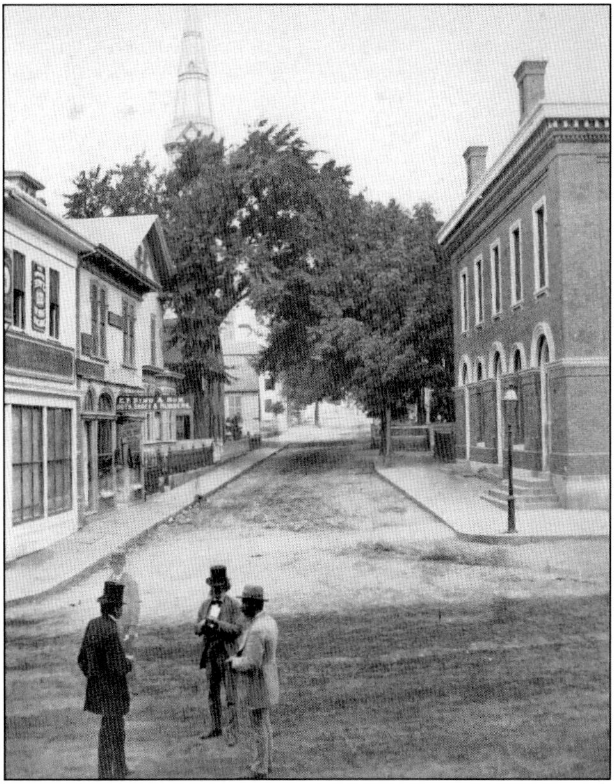

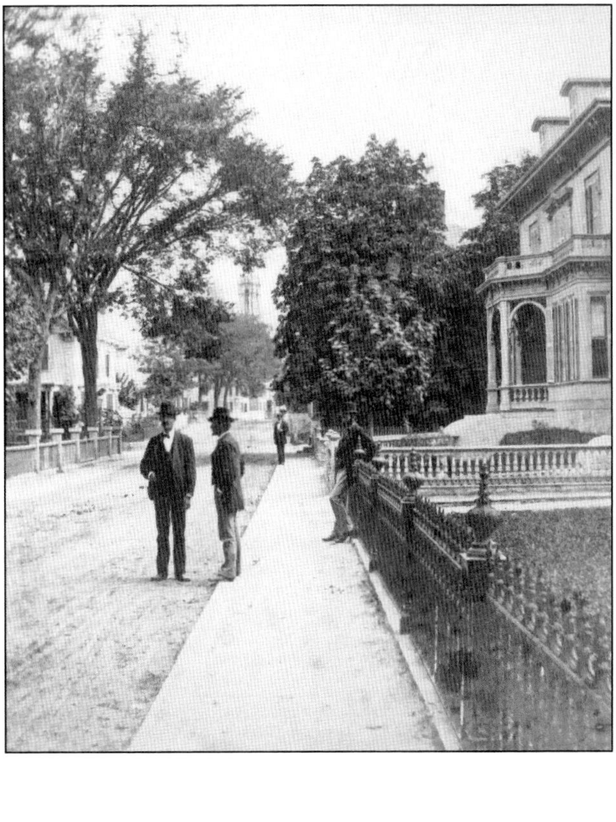

PLEASANT AND MIDDLE STREETS. Looking up Pleasant Street from Main (above), Wetherell's Drug Store is on the left and the customs house and post office are on the right. The steeple of the Baptist church looms in the rear above the trees. With two gents posed in the foreground to heighten the stereoscopic effect (left), we look east up Middle Street from Washington Street. Middle Street was graced with lovely homes of the rich and well-to-do. Both stereoviews come from a fine series of Gloucester street scenes published by E.G. Rollins.

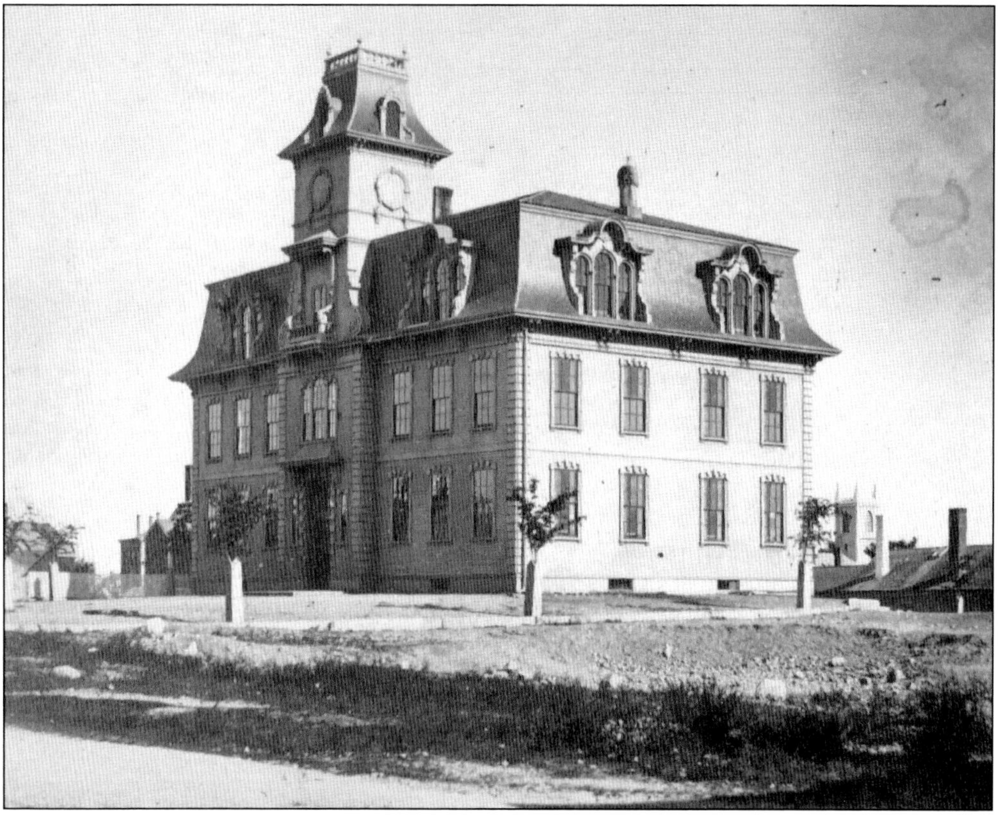

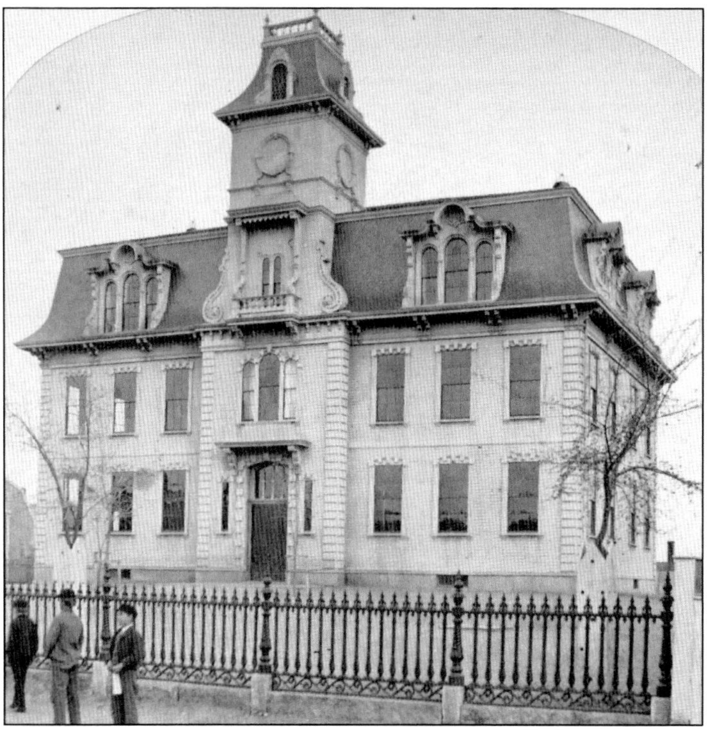

The Collins School House, Gloucester. Erected in 1864 and dedicated in September of that year, this handsome building on High Street derives its name from Madame Collins, who gave the land on which the building stands to the city. No. 97 (top) comes from a Cape Ann Scenery series published by John S.E. Rogers. The view at left comes from an 1871 series published by the Procter Brothers.

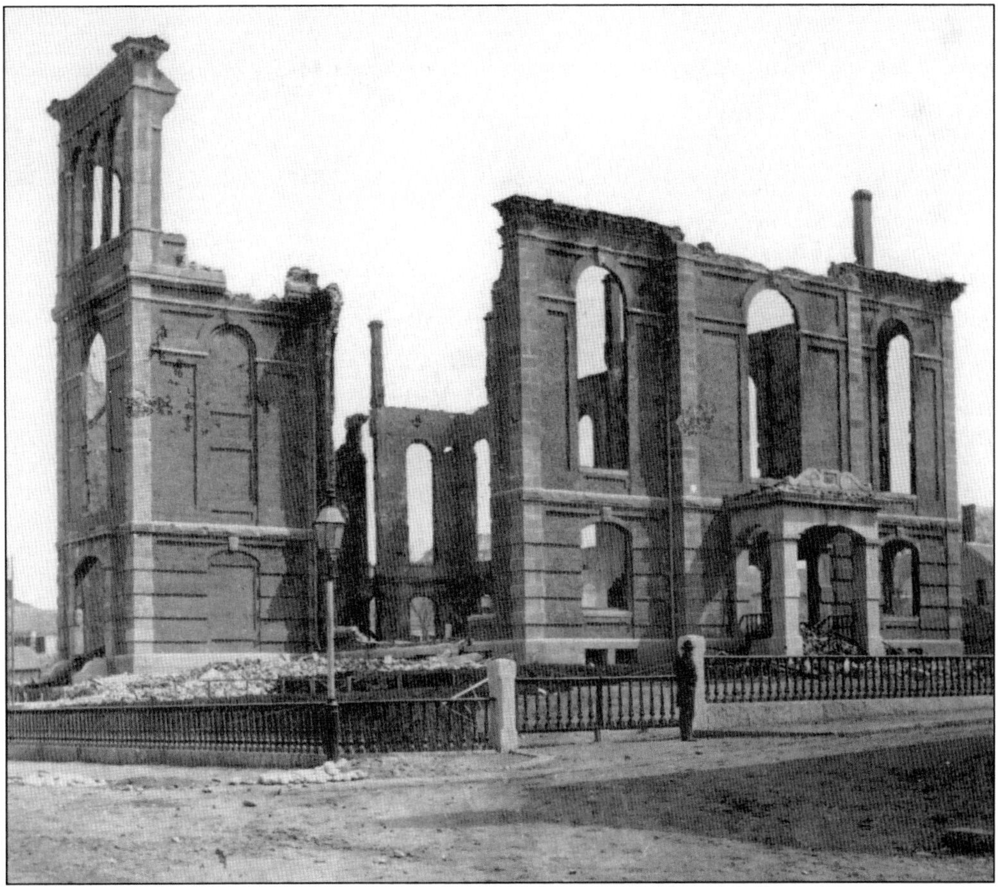

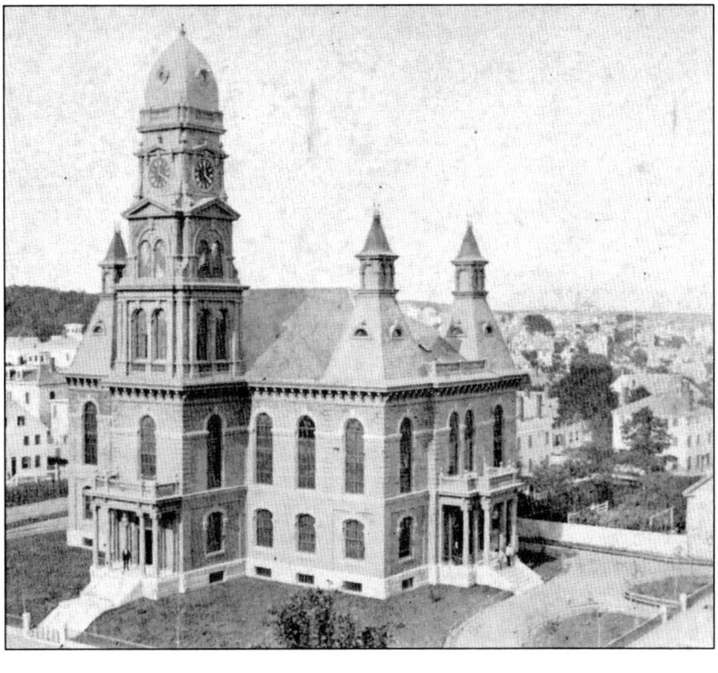

THE GLOUCESTER TOWN HALL. Just two years after this grand building was built, a fire on May 16, 1869, reduced it to a shell of its former self. Citizens of Gloucester took immediate action to rebuild, and a new town hall was dedicated on June 22, 1871. Hervey Friend photographed and published the top view. The view at right comes from a series published by John S.E. Rogers, c. 1872.

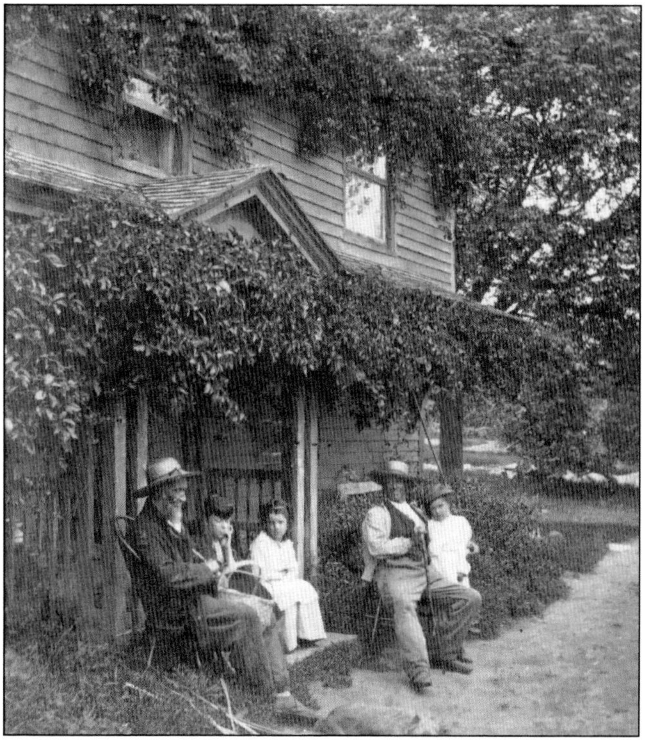

THE OLDEST HOUSE AND THE WITCH HOUSE. These early- and later-vintage stereoviews by J.W. and J.S. Moulton show the Riggs House (left), the oldest house on Cape Ann. It was built by Thomas Riggs *c.* 1660 at Goose Cove in Annisquam. Riggs was the first schoolmaster and town clerk, holding the latter post from 1665 to 1716. The Old Witch House (below) at Pigeon Cove is also known as the Babson House. It was erected *c.* 1898 by three brothers named Babson, who fled from Salem. They hid their mother here after she was accused of being a witch.

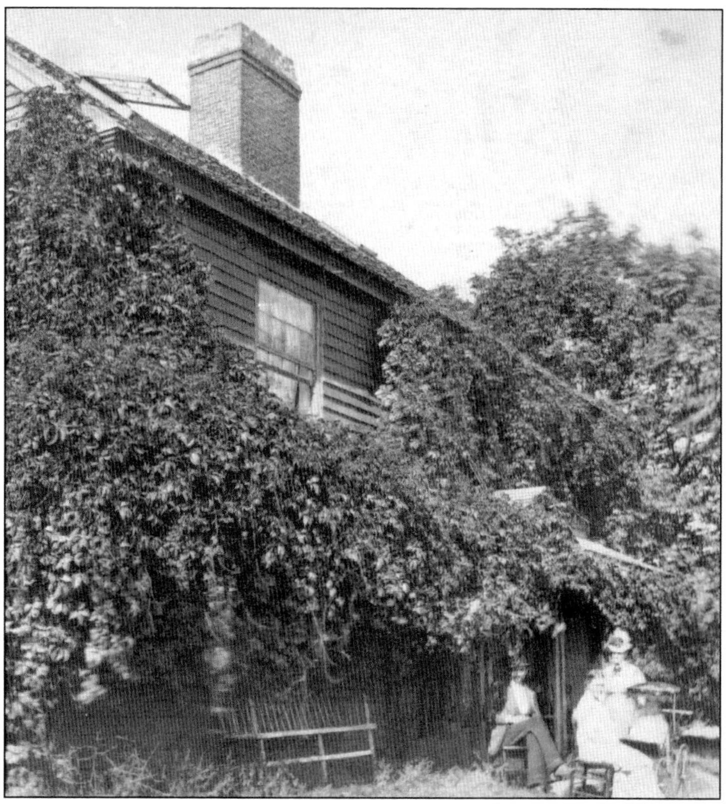

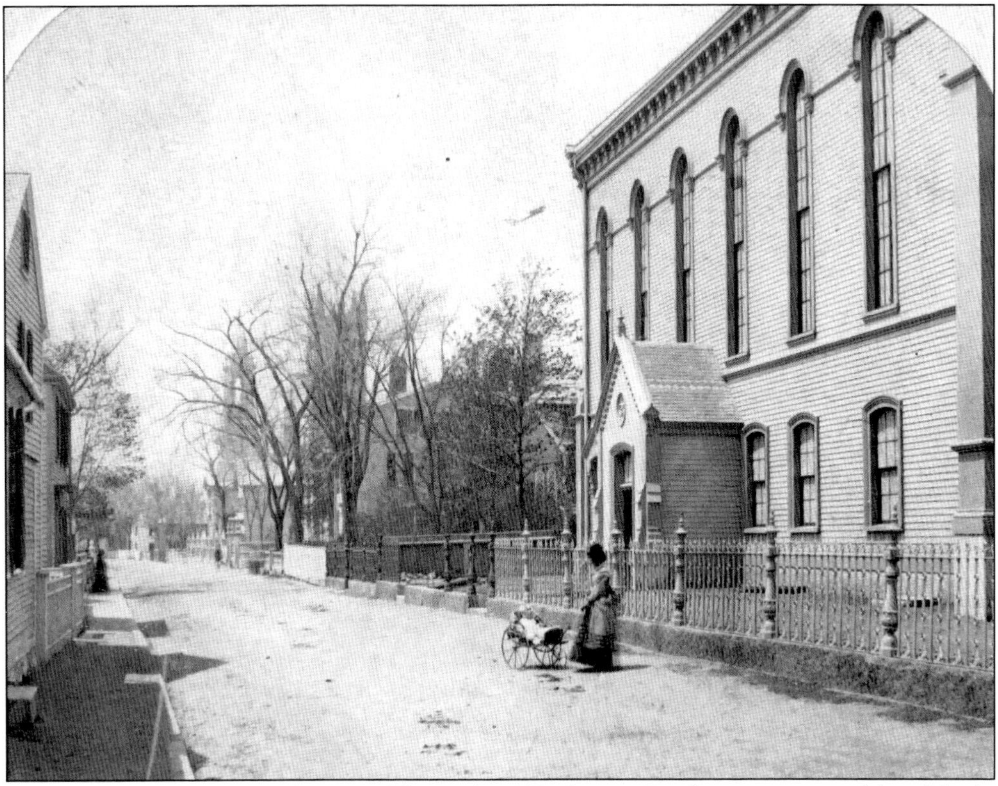

MIDDLE STREET AND DALE AVENUE. This early-1870s Procter Brothers stereoview (above) looks west at the corner of Middle Street and Pleasant Street in Gloucester. A woman and her child in a three-wheeled carriage are in the foreground. Below, in this *c.* 1910 postcard from the Leighton & Valentine Company of Dale Avenue, the Gloucester City Hall towers in the background. The Victorian buildings to the left were razed; the post office currently sits on the site.

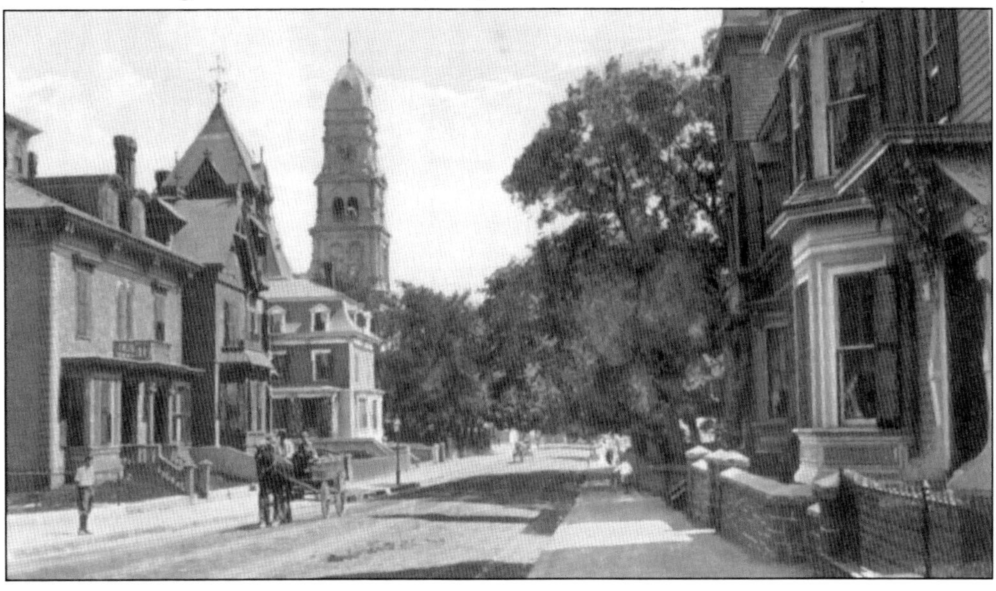

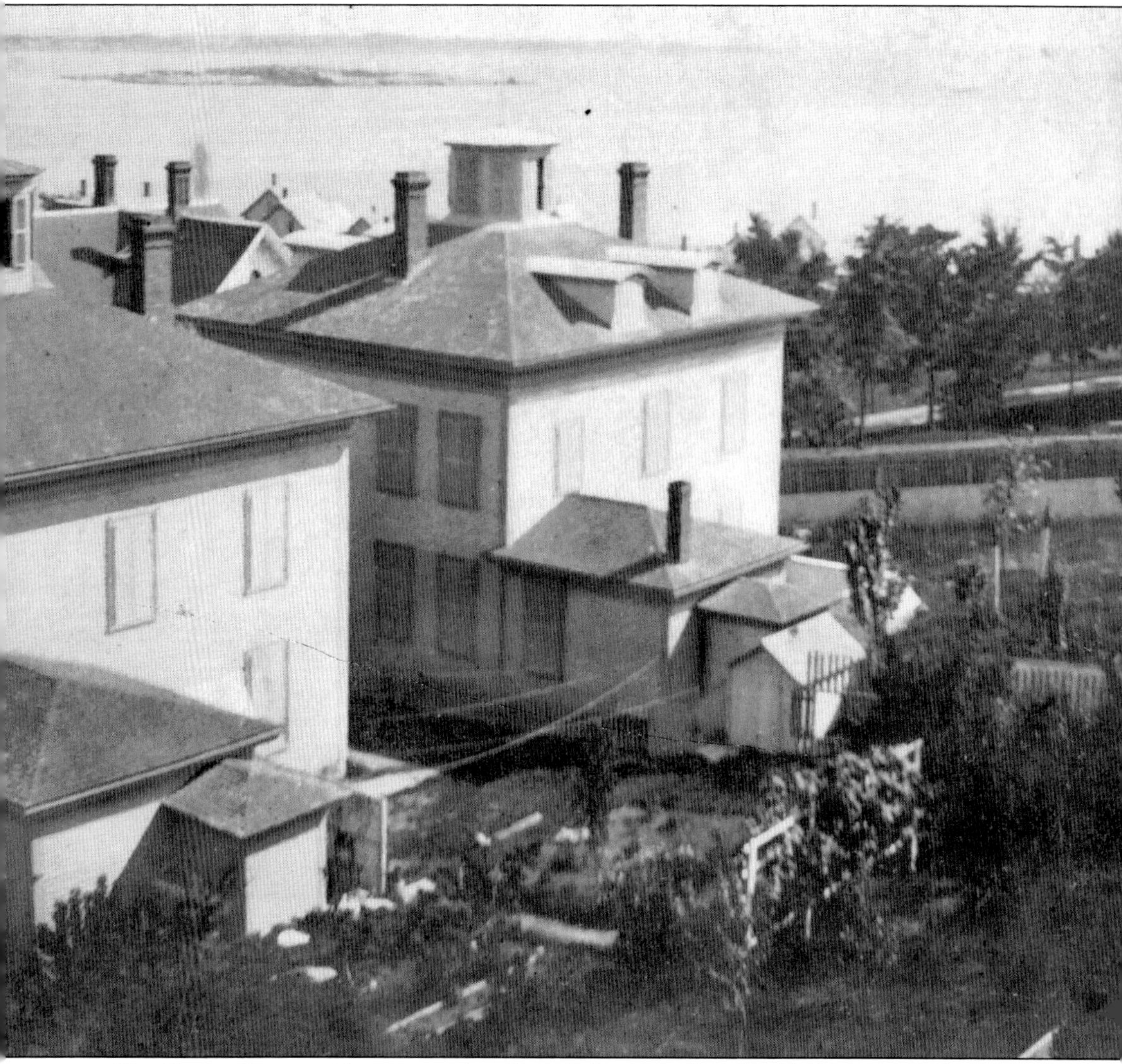

Ten Pound Island. This view, taken from Babson's Hill and published c. 1873 by the Procter Brothers, looks northeast into Gloucester harbor. Through the haze is Ten Pound Island, and beyond that is East Gloucester. Legend has it that Ten Pound Island got its name because that was the sum early settlers allegedly paid the Native Americans for it.

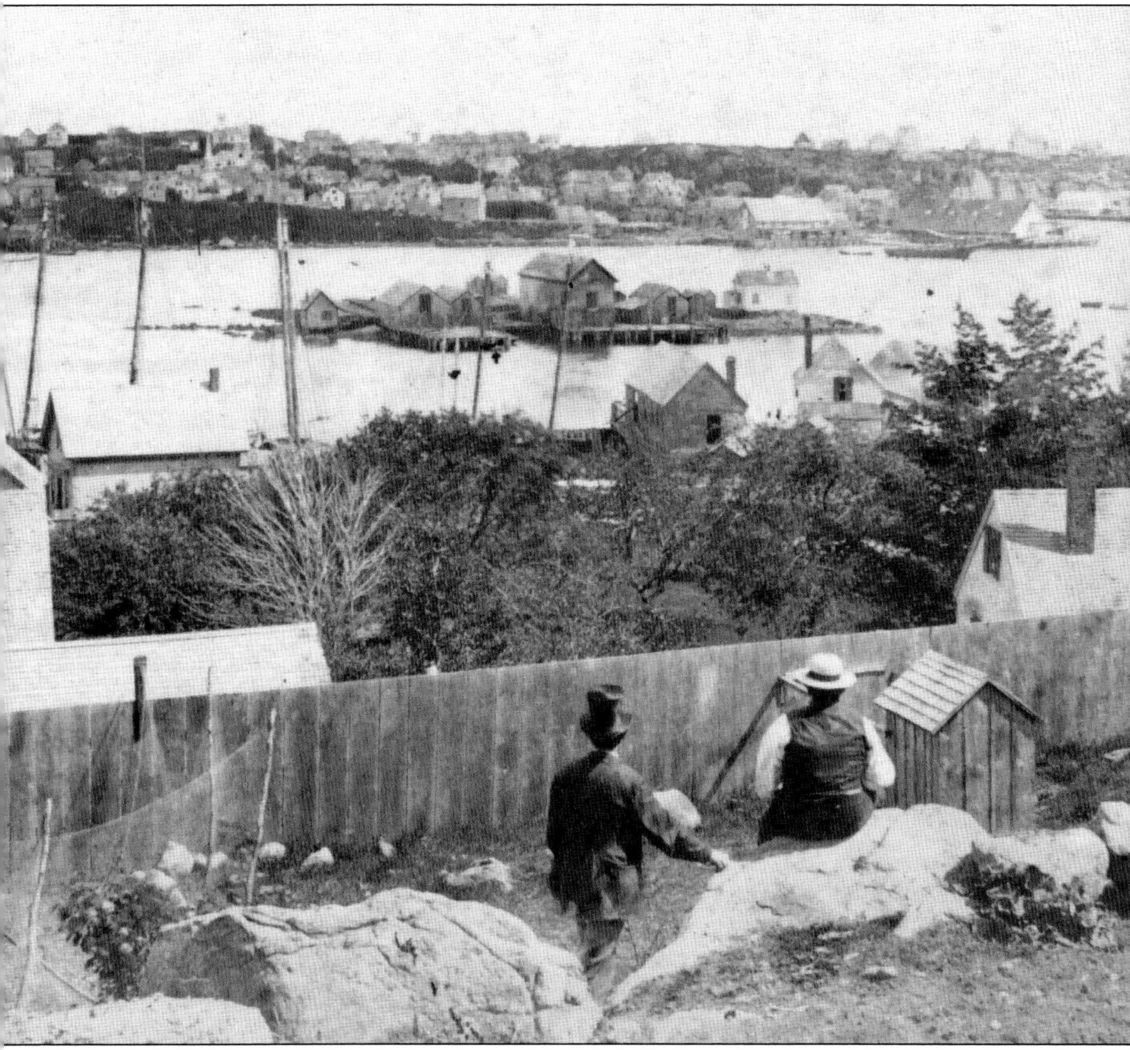

FIVE POUND ISLAND. Located in the center of Gloucester's inner harbor is Five Pound Island, which also takes its name from a transaction with the Native Americans. Here, in this magnificently composed c. 1880s stereoview by J.W. and J.S. Moulton, two gents in the foreground look out upon the island and its fish houses and piers.

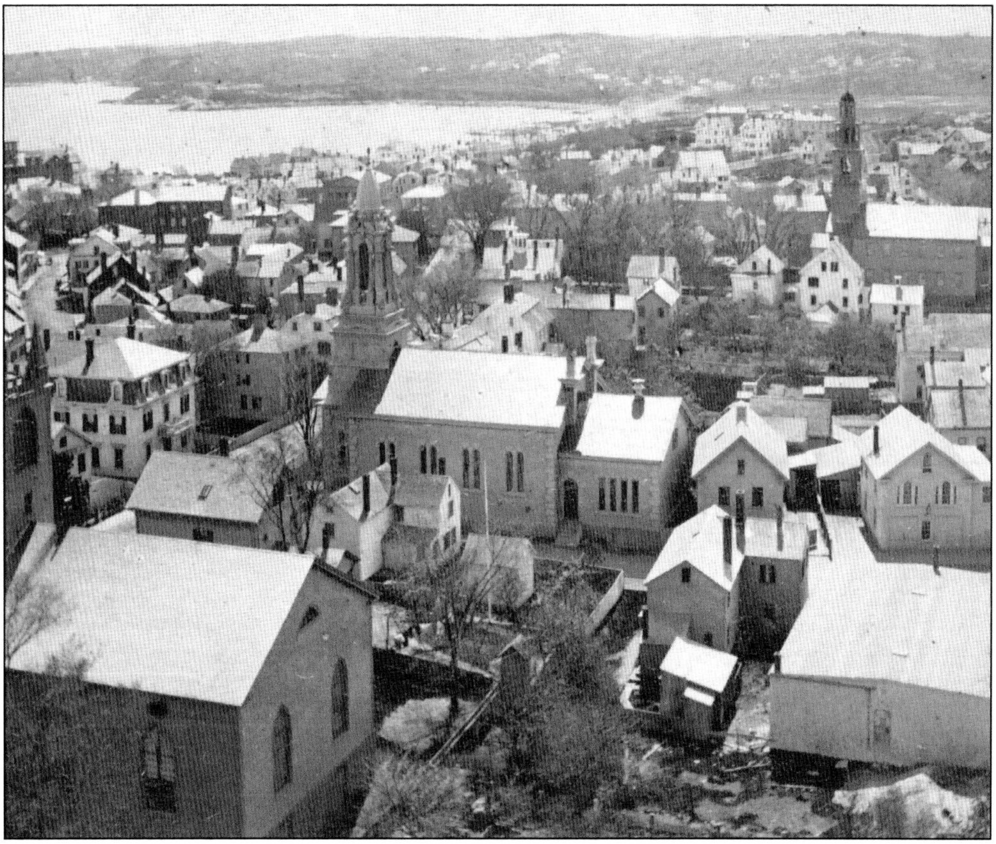

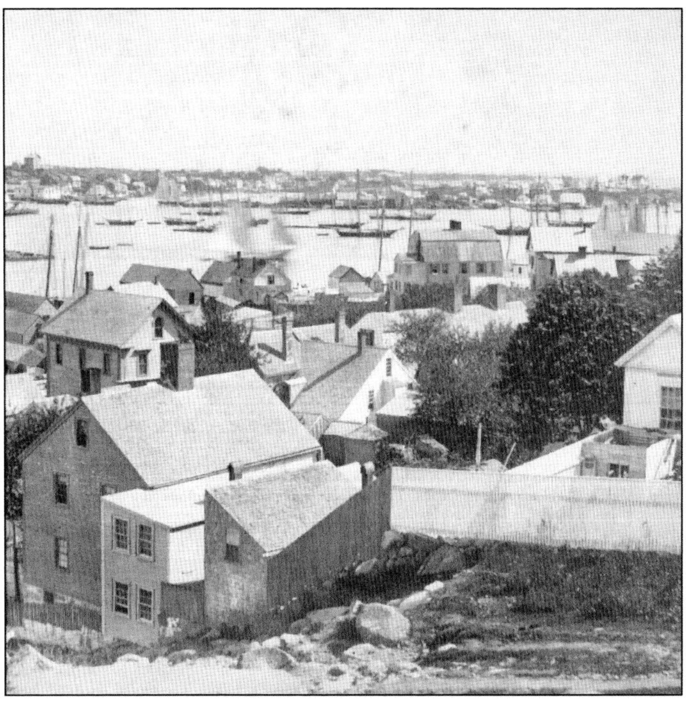

FROM LAND. The early-1870s vista above, photographed by the Procter Brothers from the Gloucester City Hall tower, looks west. The church at left center is the Congregational church. At right is the Universalist church and meetinghouse. The photograph (left) shows a busy harbor from an unidentified maker; it may be a "pirated" Rogers or Procter Brothers view.

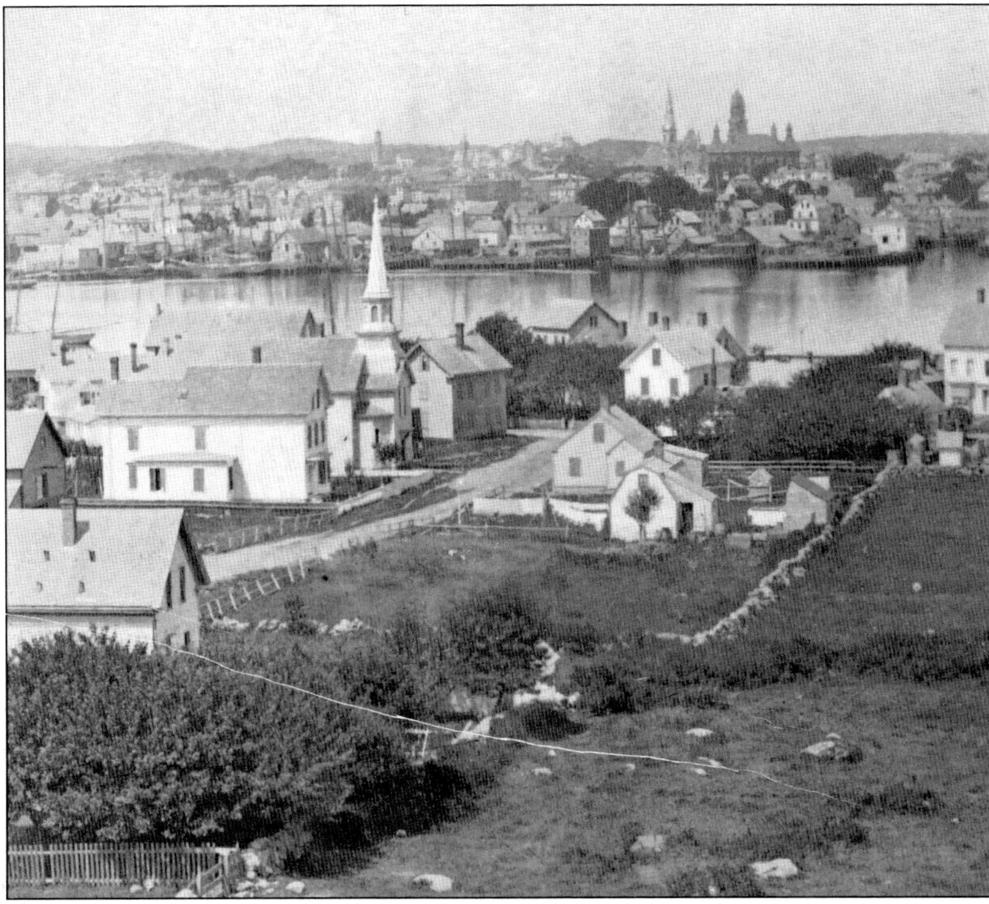

FROM EAST AND WEST. This John S.E. Rogers view (above) of Chapel Street in East Gloucester looks west across the harbor into the city. Prominent in the background are the church steeples on Middle Street and the city hall tower. Pausing during a day's outing, a well-dressed group (right) enjoys a view of the city from Beacon Hill looking southeast. The Procter Brothers produced this card in the mid-to-late 1880s.

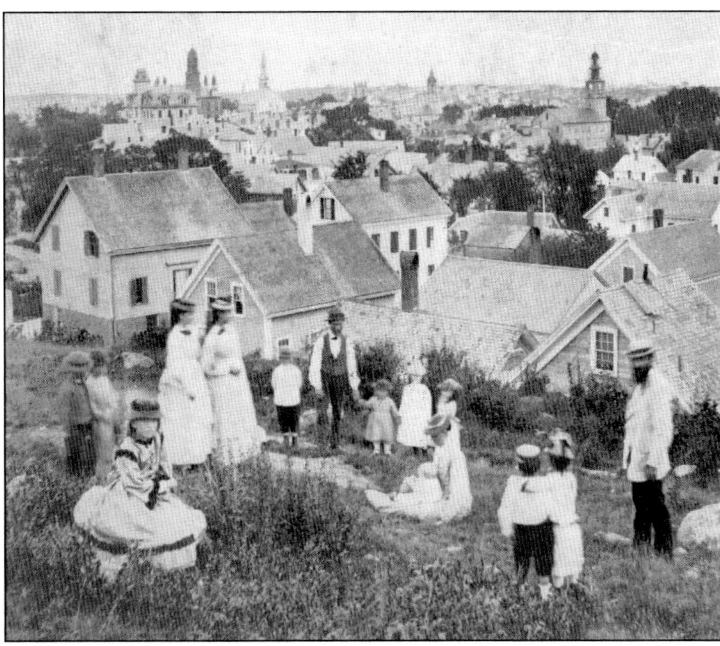

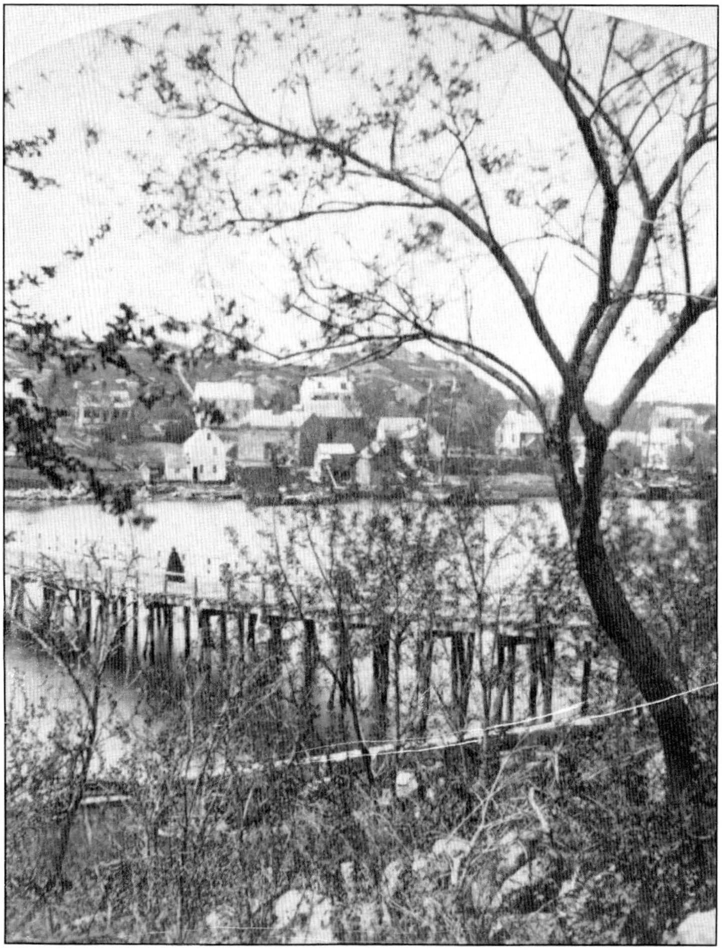

ANNISQUAM. The quaint, picturesque village of Annisquam, with its rustic overlooks, beautiful summer homes, beaches, dunes along the Annisquam River, and coves is the oldest settled section of Gloucester. The village derives a part of its name from *squam*, said to be a Native American word descriptive of a harbor in the mouth of a river. The Procter Brothers produced the early stereoview at left. The early-1900s real photo postcard below shows Squam's Lobster Cove and the village church, originally built in 1728, at the head of the cove.

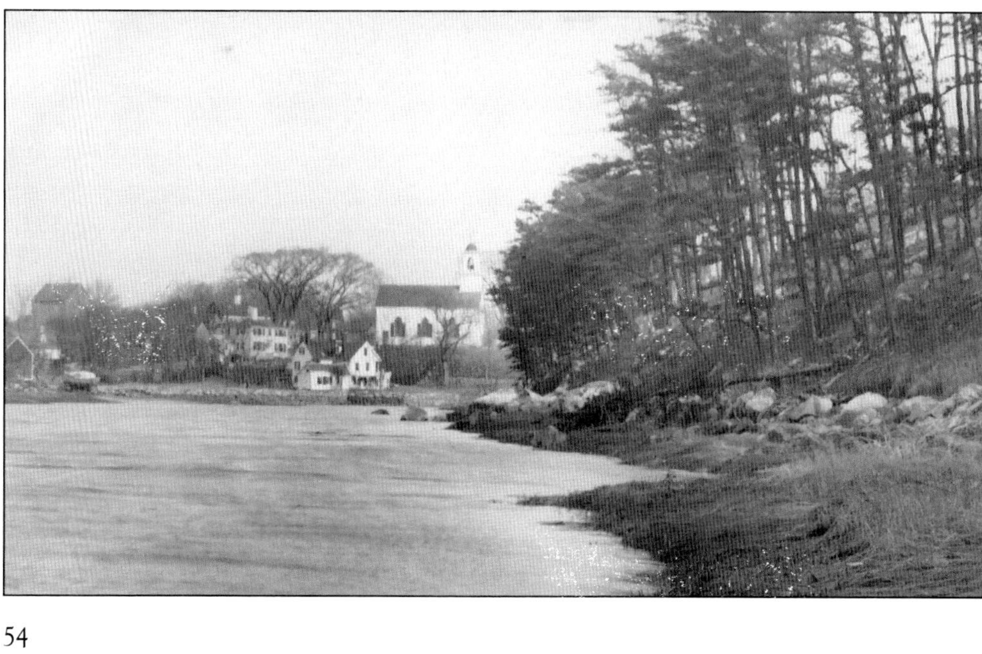

RIVERDALE. A couple of boys (right) take advantage of the view from "the Poles," or Poles Hill as it was called, and gaze upon the Mill River and tidal dam in background at Riverdale. Here, the oldest of Gloucester's mills were built over the river in the mid-1600s. The first one was a sawmill, followed later by a corn mill, as shown in these two stereoviews. E.G. Rollins produced the photograph at right c. 1875. The bottom photograph was copied, or "pirated," from an unknown maker.

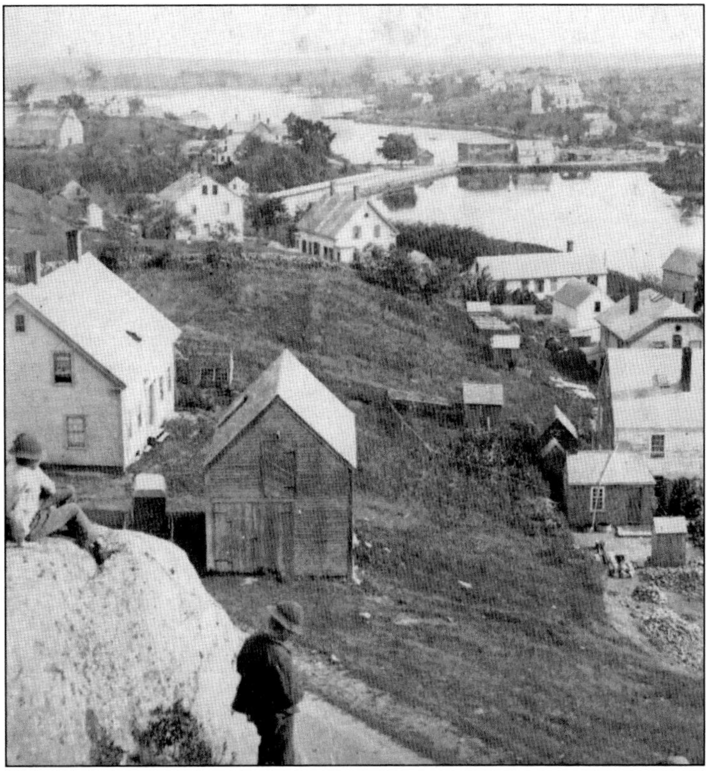

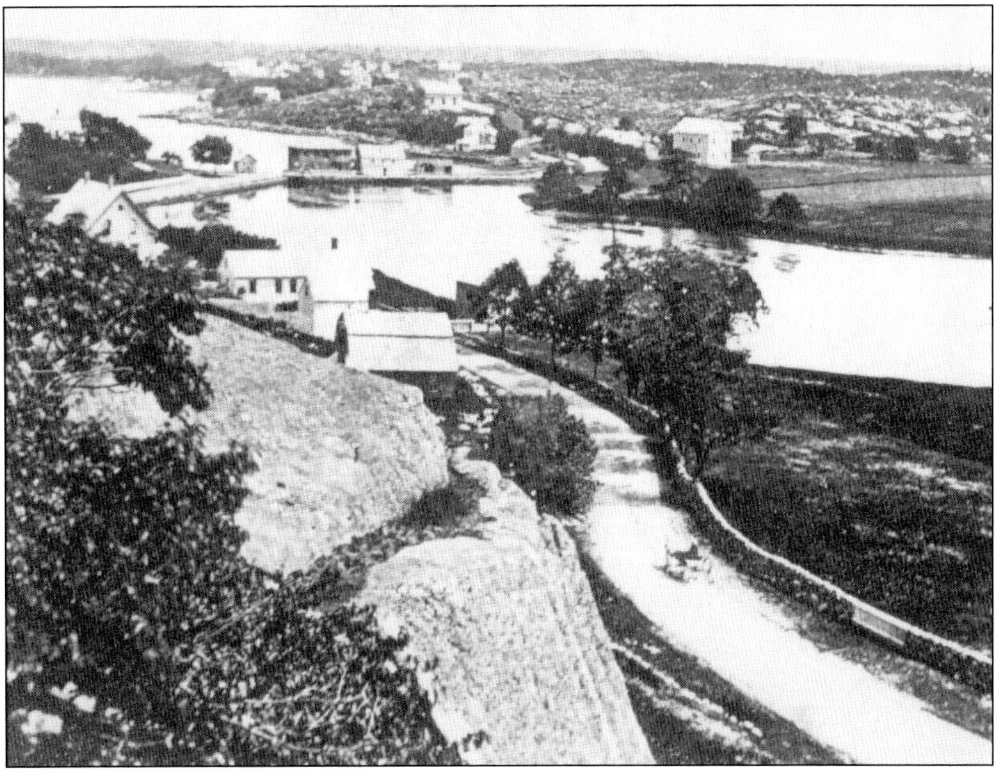

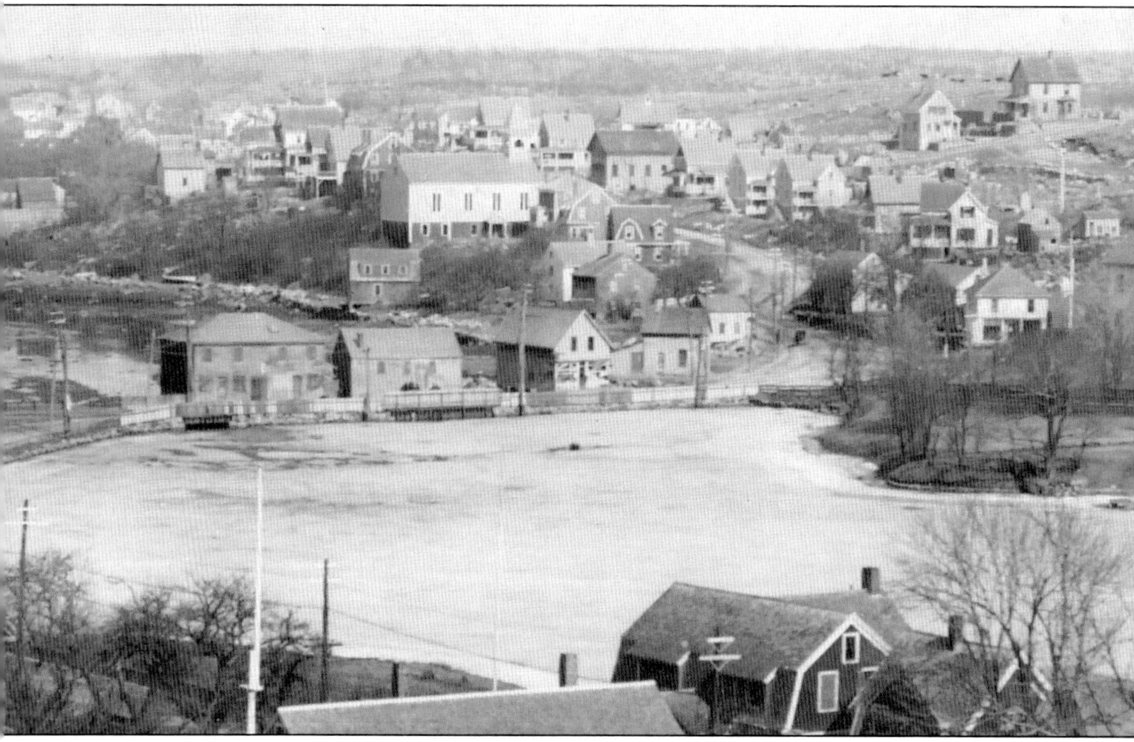

A Closer Look. The old corn mill at Riverdale was probably still in operation when this early-1900s real photo postcard was taken. The dam and the sluiceway are visible before the storehouse, at left center, and adjacent milling building.

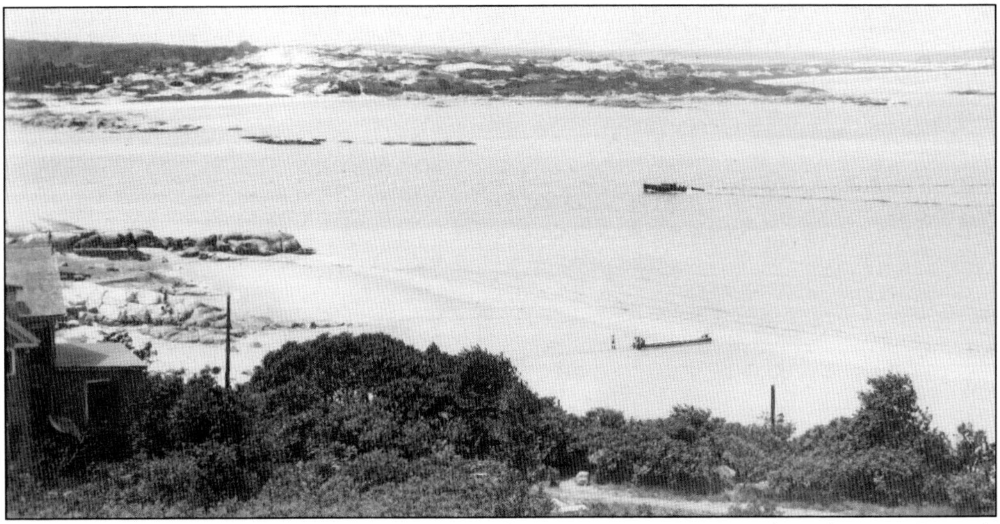

SQUAM'S BEAUTY AND GRACE. The beauty of the Annisquam River and its dunes at Ipswich Bay (above, in an early-1900s postcard) has attracted many a summer visitor; the shores are lined with magnificent summer homes and cottages. A penciled notation on the verso of the Procter Brothers stereoview below says this pleasant home-cottage was in Annisquam. Notice the quite distinctive gazebo at left; its base and stairway fit into the huge rock. Three women, a child, and a housemaid enjoy the surroundings.

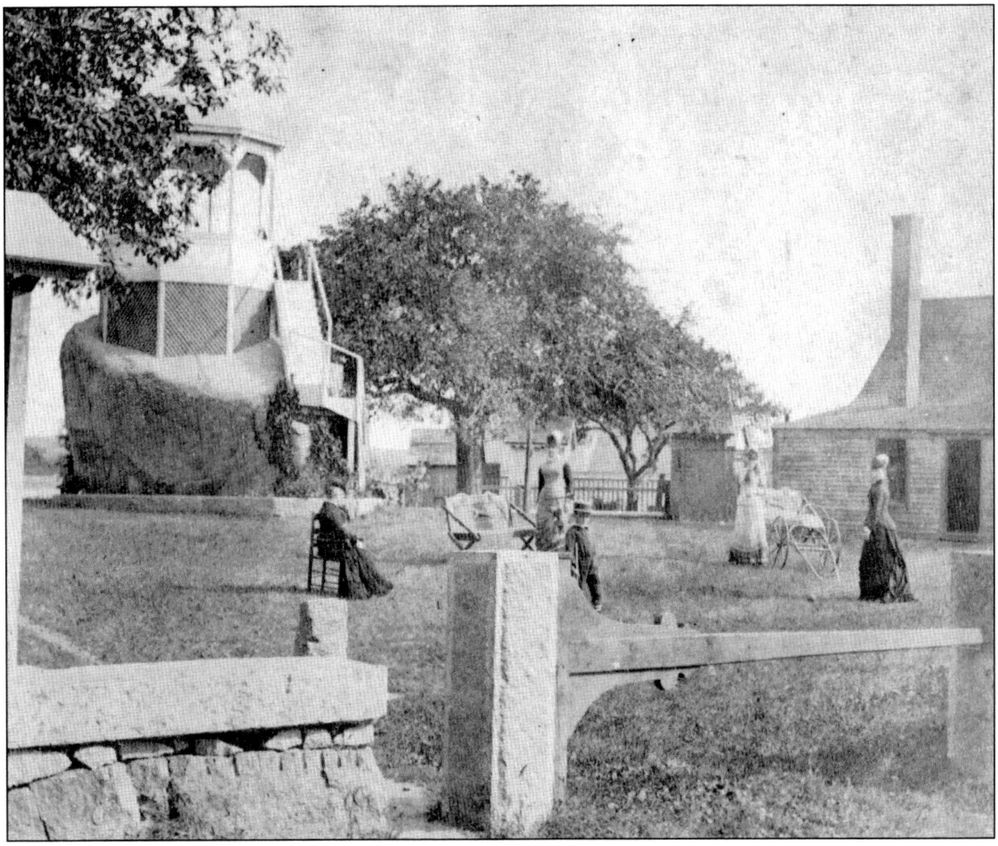

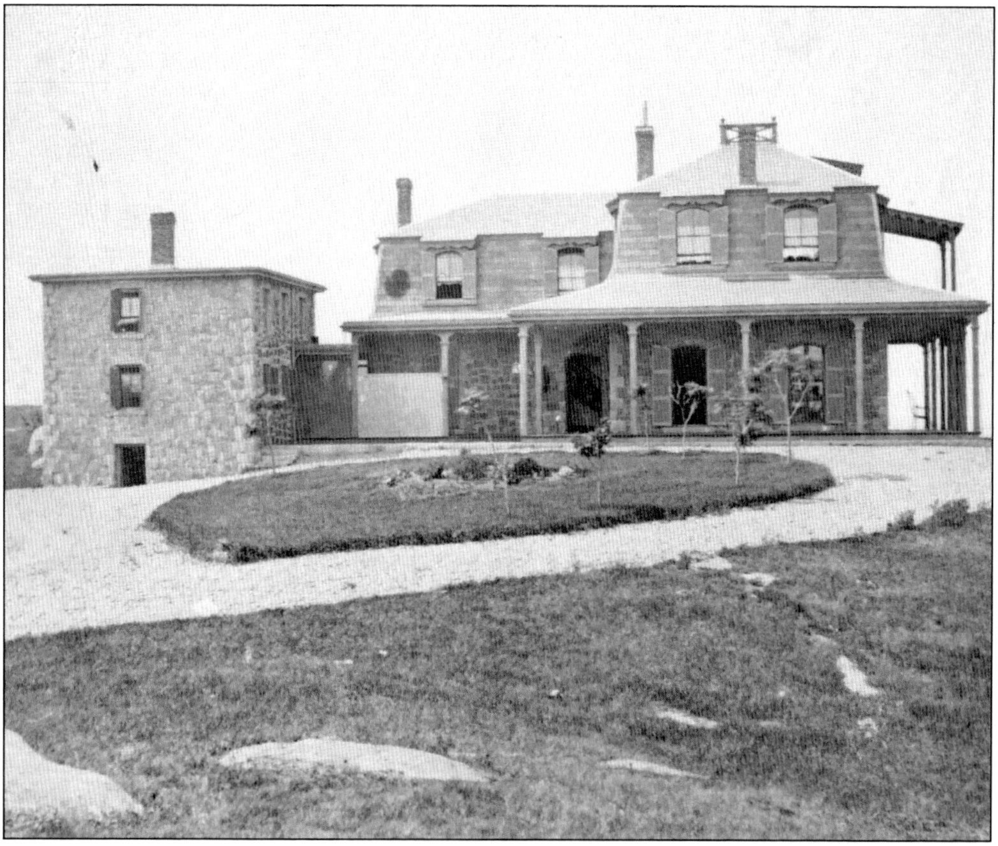

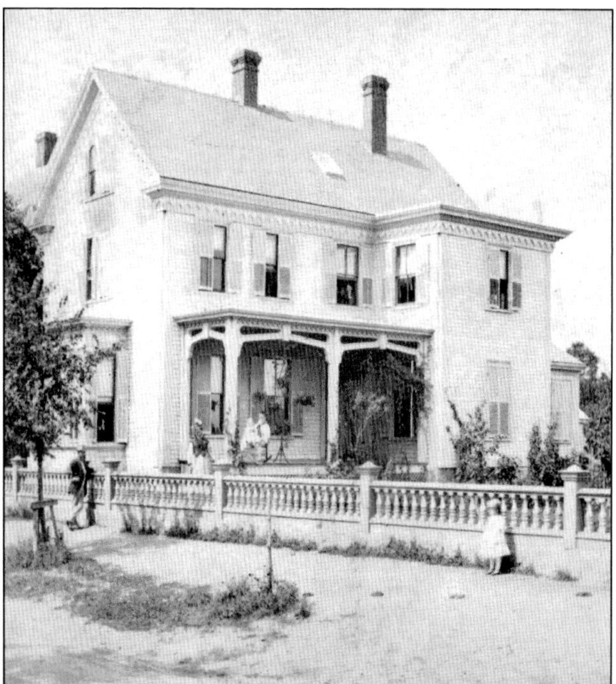

The Well-to-Do. The Procter Brothers stereoview (above) shows the Gen. Benjamin F. Butler's residence. Butler named the house Bay View because it overlooked Hodgkin's Cove and Ipswich Bay. Butler, a Civil War general of considerable note, was a congressman and later a governor of Massachusetts. Butler and his old comrade Col. Jonas H. French organized the Cape Ann Granite Company. J.W. and J.S. Moulton stereoview (left) shows the Washington Street residence of Capt. Fitz J. Babson, who compiled a meritorious record during the Civil War. Babson later distinguished himself as a state legislator and as one of the staunchest defenders of U.S. fishing interests against Canadian aggression.

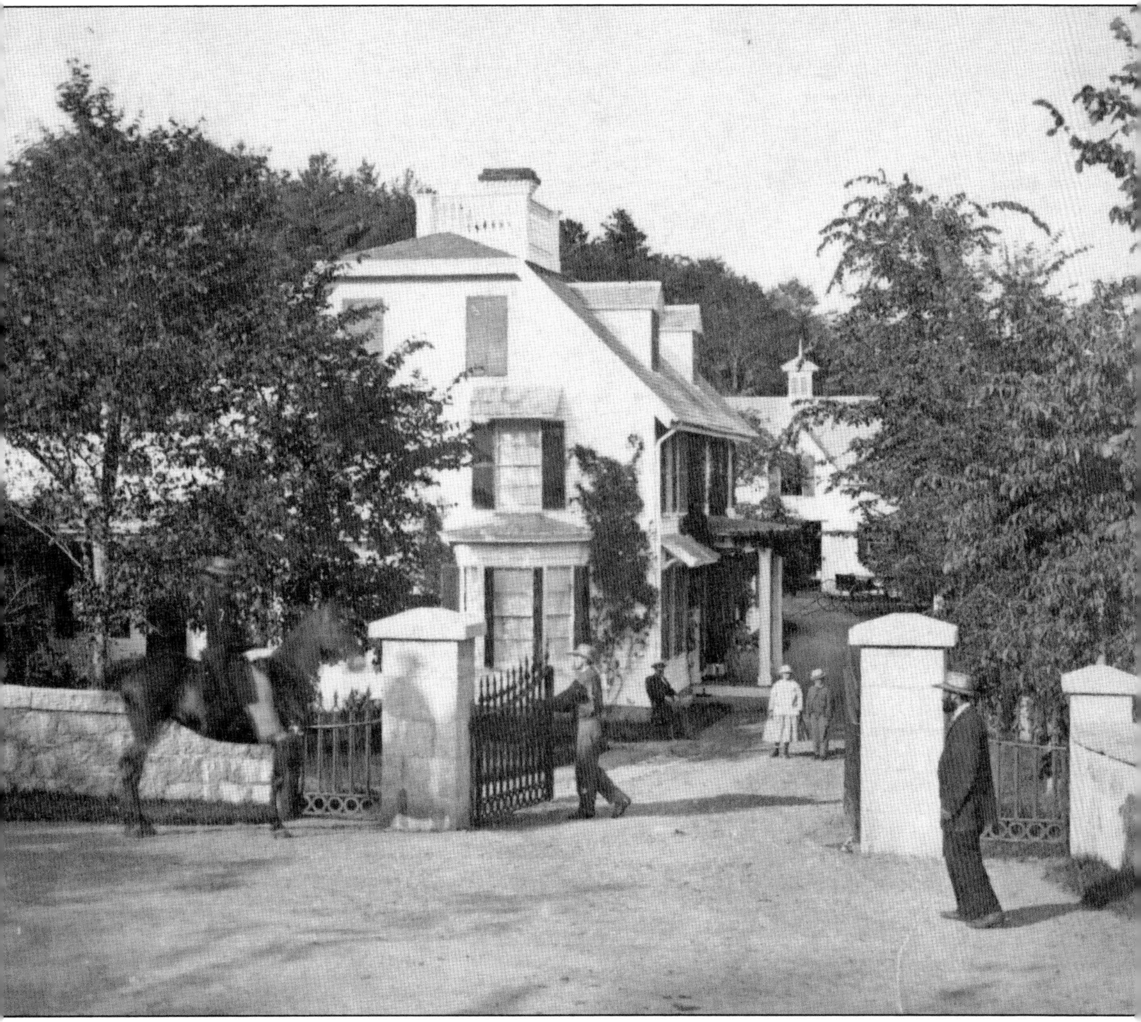

BROOKBANK AT FRESHWATER COVE. This early-1860s stereoview by John Heywood of Boston shows the entrance to Brookbank, the family homestead of Samuel Sawyer. A prominent and prosperous Boston merchant, Sawyer was one of Gloucester's biggest benefactors. His gifts to the city included the land for Ravenswood Park and the house at Middle Street and Dale Avenue, which Sawyer purchased in 1884 for $20,000 and which today is the Sawyer Free Library. (See related image, page 117.)

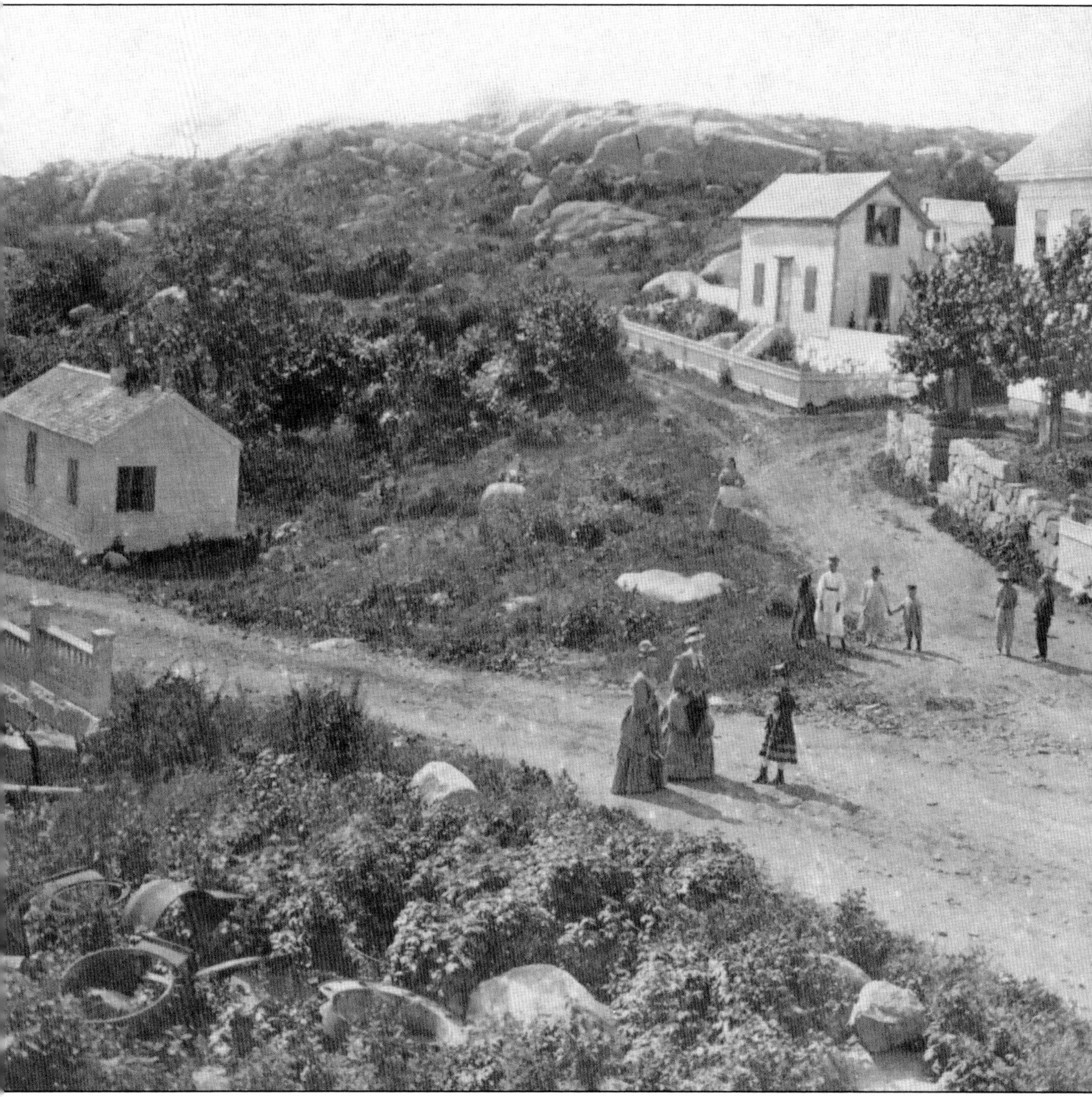

AT GOVERNOR'S HILL. This early-1870s Procter Brothers stereoview shows the junction of what was then known as Granite Street and the old road. The Lakeman House at the foot of Bellevue, or Governor's Hill as it was later called, can also be seen. Vistas of the city and its harbor from the summit lying west of Gloucester's central section were quite sweeping.

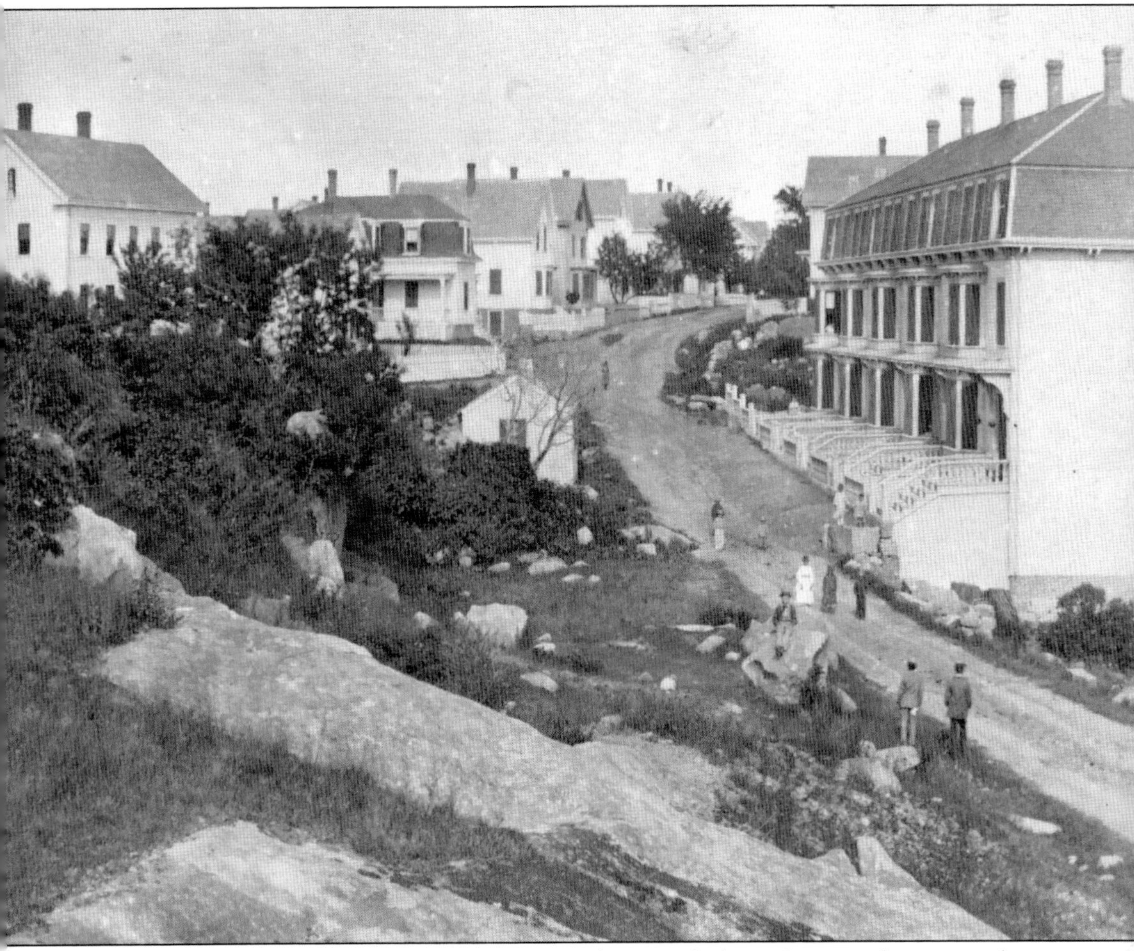

Babson's Block. Related to the Procter Brothers photograph from the preceding page, this image is listed as Babson's Block, Granite Street, and looks southeast from Bellevue (Governor's Hill). Well-kept and neatly arranged homes on both sides of the street lead down into the harbor village beyond. Entranceways to large building at right prove especially interesting.

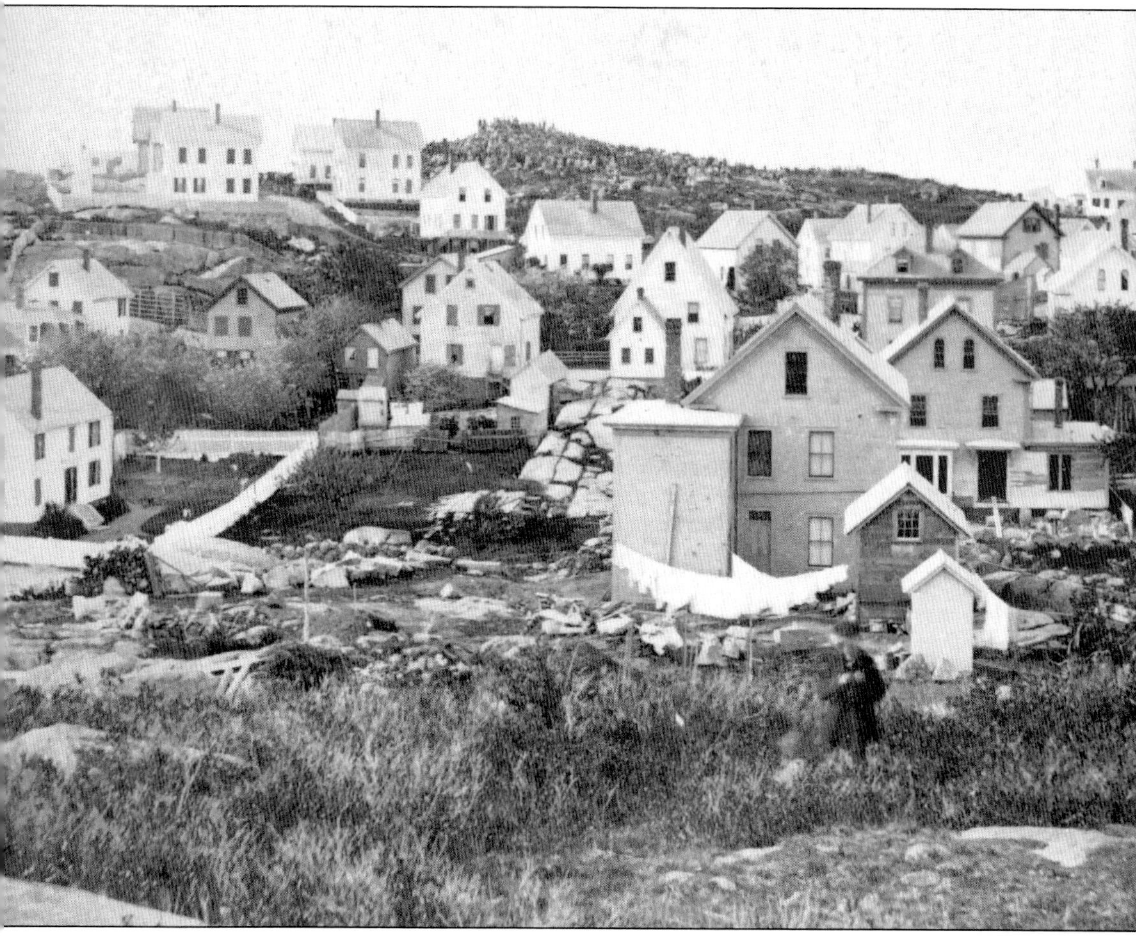

Beacon Pole Hill. Governor's Hill was also called Beacon Pole Hill. This John S.E. Rogers view was taken from the south side of the summit on May 30, 1870, during final ceremonies for Commemoration Day. The area is quite built up. Note the laundry hanging out to dry in the foreground.

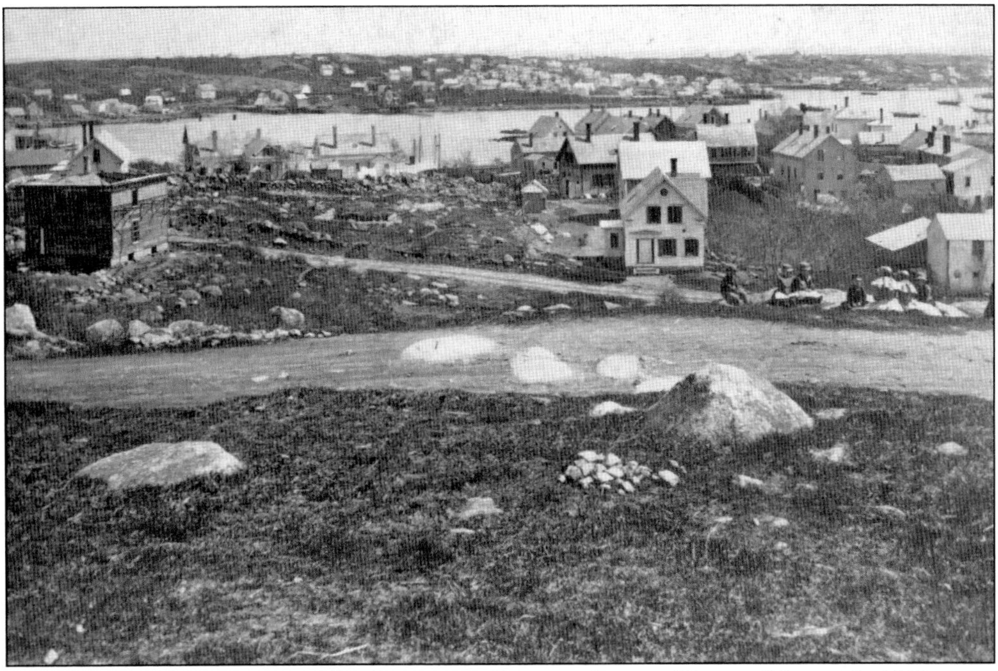

PERKIN'S HILL (PORTUGUESE HILL) AND THE BABSON-ALLING HOUSE. This early-1860s view (above), photographed by John Heywood and published by Hervey Friend of Gloucester, was taken of East Gloucester from Perkin's Hill. The area reaches the highest elevation on Gloucester's east side and was the home for growing numbers of the working class. Since many of them were Portuguese fishermen and their families, the name Portuguese Hill became associated with the neighborhood. The Cook & Friend stereoview (below) is misidentified on the verso as the Murray Meeting House. The house beyond the barn complex in the foreground is more likely the Babson-Alling House, which was erected *c.* 1740.

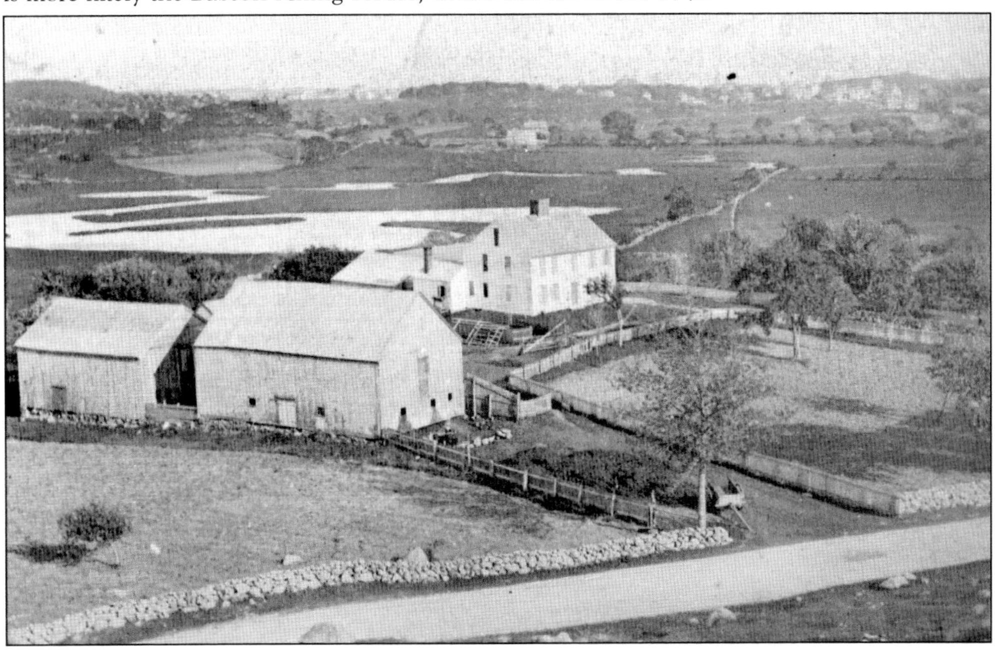

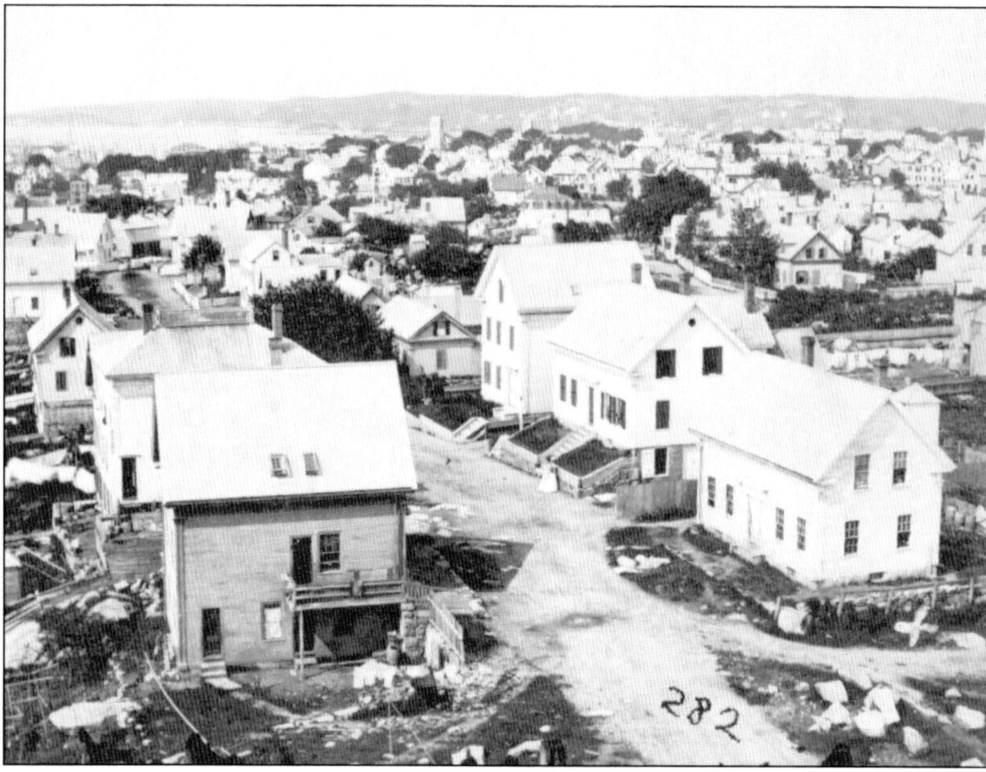

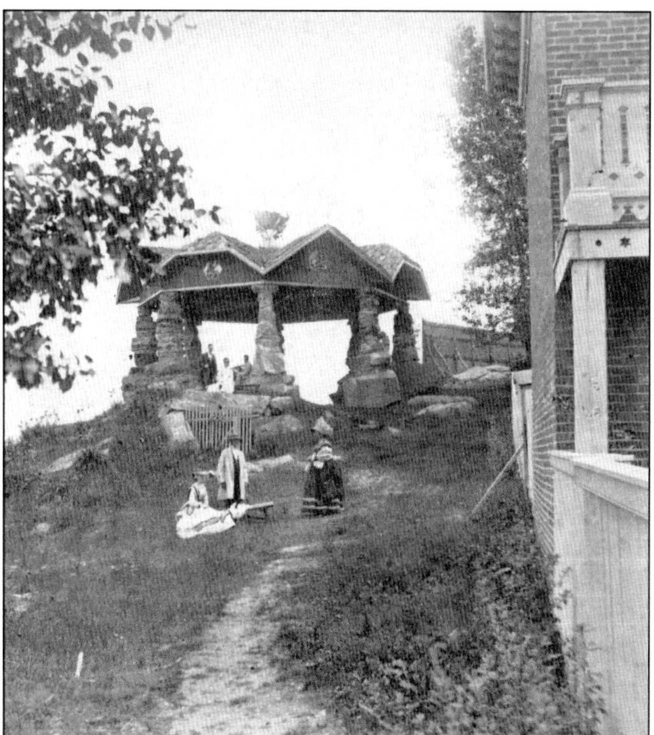

The Other Way. Although not identified on the back, the stereoview above was probably produced by Cook & Friend. The Gloucester image looks south from Portuguese Hill. Church steeples and the city hall tower are visible in the distance. No maker or site was noted for Cape Ann photograph at the left. Notice the stone-pillared gazebo with a huge clamshell on top; a gentleman at the distant right appears seated before a telescope.

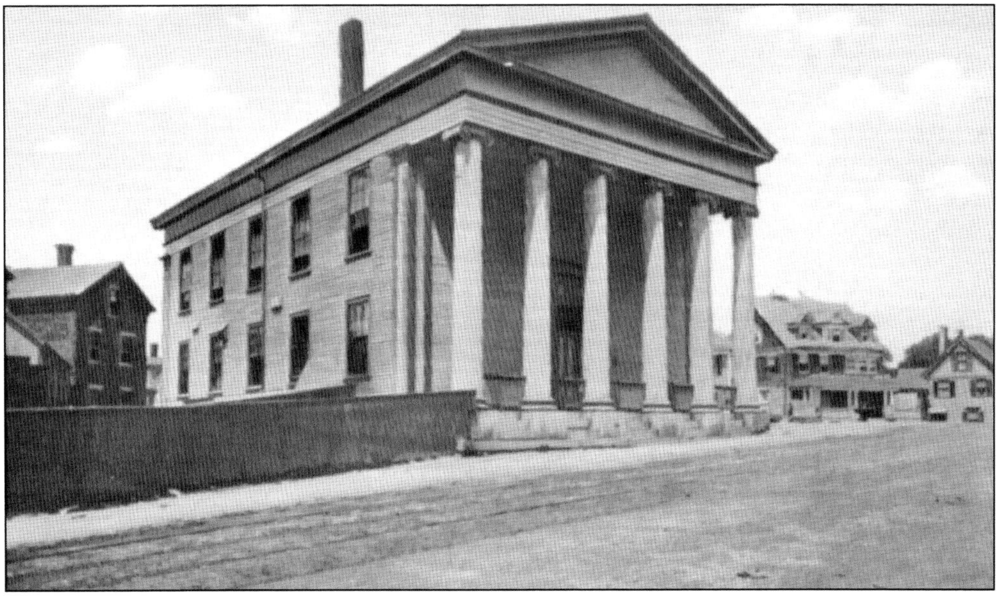

The Forbes School and the Old High School. These early-1900s postcards show the Forbes School on Washington Street (above) and the old high school (below). The Greek Revival–style Forbes School was Gloucester's first town hall in 1844. When a new town hall was erected in 1867, the school occupied the old building; it is now the American Legion Post. The old high school on Dale Avenue was built between 1888 and 1889 at a cost of $100,000, including land. Constructed of brick with granite trim, it was considered one of the most imposing structures of its kind.

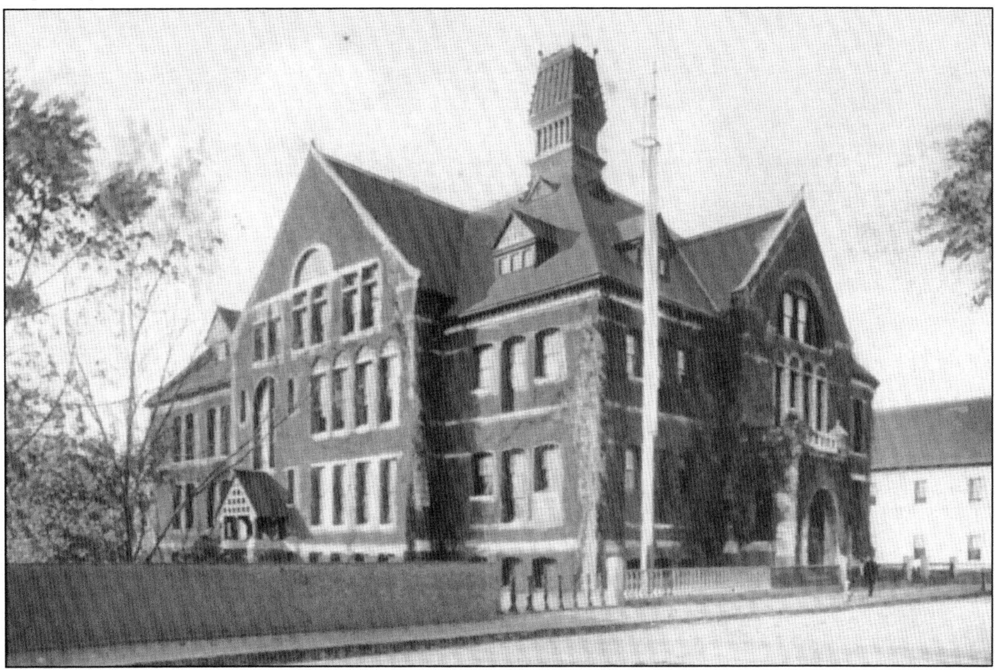

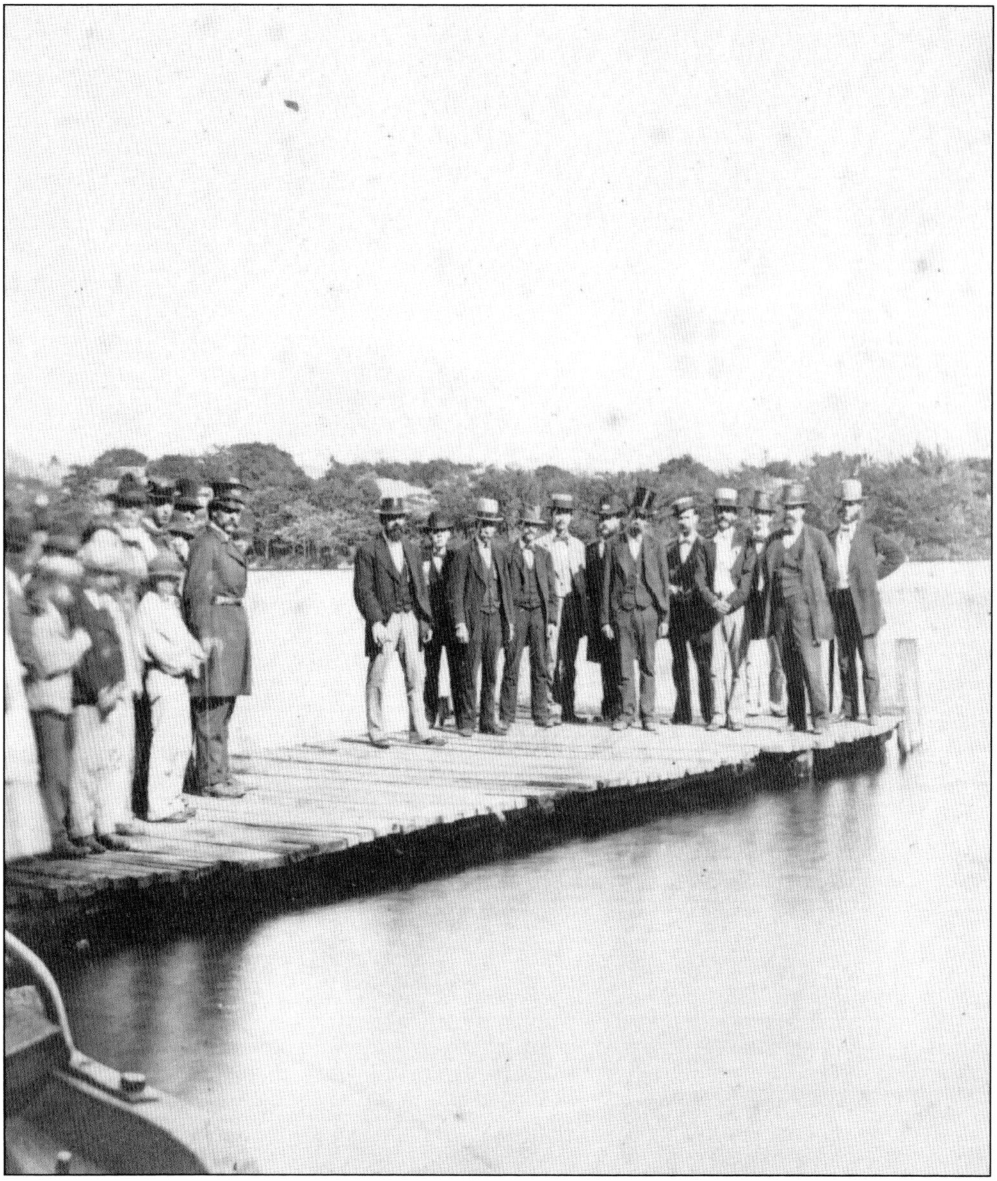

THE 1875 CENTENNIAL CELEBRATION. This rare image, taken from a Procter Brothers stereoview, shows members of the Massachusetts Press Association and reporters posed on the wharf at Cape Pond Grove. This August 9, 1875 patriotic gathering was part of the ceremonies marking the repulse by Gloucester citizens of a British warship's attempt to bombard and destroy the town. (See related image, page 116.)

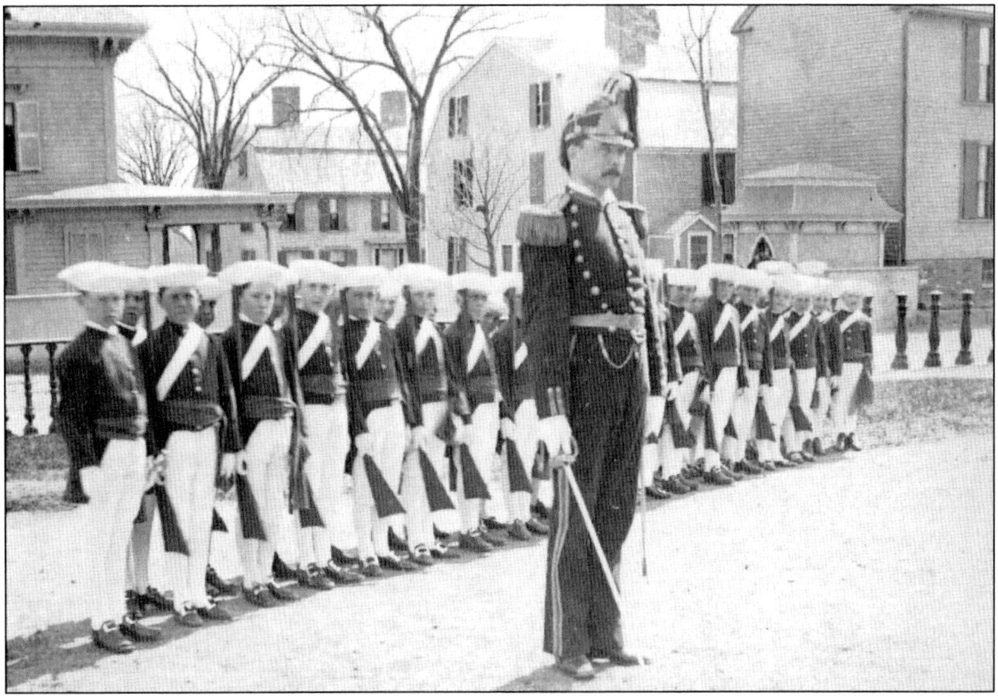

THE 1876 CENTENNIAL SPECTACLE. This pair of stereoviews published by E.G. Rollins shows a corps of uniformed boys being drilled by Capt. Richard C. Lawrence Jr. of the 8th Massachusetts Regiment. An imprint on the verso identifies the unit as the "Gloucester Centennial Light Infantry to participate in a Grand Centennial Spectacle at Gloucester City Hall on Thursday Evening, Apr. 20th, 1876." On July 4, 1876, a grand celebration took place in Gloucester. It included a trades and civic procession, an antique and horribles parade, and a gala yacht race.

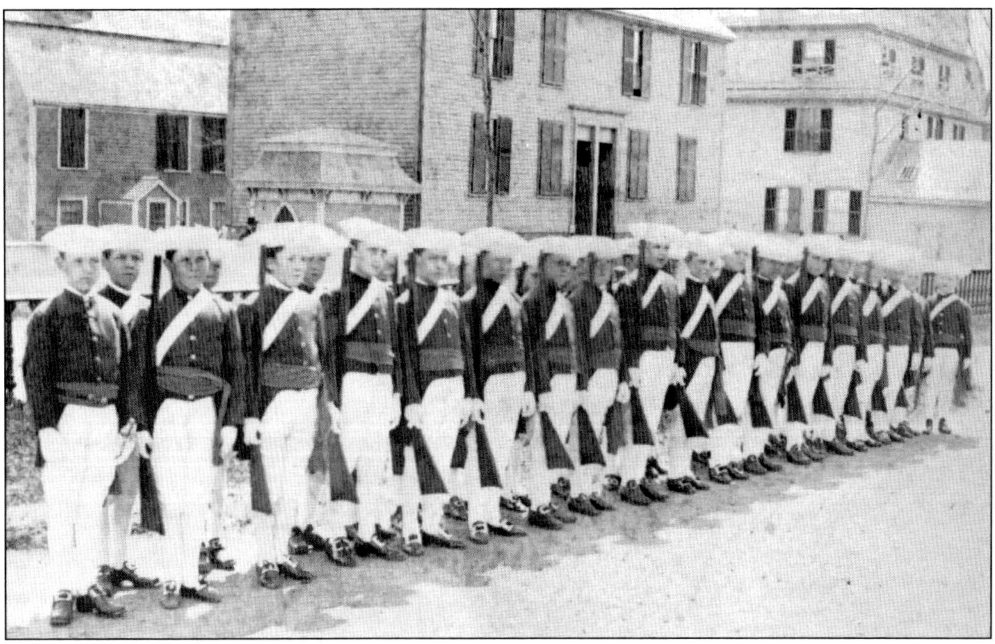

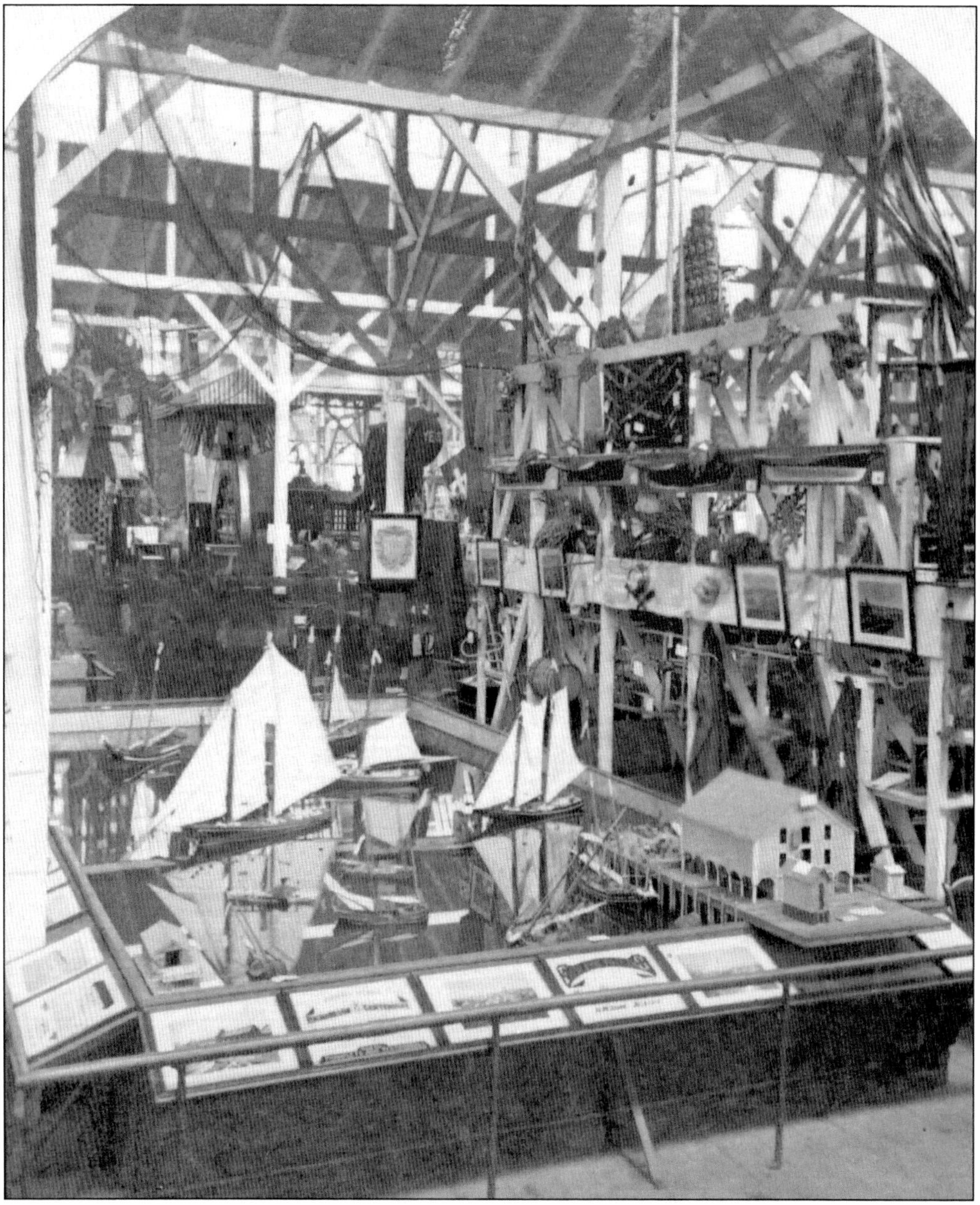

THE INTERNATIONAL EXPOSITION. This Centennial Photo Company stereoview shows the display presented by the fisheries of Gloucester at the Centennial International Exhibition of 1876, which was held in Philadelphia. In a large water-filled tank were exact-scale models of various Gloucester fishing ships. Also featured were models of wharves, miniature fishermen, ship designs, and other artifacts related to fishing and fish processing.

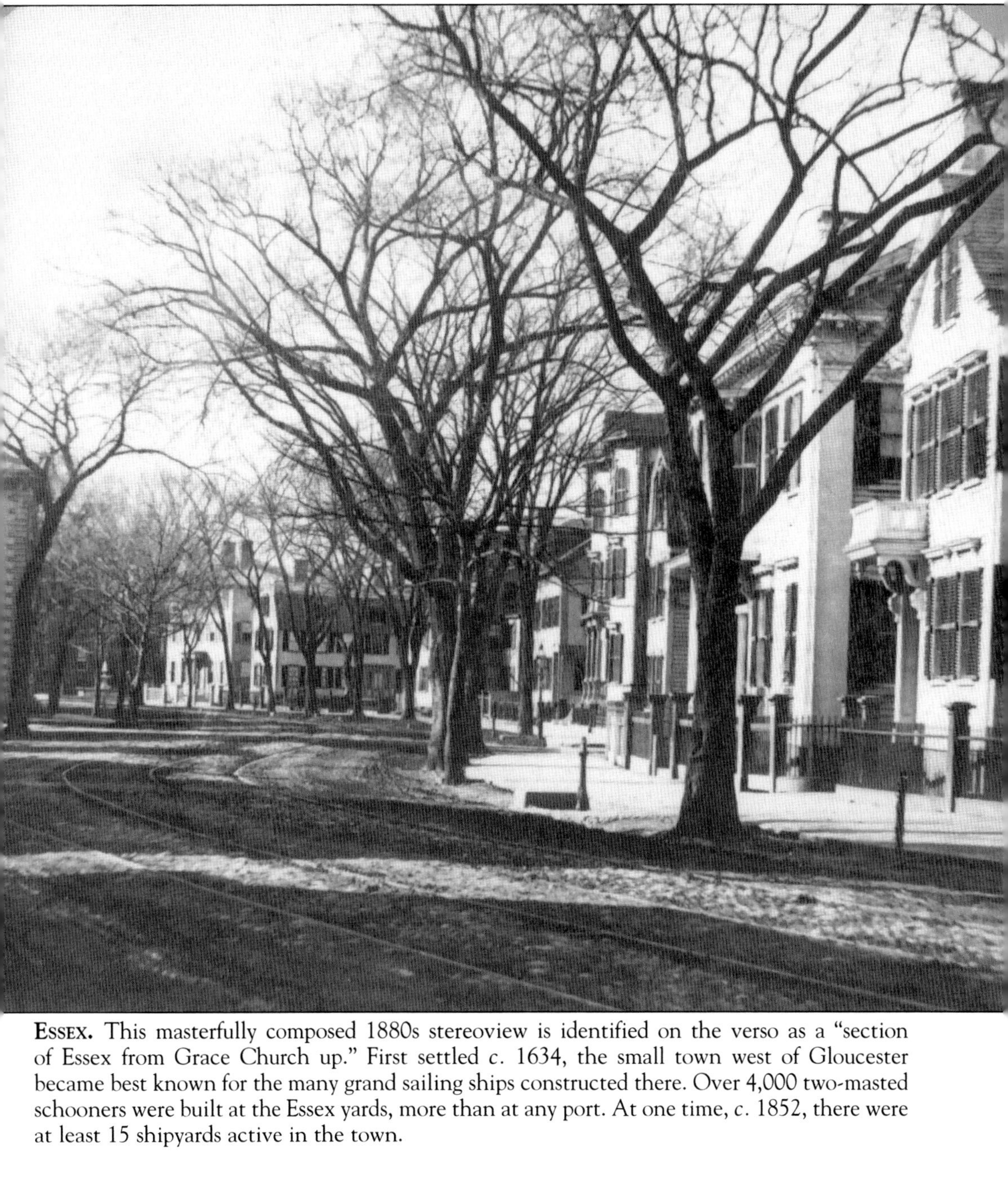

ESSEX. This masterfully composed 1880s stereoview is identified on the verso as a "section of Essex from Grace Church up." First settled *c.* 1634, the small town west of Gloucester became best known for the many grand sailing ships constructed there. Over 4,000 two-masted schooners were built at the Essex yards, more than at any port. At one time, *c.* 1852, there were at least 15 shipyards active in the town.

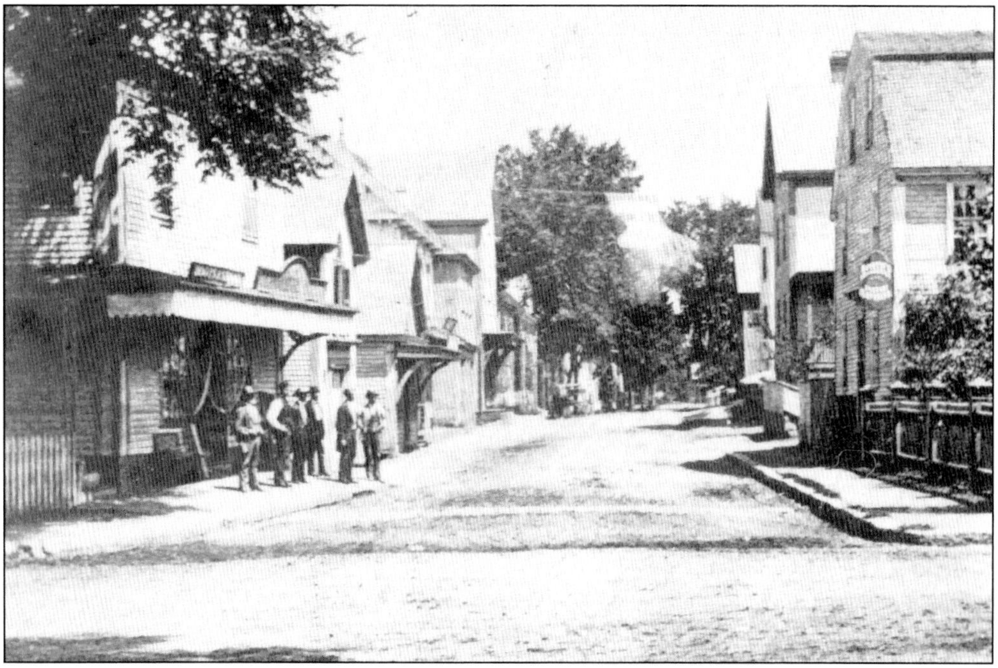

MANCHESTER-BY-THE-SEA. These two copy stereos from American Scenery's Best Series show Manchester (Manchester-by-the-Sea). Gloucester's seacoast neighbor to the west was incorporated in 1645 and was the home to some of Cape Ann's finest mariners, merchants, and others of wealth. The well-to-do from Boston and New York turned the area into a fashionable summer community. The street scene above was photographed *c.* 1885. The view below shows Black Cove Beach.

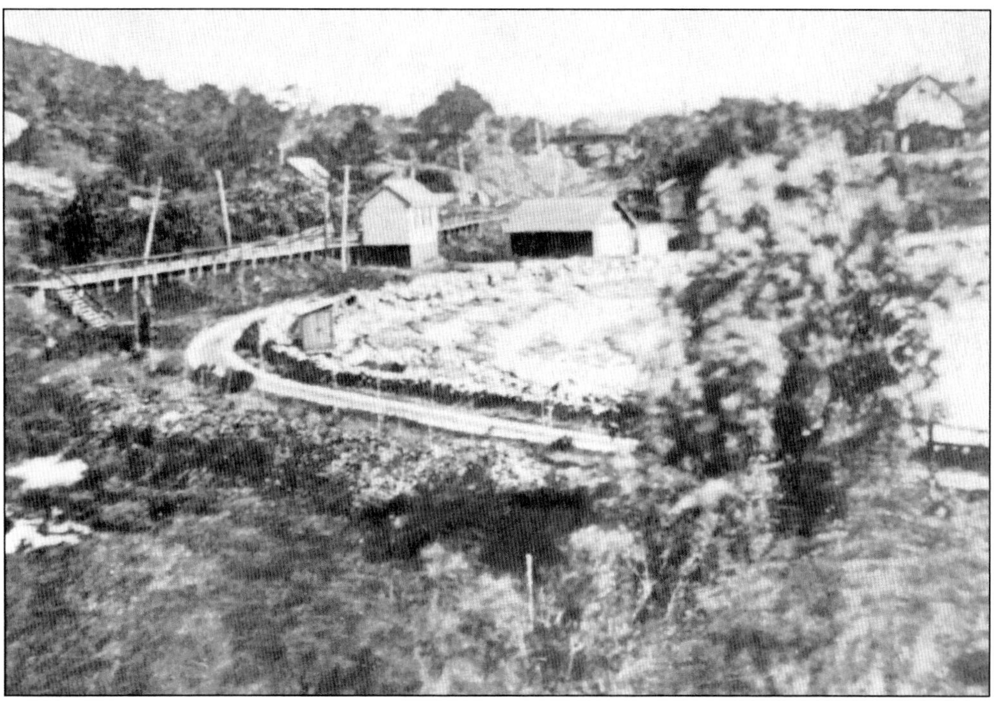

Four

ROCKPORT AND GRANITE

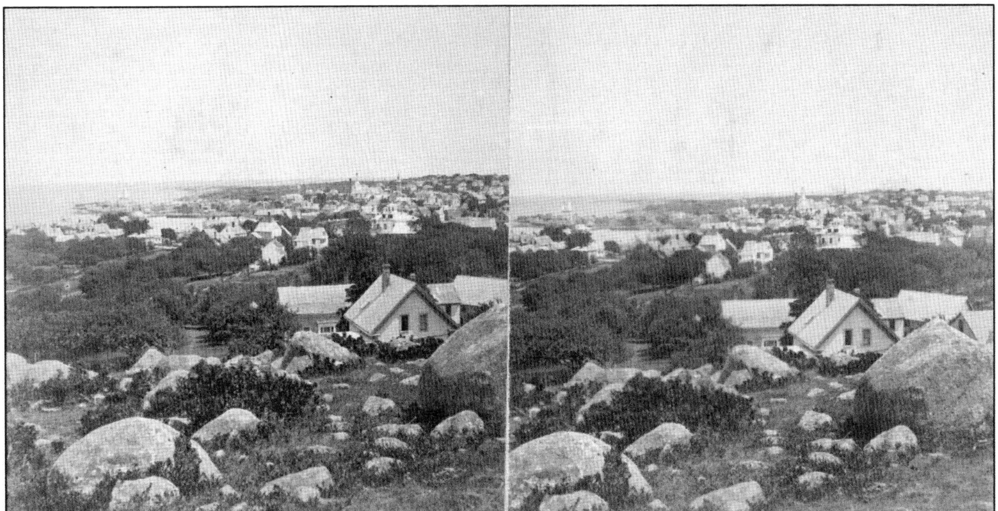

ROCKPORT FROM 'SQUAM HILL. This early-1870s stereoview from John S.E. Rogers looks down on Rockport's South Village and the Sandy Bay Pier Company. Straitsmouth Island and its lighthouse is faintly visible in far distance.

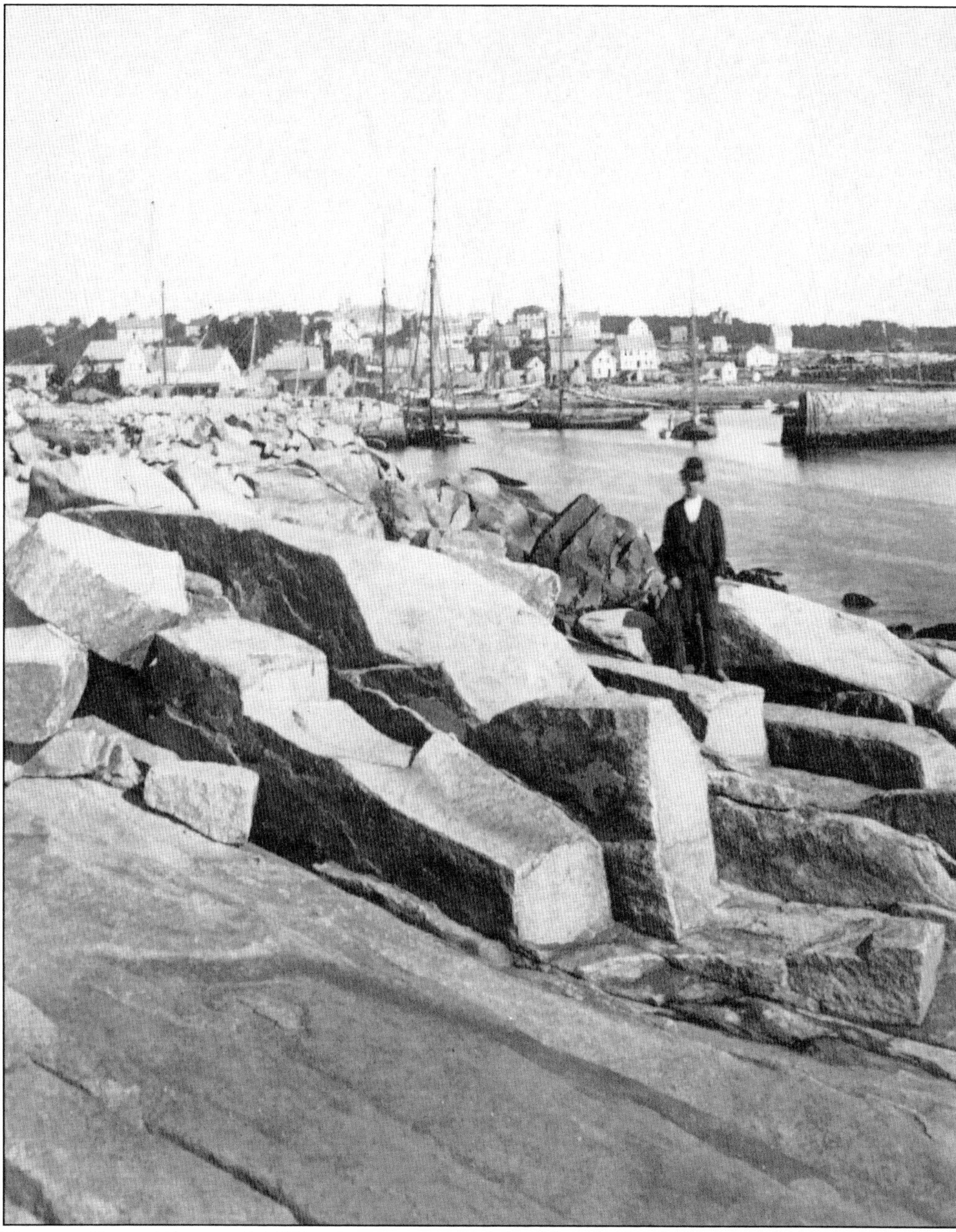

PIGEON COVE. This mid-1870s stereoview, published by the Henry C. Ropes & Company of New York, looks into the harbor at Pigeon Cove. Ropes was active between 1865 and 1880, indicating that the scene could be of earlier vintage. Some of the earliest granite quarrying on Cape Ann took place here.

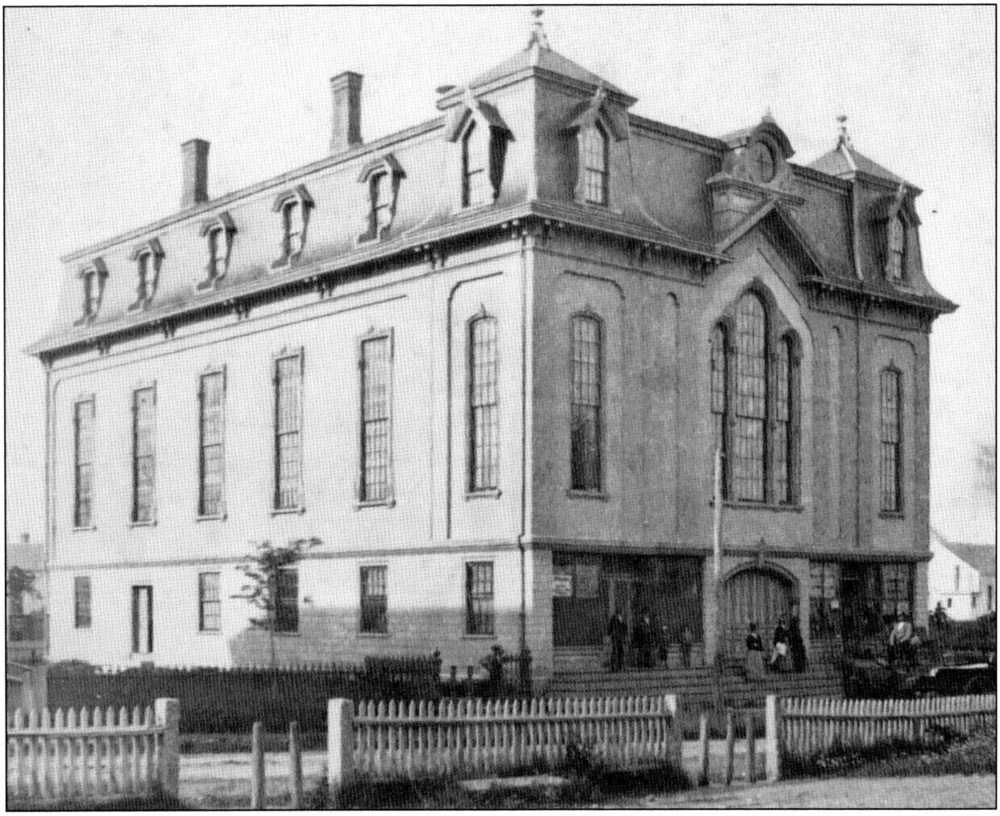

ROCKPORT TOWN HALL AND KNOWLTON'S WHARF. This early-to-mid-1870s stereoview from E.G. Rollins of Gloucester (above) captures the Rockport Town Hall on Broadway Avenue. The building was erected in 1869, and town offices moved onto the first floor, to the sides and rear of the stores that flanked the entranceway. A large auditorium took up the second floor. The mid-1870s stereoview below shows Knowlton's Wharf at the corner of Beach Street; the first shipments of Rockport granite were made from this area. The town is in the background.

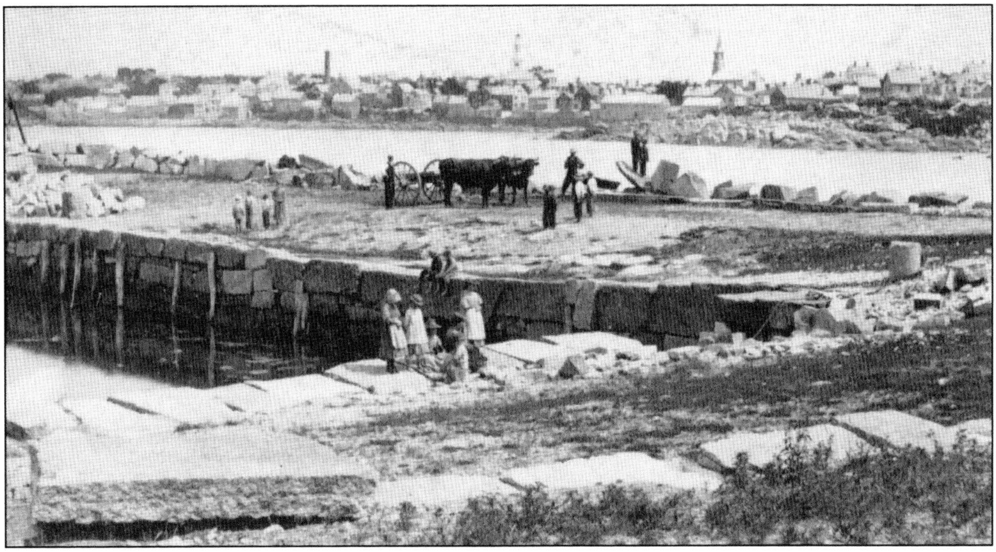

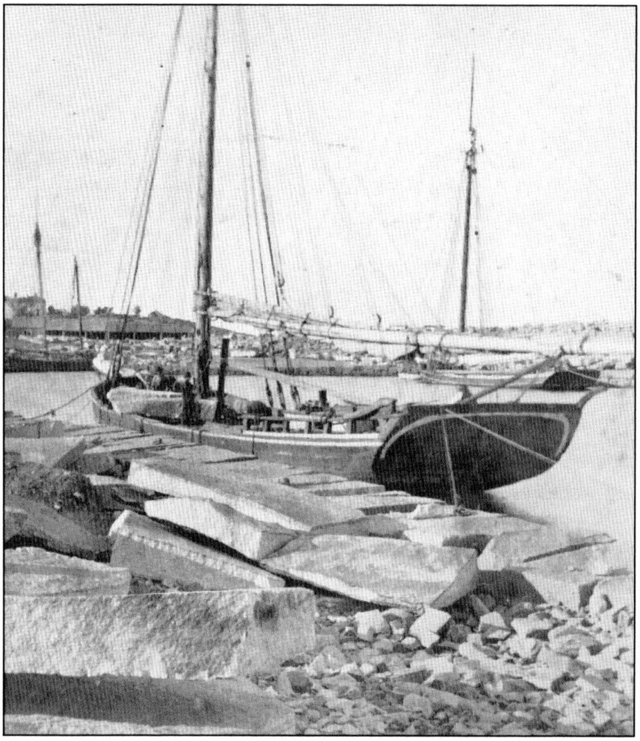

THE WHARF AND SHIPPING. Above, a huge granite slab is loaded aboard a lighter at the Rockport Granite Company pier at Pigeon Cove. At right, Men prepare to load some paving blocks at the same pier. The lighters would then transfer their cargoes to granite sloops anchored beyond the harbor in deeper waters. Both stereoviews were produced by E.G. Rollins, *c*. 1875.

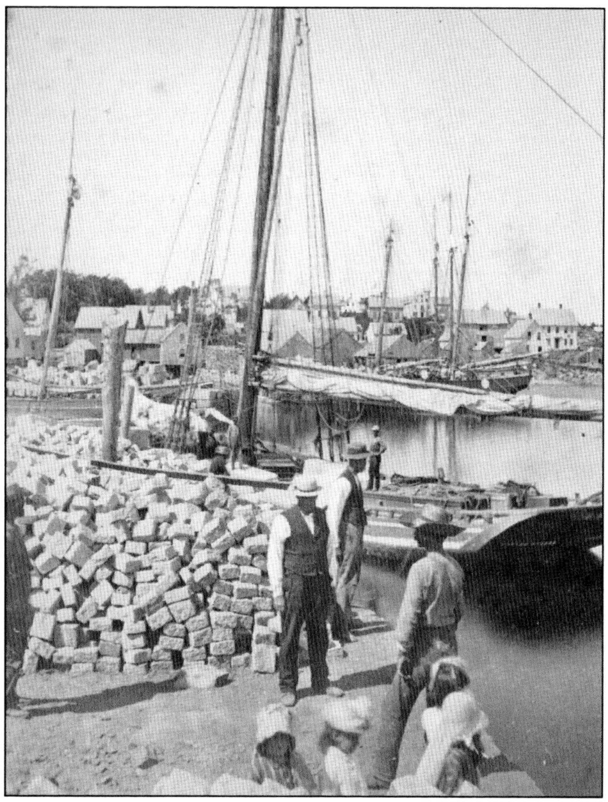

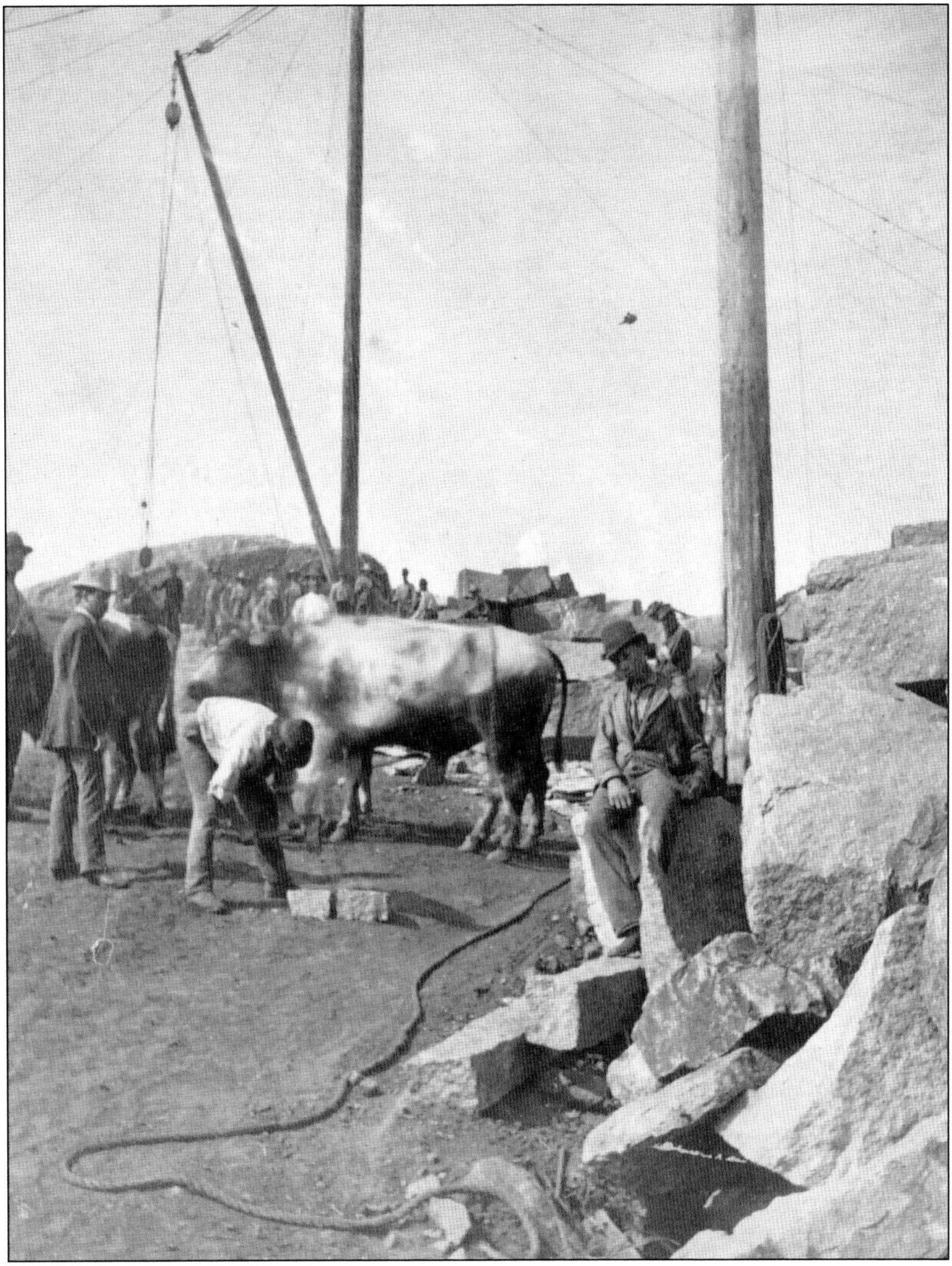

AT THE PIT. With hoisting derricks towering above them, workers begin hitching up oxen to wooden wagons called garymanders, which were used to haul away huge granite stones cut from the quarry pits. The Procter Brothers published this stereoview in the mid-1870s.

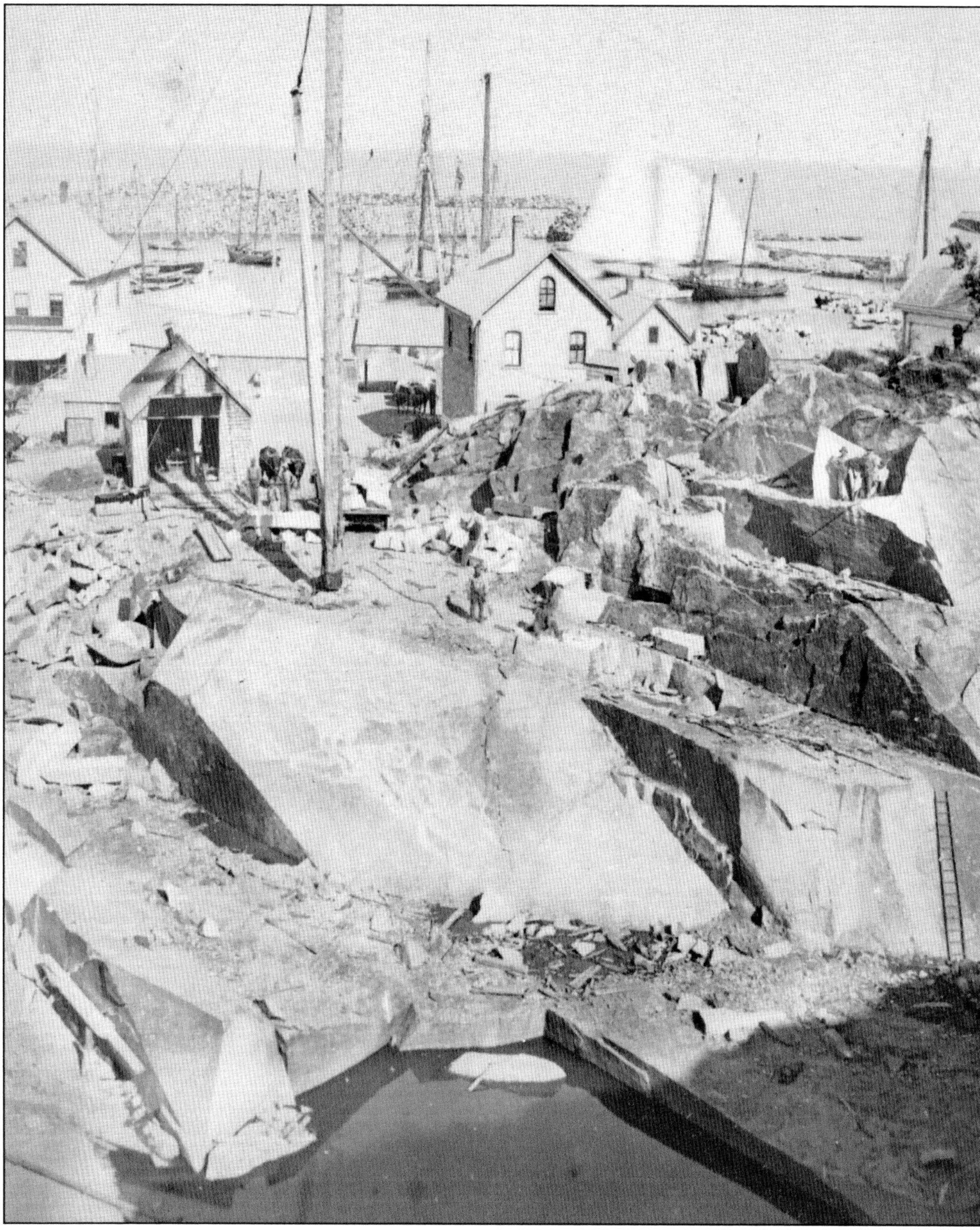

PIGEON COVE GRANITE COMPANY QUARRY. This busy mid-to-late-1880s stereoview (probably E.G. Rollins) provides us with a sweeping look at quarrying operations carried on by the Pigeon Cove Granite Company. Ships in the background await their heavy cargoes, which have been cut and hauled from the massive ledge in the foreground. The Pigeon Cove Granite Company also had a quarry in West Gloucester.

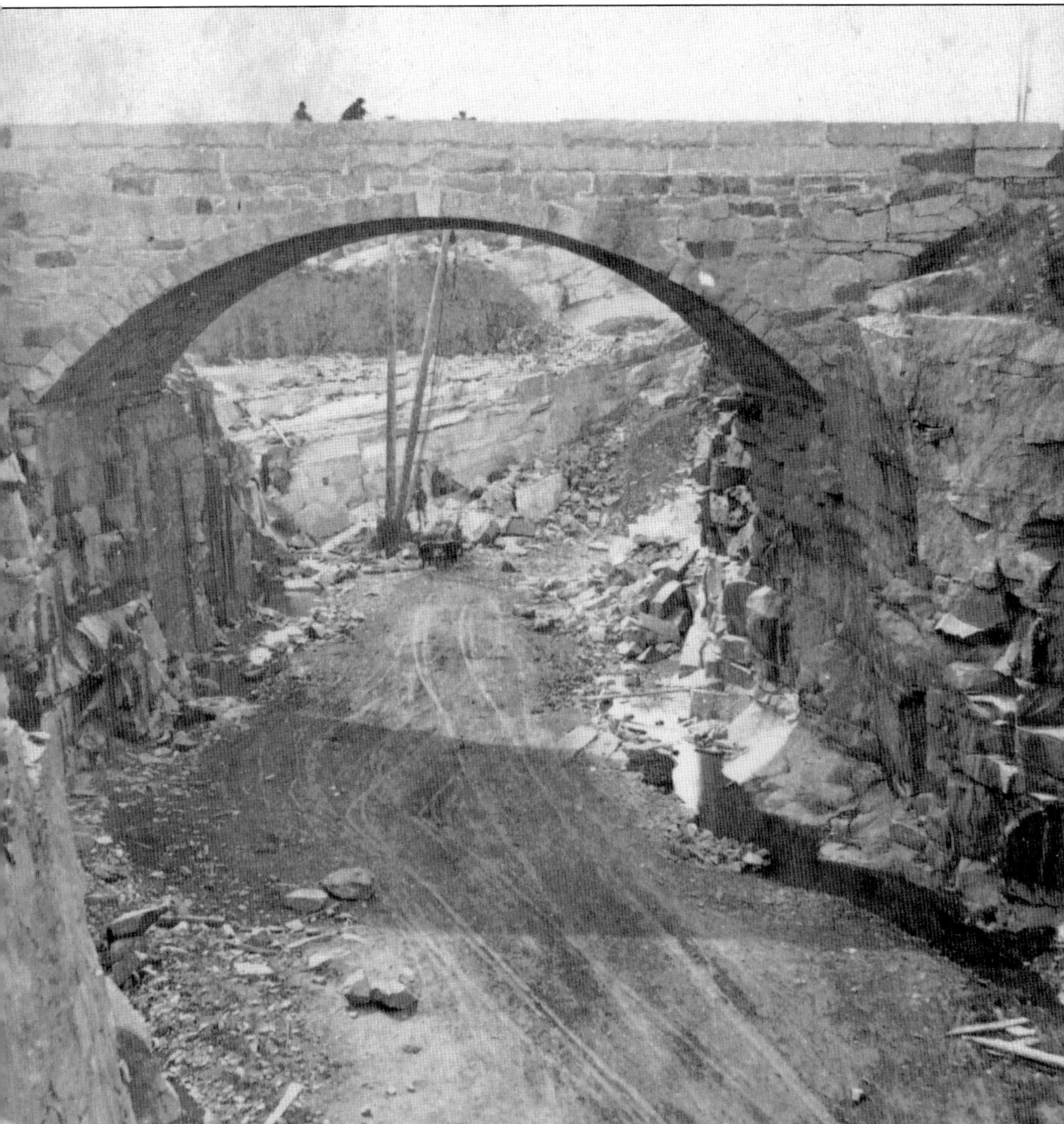

The Great Arch. This *c.* 1872 E.G. Rollins stereoview captures the Stone Bridge, also called the Great Arch, which was built by the Rockport Granite Company. The four-year project that built the tunnel and roadway below the span was designed to connect the company's two quarries and to provide a straight (and quicker) run to the wharf.

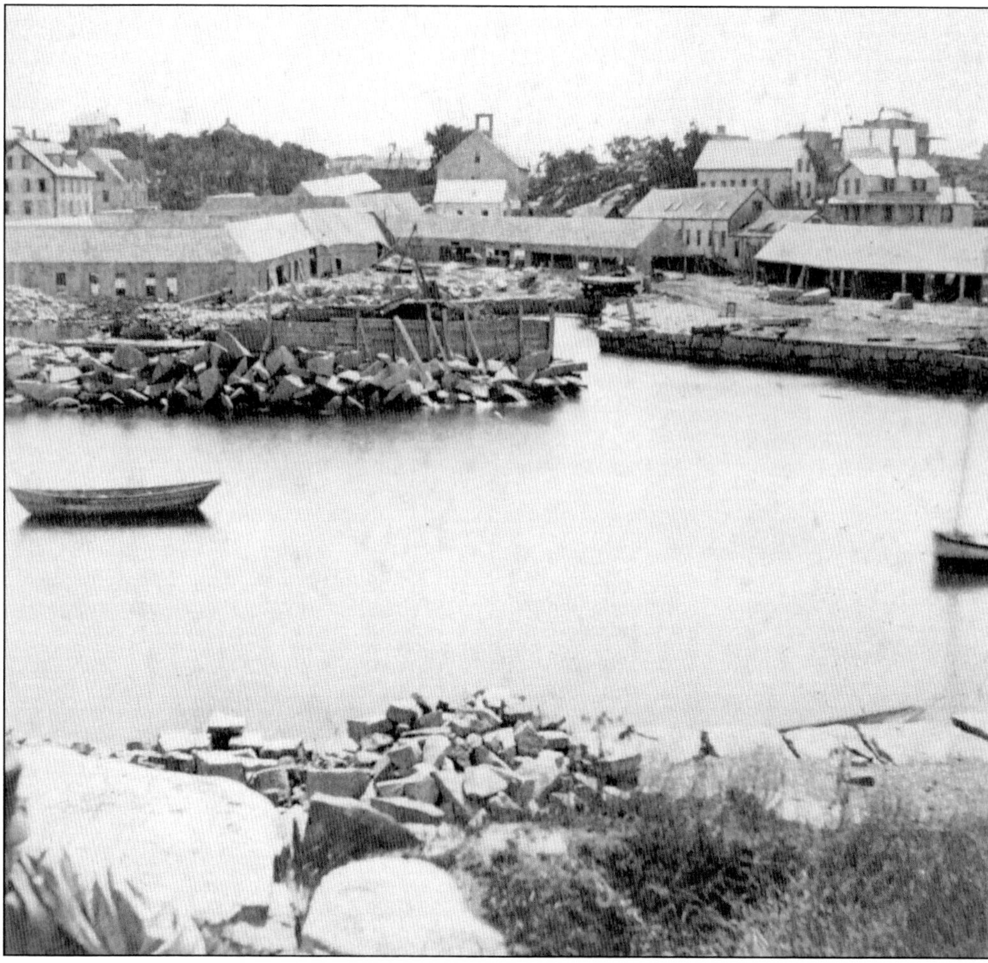

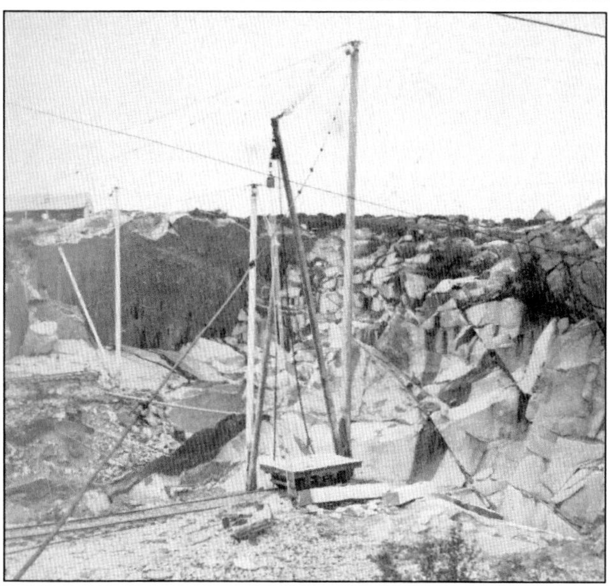

THE CAPE ANN GRANITE COMPANY. Two more Rollins views show the Cape Ann Granite Company at Bay View. Organized by Gen. Benjamin F. Butler and headed up by Col. Jonas H. French, the firm employed hundreds of men. Its processing and loading works were located at Hodgkin's Cove (above). The photograph to the left shows the interior of one of the company's pits. A large derrick and flatcar are on the track at center.

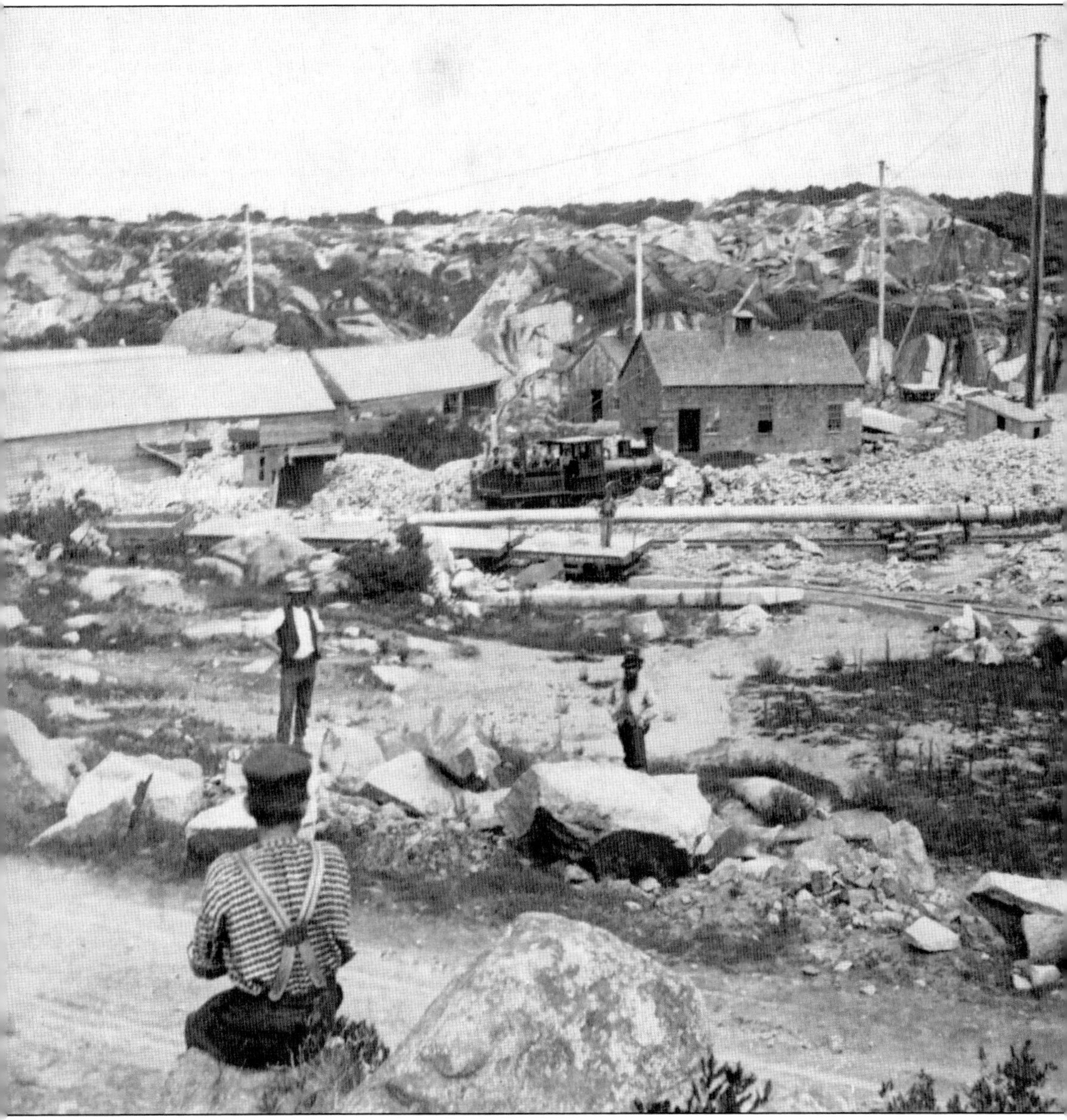

Polyphemus No. 1. The locomotive in the center of this mid-1870s E.G. Rollins stereoview is quite likely Polyphemus No. 1, which hauled stonecars at the Old Pit quarry at Bay View. This 10-ton engine was followed later (1879) by a 20-ton giant, Polyphemus No. 2, which was in continuous use through 1930, when the granite industry collapsed along with other industries killed off by the Great Depression.

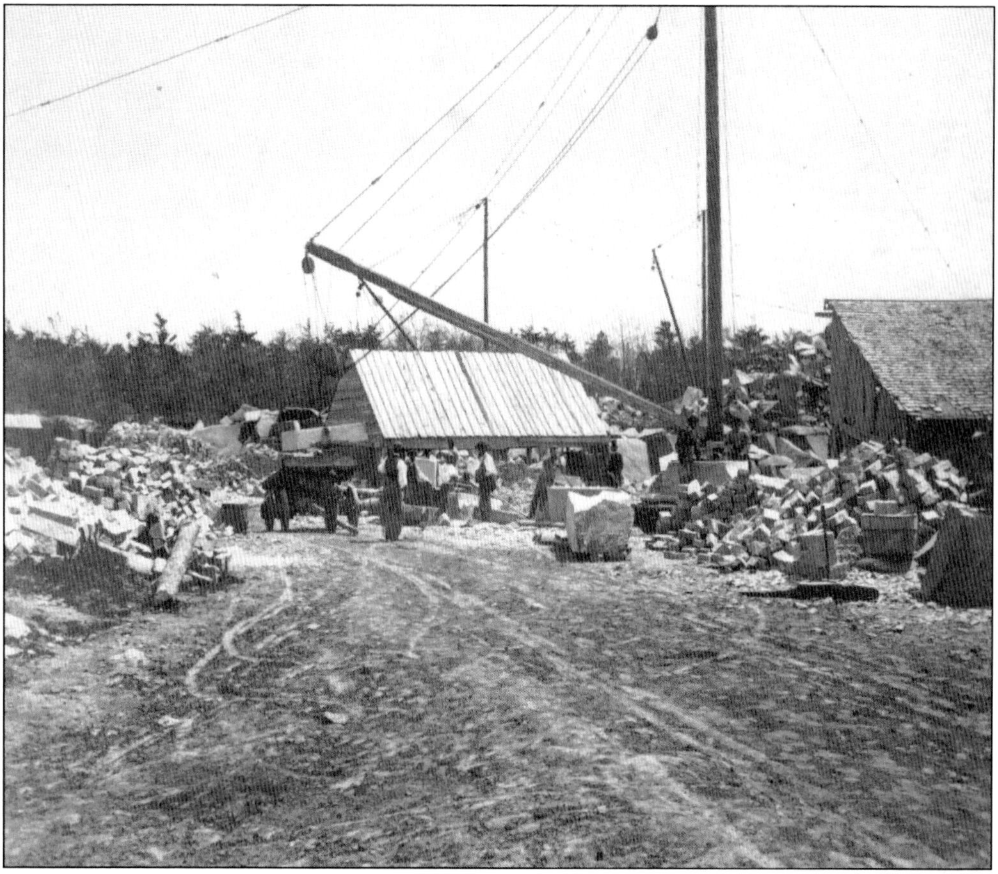

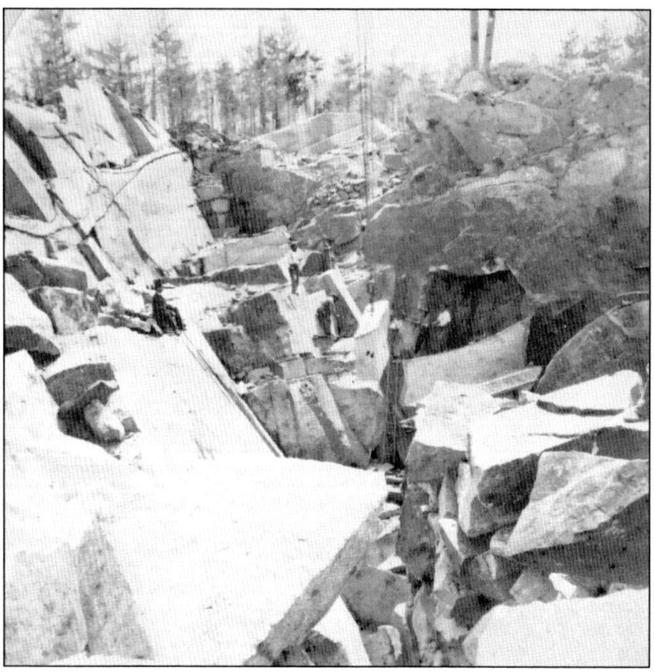

The Quarries at Lanesville. This mid-1860s stereoview from Boston's John Heywood (above) shows quarrying at the Cape Ann village of Lanesville. The first of the Lanesville quarries opened *c.* 1828. Lanesville was also settled by many hardworking Finns who flocked to Cape Ann to labor in the pits. The image at left, also issued by Heywood, shows a large granite slab being hoisted out of a deep pit in Lanesville. A well-dressed gentleman left of center supervises the operations.

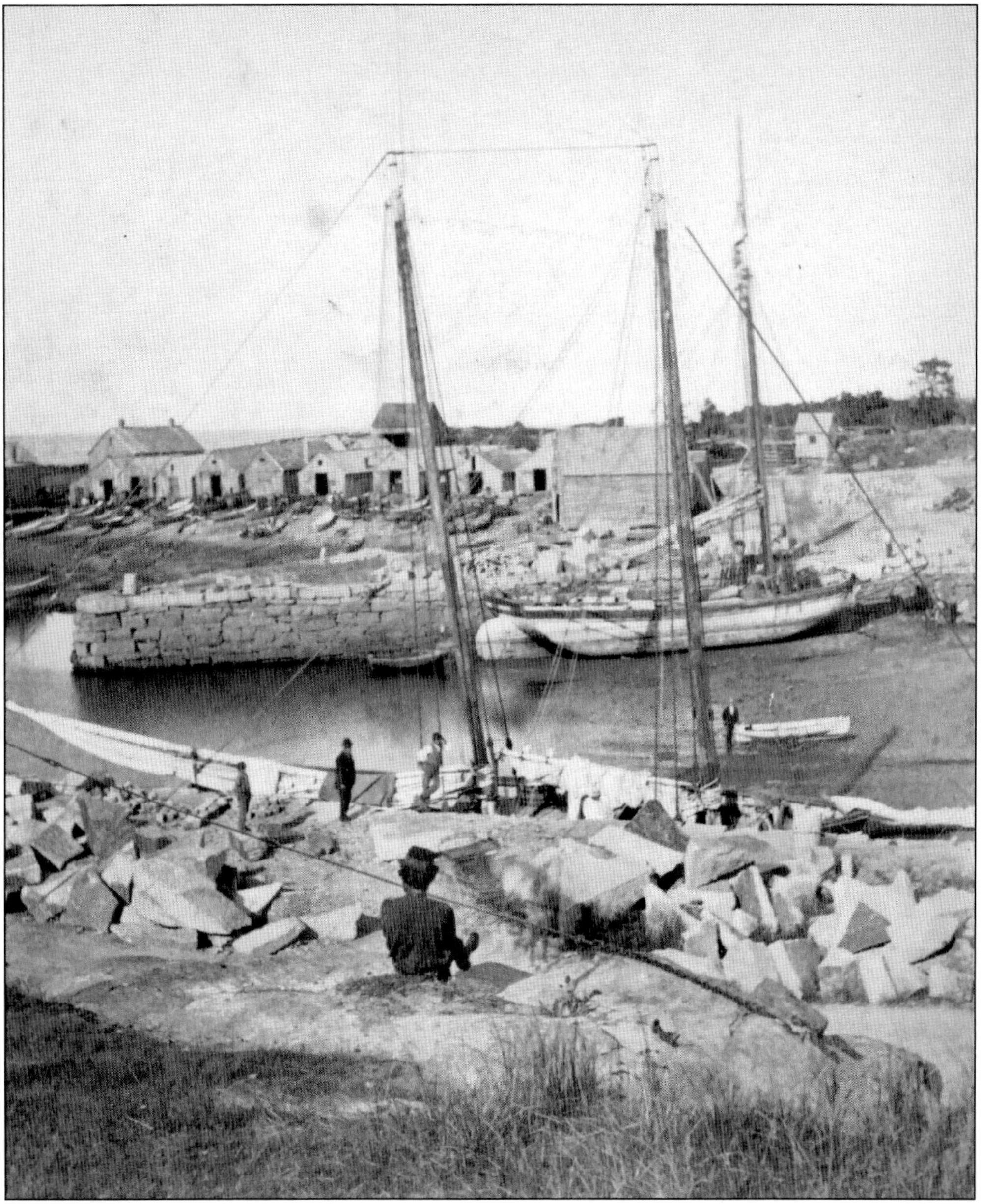

Loading Granite at Lane's Cove. The two-masted granite sloop in the foreground is being loaded at Lane's (Flatstone) Cove, Lanesville, in this late-1870s E.G. Rollins stereoview. A pier company formed in 1828 finally managed to build a breakwater at the cove's entrance, creating a small harbor just snug enough for a vessel to get through the 52-foot-wide gap. Notice the old fish houses in the background.

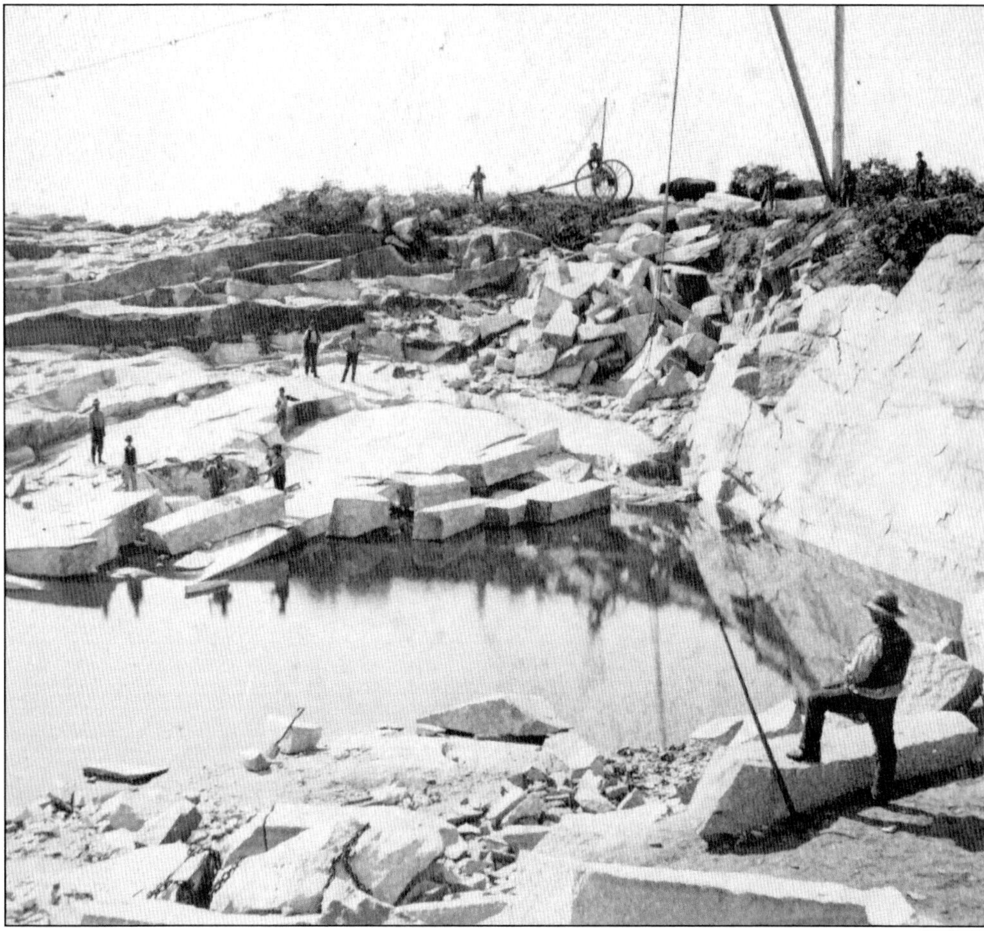

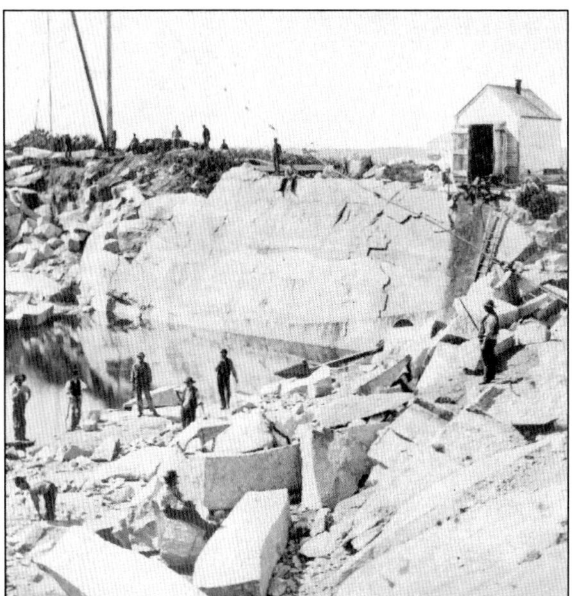

The Eastern Point Granite Company. The seldom seen 1870s stereoviews on this page and the next that were published by E.G. Rollins show stonecutters at work at the Niles quarry of the Eastern Point Granite Company in Gloucester. A good-sized garymander and its team of oxen wait on top of the slope to hoist up a load in the photograph above. There are reports of an earlier quarrying operation on land acquired from the Niles family, but it allegedly lasted only seven years (1836–1843). Workers in the photograph at left pause during a break in their labors; much work was done by hand, using only chisels, shims, wedges, and hammers.

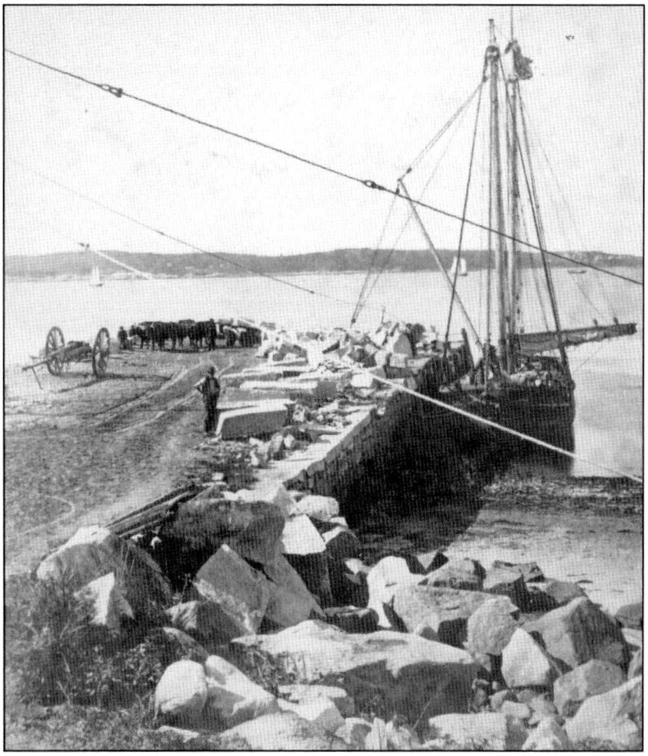

LOADING AT STONE WHARF. The granite-hauling schooner (right) is loaded with stone from the Niles quarry at Eastern Point. Teams of oxen and a small platform cart are on the left, along with a garymander and its 8-foot wheels. Another view (below) of the Niles quarry pit was taken from a slightly different angle than those on the preceding page.

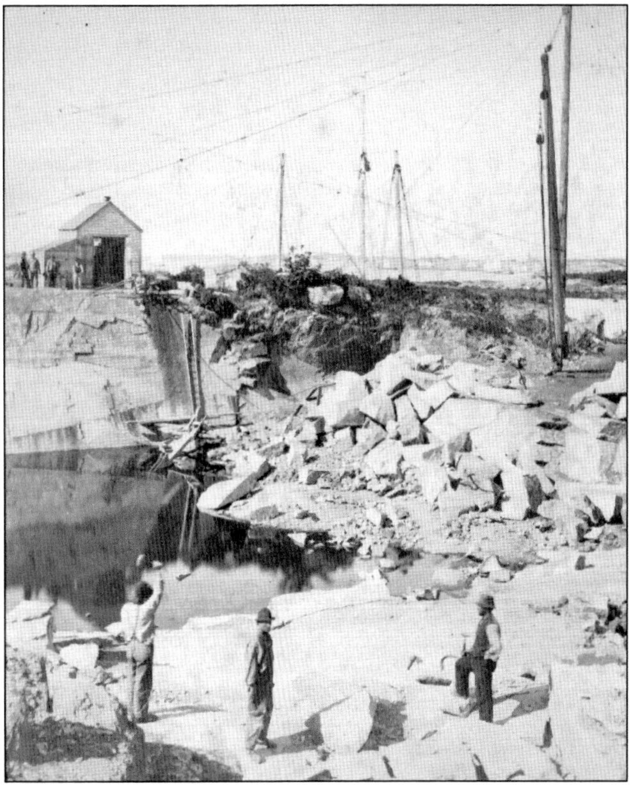

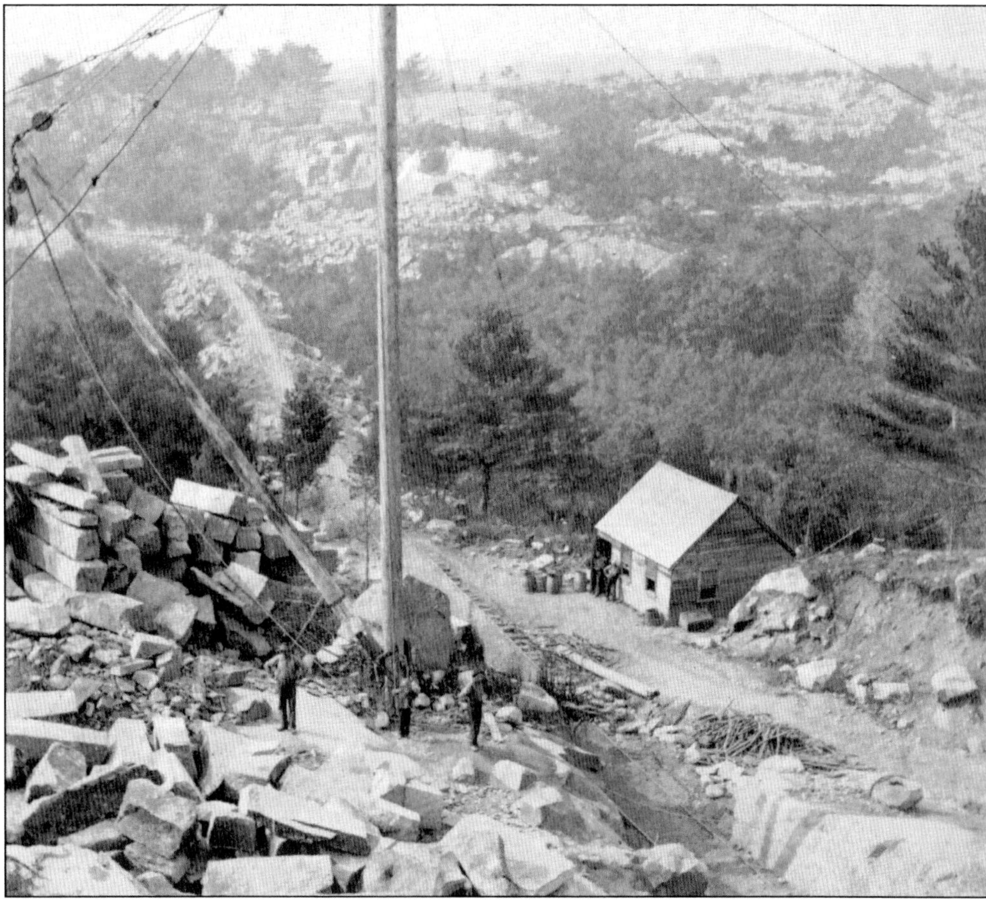

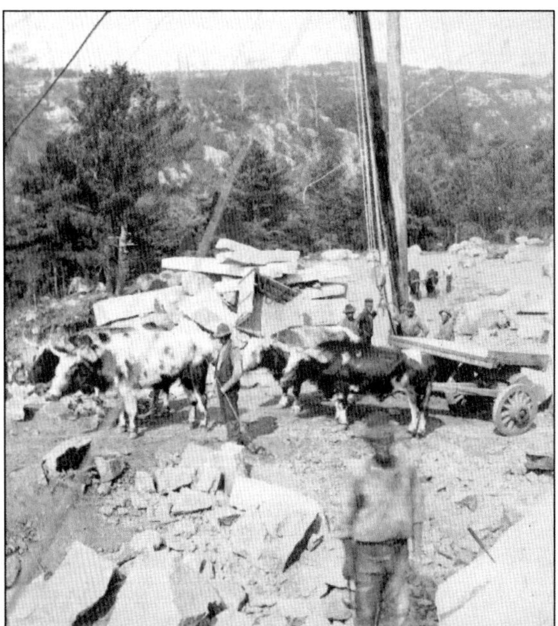

The Gloucester Granite Company. West Gloucester's forested hills and rocky ledges near Stoney Cove served as the setting for the quarrying done by the Gloucester Granite Company. The company began *c.* 1870 with Solomon T. Trumbull, Charles A. Chadwick, and John Todd as partners. The mid-1870s stereoviews on this page and the next, published by E.G. Rollins, show a towering, hoisting derrick and long granite slabs (above). A closer view from the same site (left) reveals a cart pulled by four oxen.

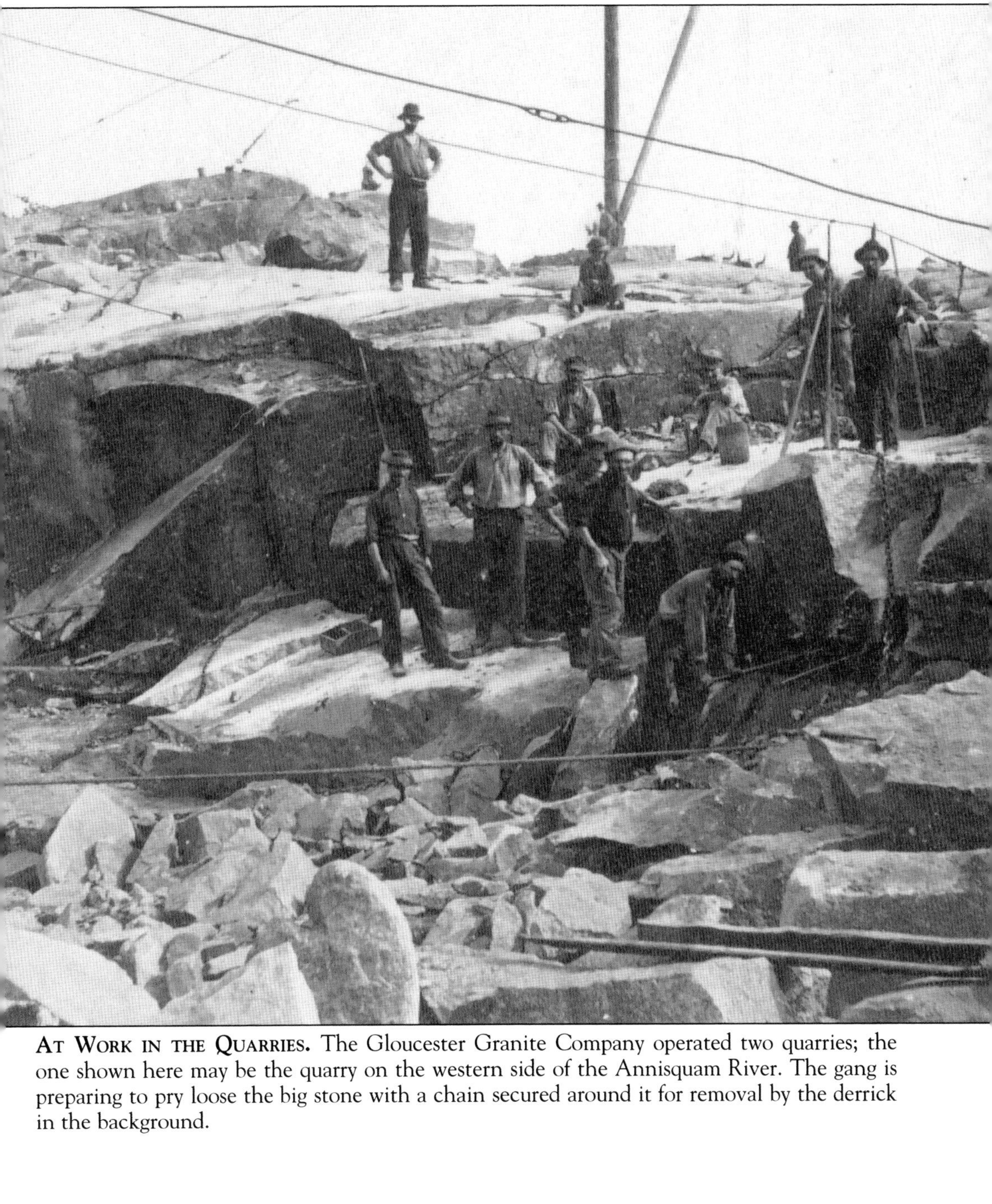

At Work in the Quarries. The Gloucester Granite Company operated two quarries; the one shown here may be the quarry on the western side of the Annisquam River. The gang is preparing to pry loose the big stone with a chain secured around it for removal by the derrick in the background.

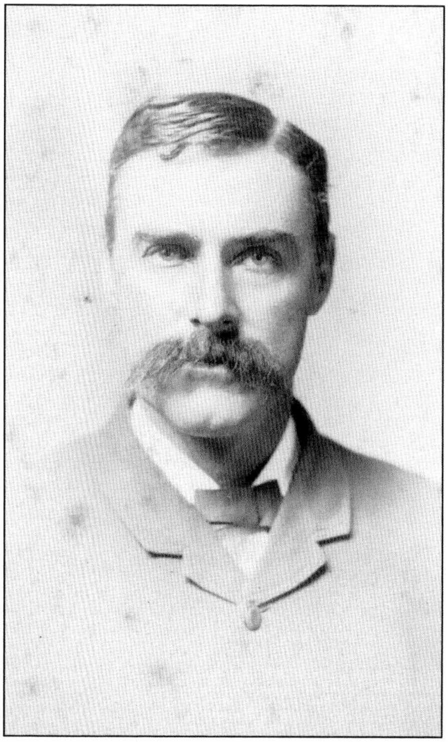

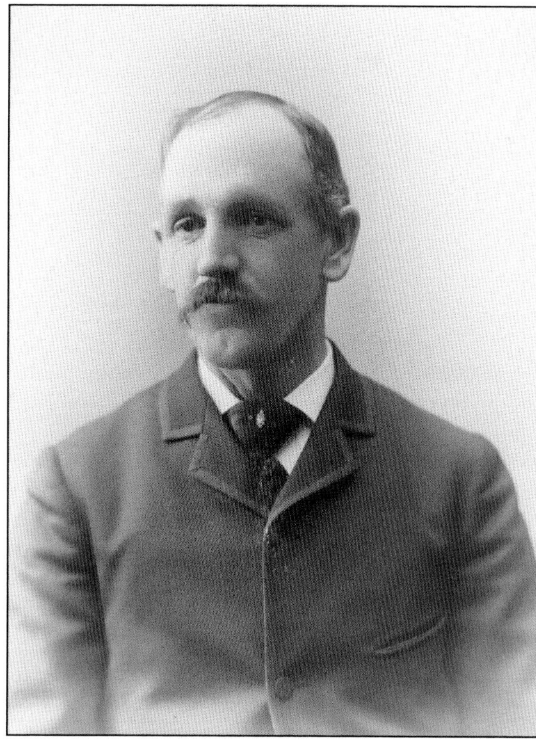

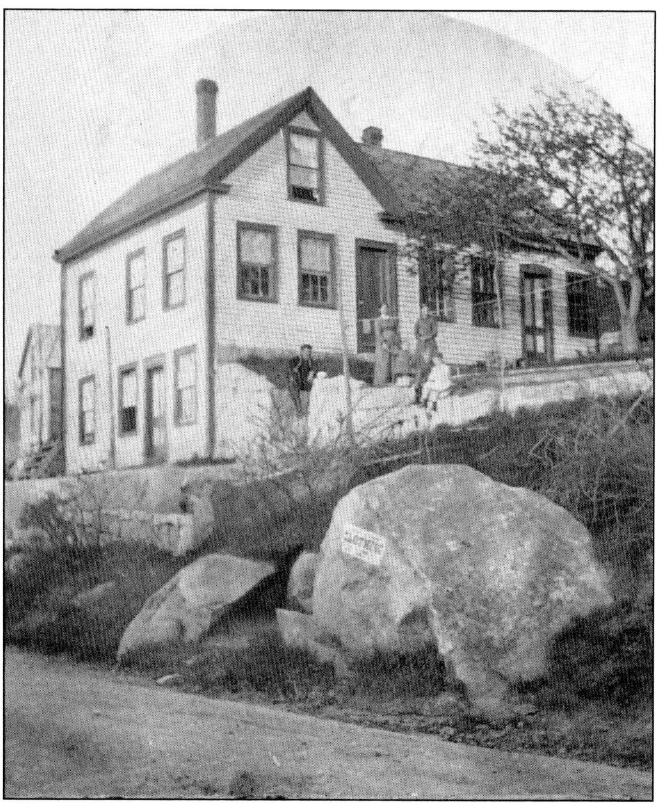

Forty Years at the Helm. One of the most famous Cape Ann granite sloops was the *Albert Baldwin* out of Bay View, which carried stone for the Cape Ann Granite Company and later for the Rockport Granite Company. Known as the "floating ledge," the *Baldwin* was built in Essex in 1890. It could carry very heavy loads and was faster than others of its time. The only skipper that the *Baldwin* ever had was Capt. William Howard Poland Sr. (top left) of Gloucester, who was at the helm from 1890 to 1920. Nathaniel Lane (top right) was one of the crewmen who served under Poland on the *Baldwin*. The stereoview (left) shows the Poland homestead on Washington Street in Annisquam.

Five

Lighthouses and Lifesavers

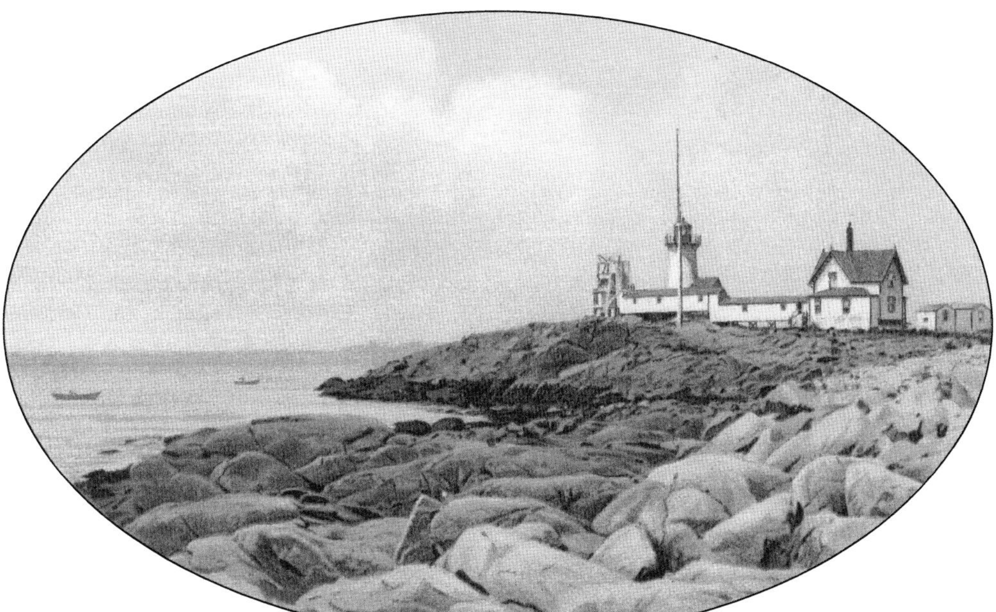

Eastern Point Light. The beacon at the entrance to Gloucester harbor has been a landmark for seafarers past and present. This early-1900s postcard comes from a series titled "New England Views on Boston & Maine R.R."

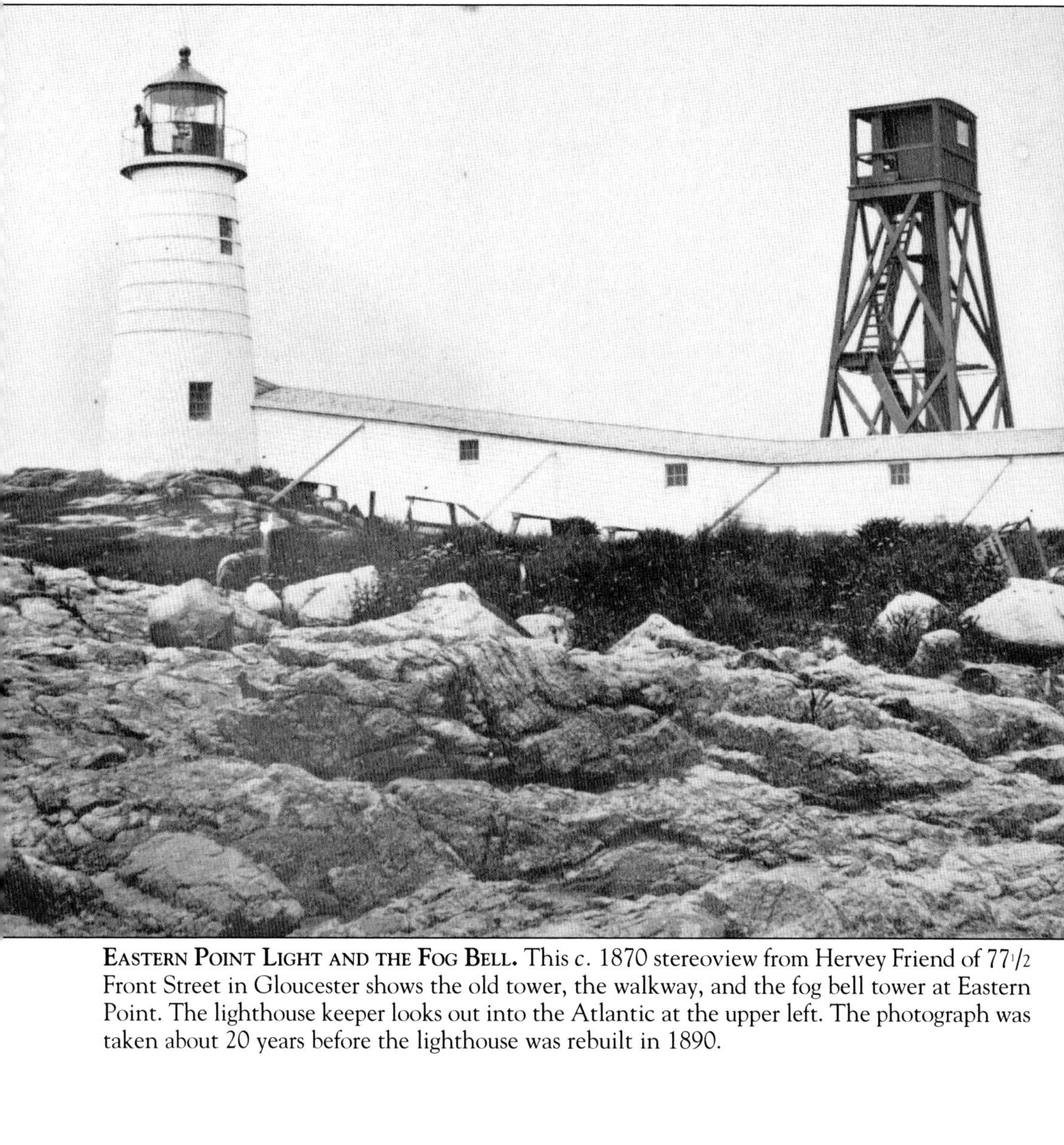

EASTERN POINT LIGHT AND THE FOG BELL. This *c.* 1870 stereoview from Hervey Friend of 77 1/2 Front Street in Gloucester shows the old tower, the walkway, and the fog bell tower at Eastern Point. The lighthouse keeper looks out into the Atlantic at the upper left. The photograph was taken about 20 years before the lighthouse was rebuilt in 1890.

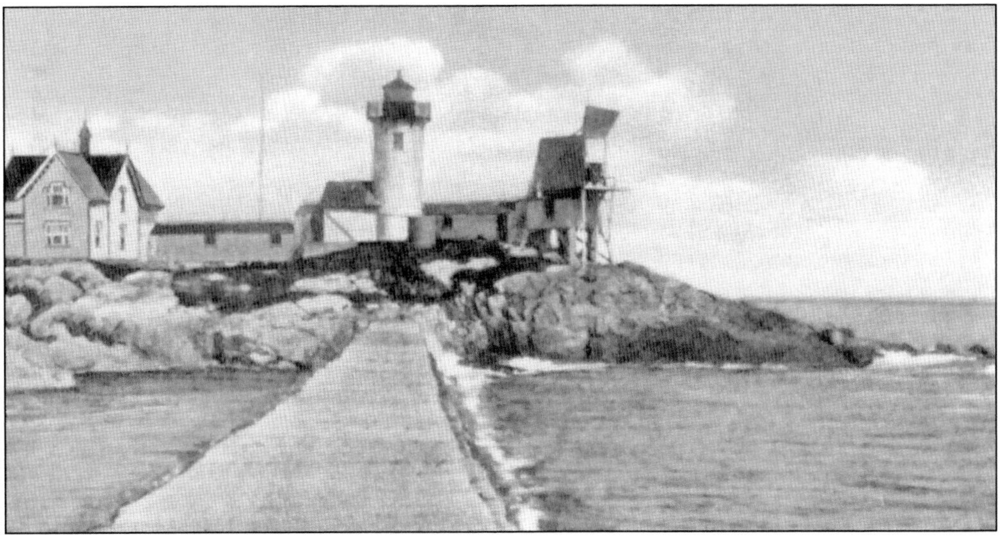

THIRTY OR SO YEARS LATER. These turn-of-the-century postcards show Eastern Point Light after is was rebuilt in 1890. The revolving lantern and fog bell were first operated by hand-wound devices. In the foreground of the view above is a portion of Dog Bar Breakwater, constructed between 1894 and 1905. The closeup photograph below, taken *c.* 1910, shows the fog bell on the right, which was later replaced by electrically operated horns.

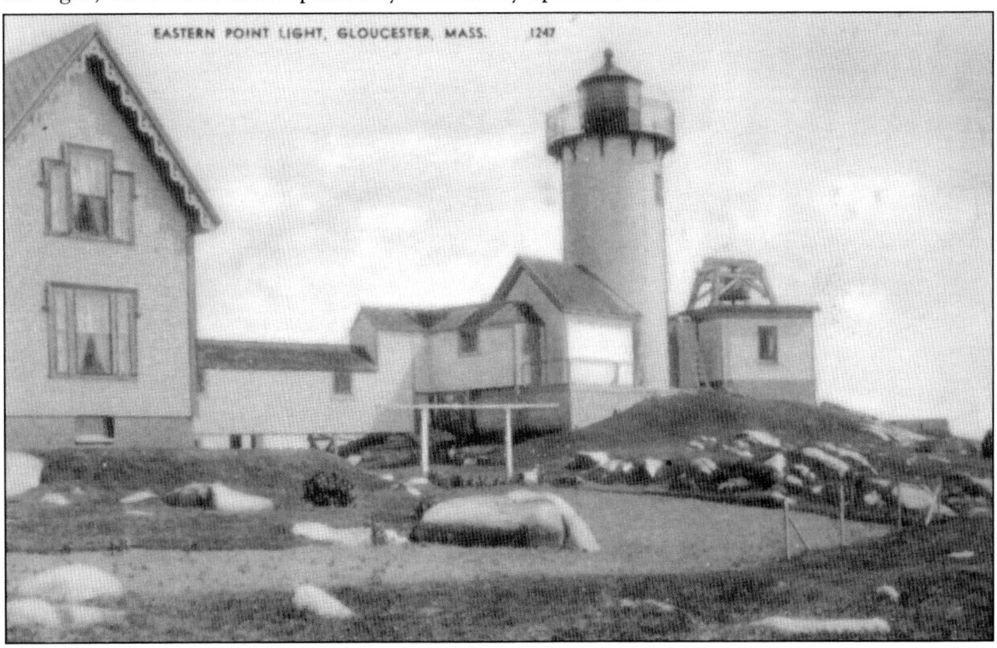

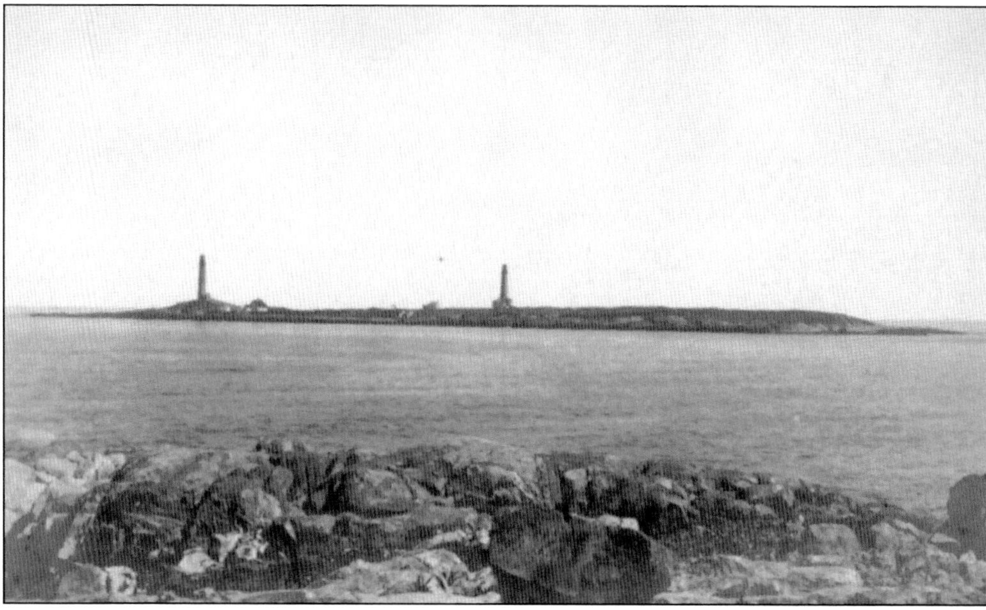

THE TWIN LIGHTS ON THACHERS ISLAND. These early postcards illustrate the Twin Lights on Thachers (also spelled Thatcher's) Island off the coast of Rockport. Purchased by the colonial government in 1771, two lighthouses were immediately put up on the island, along with a caretaker's building. The old lights were replaced by newer ones in 1861. (Above, real photo postcard from *c.* 1905. Below, *c.* 1915 closeup view.)

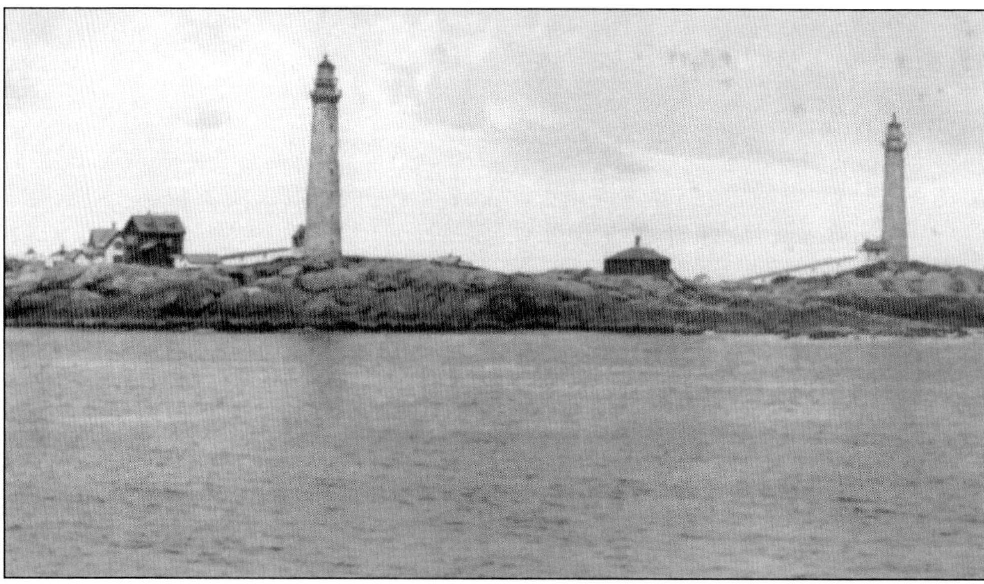

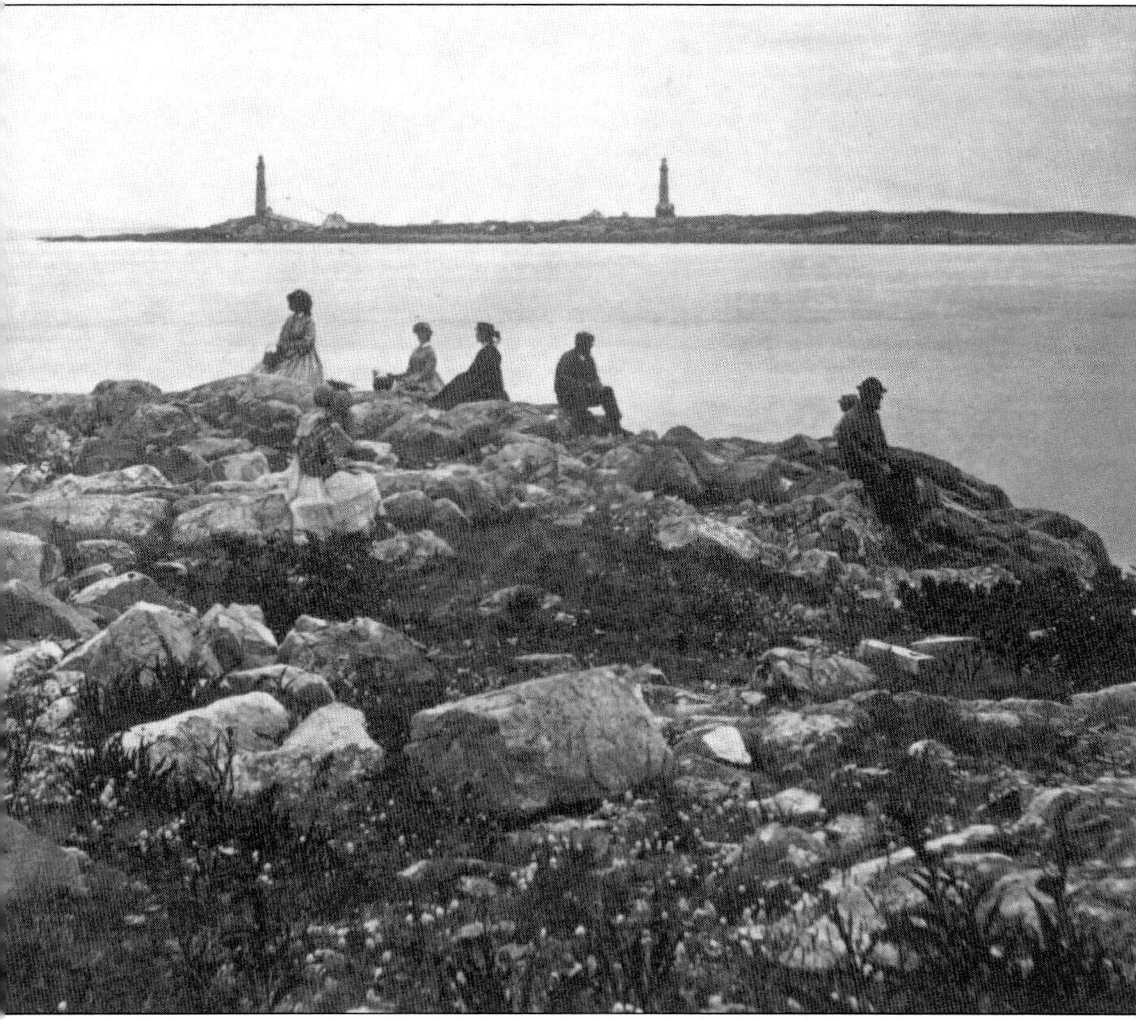

THACHERS FROM THE ROCKS. This mid-1860s stereoview, photographed by John Heywood of Boston and published by Hervey Friend & Company of Gloucester, is among the earliest known photographs of the lights shortly after they were put up by the federal government in 1861. The lighthouse towers are the tallest in the area. The island is also a prolific breeding ground for gulls. (Stereoview courtesy of Larry Gottheim.)

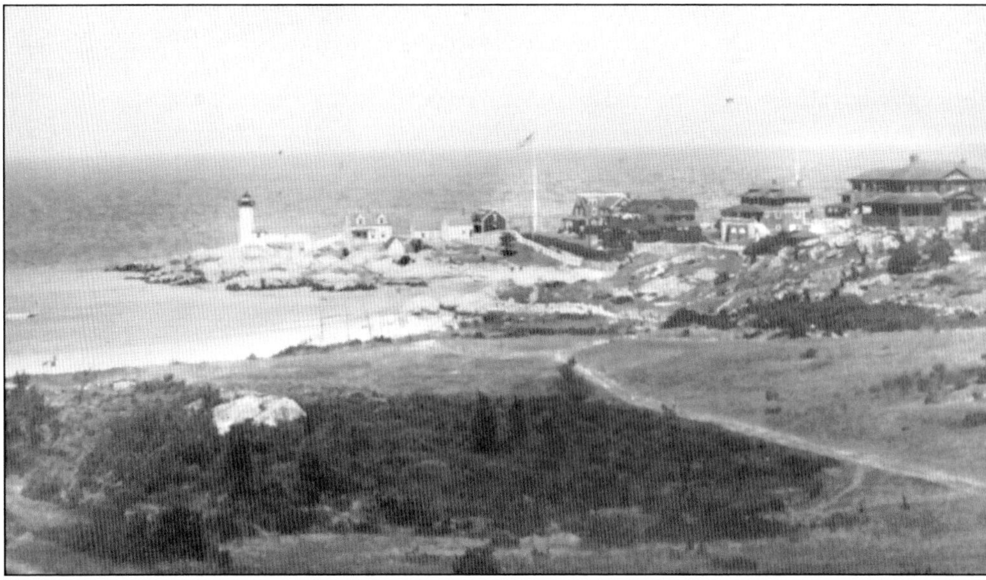

Squam Light and a Lifesaving Drill. This early-1900s real photo postcard (above) shows Annisquam Light and Ipswich Bay beyond. First erected on Wigwam Point in 1801, the old wooden lighthouse was rebuilt of brick in 1897. A lifesaving crew (below) drills at Dolliver's Neck in this early postcard from the Leighton Company of Portland, Maine. Dolliver's Neck, just south of Freshwater Cove in Gloucester, was once the base for the U.S. Coast Guard from 1900. A new U.S. Coast Guard station opened in 1973, uptown near the Harbor Loop, where it is located today.

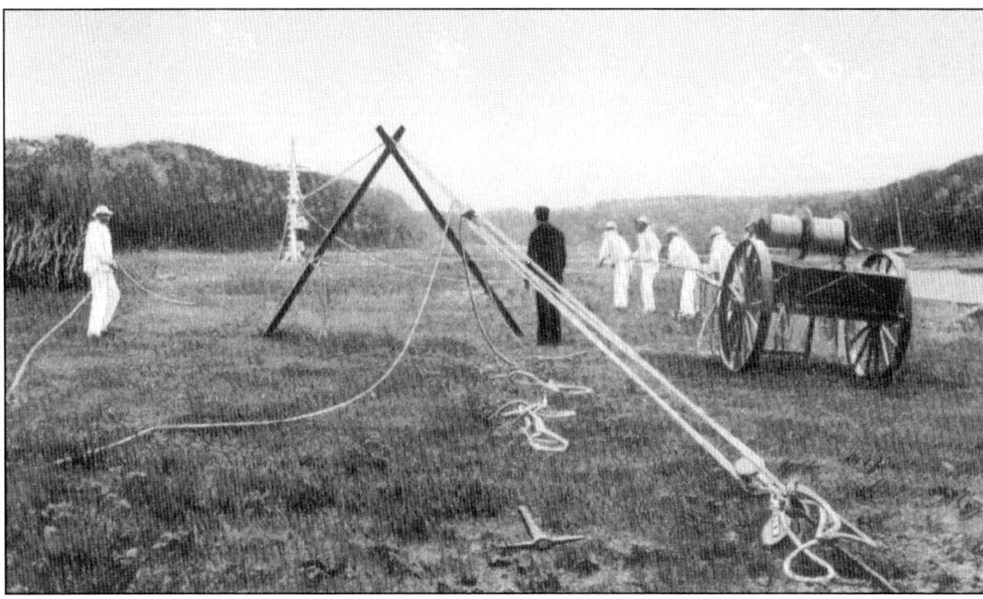

Six

HOTELS AND TOURISM

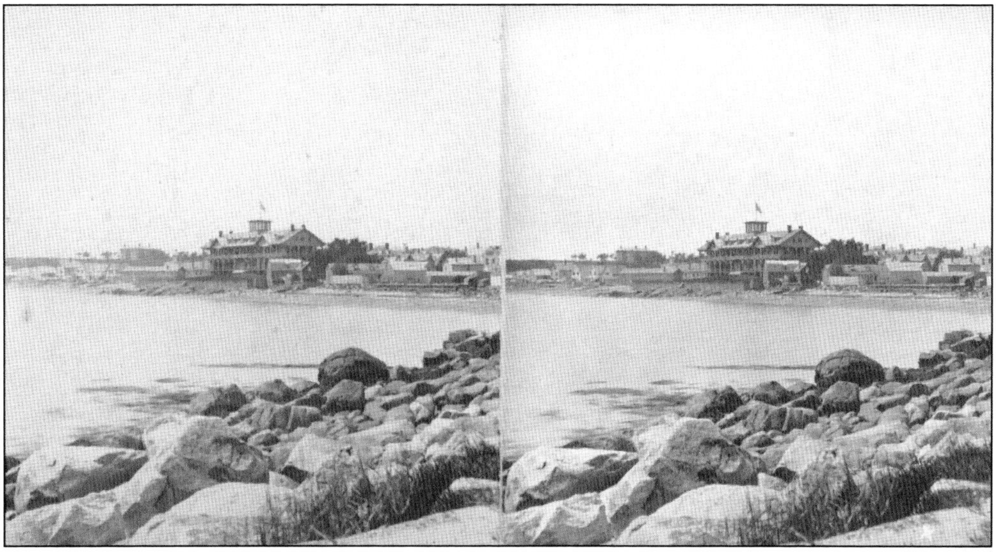

PAVILION BEACH, GLOUCESTER. This *c.* 1870 stereoview from John S.E. Rogers shows Gloucester's Pavilion Beach with the grand Pavilion Hotel in background.

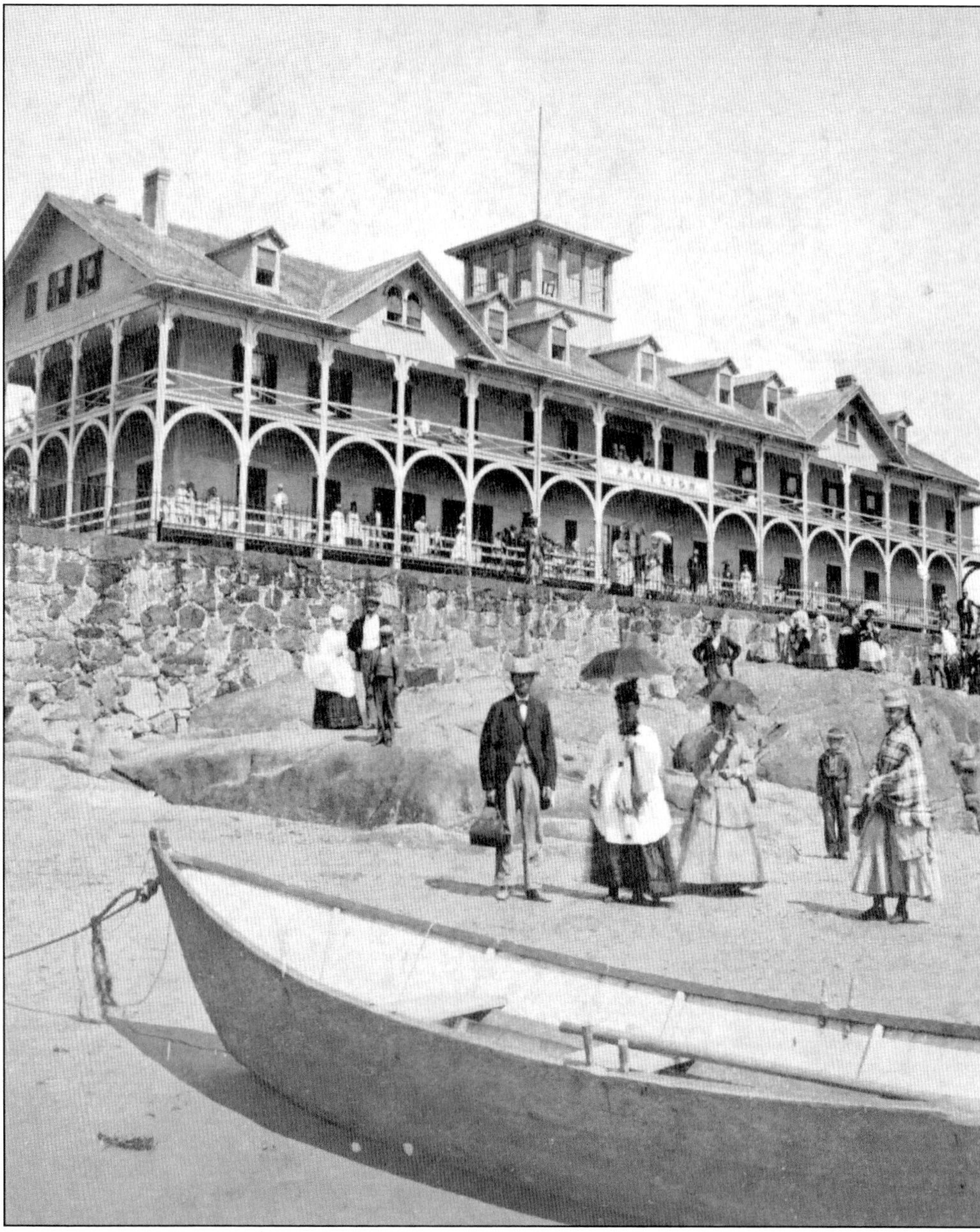

THE PAVILION HOTEL. Gloucester's conspicuous and first strictly summer hotel opened in 1849. It was later known as the Surfside (which burned in 1914) and even later as the Tavern. The Pavilion lured its guests with broad vistas of the Atlantic to the east. The once grand structure is now a professional office building. J.W. and J.S. Moulton of Salem produced this stereoview, c. 1875.

TIDE'S OUT. This interesting pair of mid-1870s stereoviews shows very similar scenes of the Pavilion beach and the hotel in the background at right. The woman in white (right, Moulton Brothers stereoview) is pretty much by herself. In the Rollins photograph below, she is joined by several others at the water's edge, including what appears to be a photographer and his wagon near the small boat.

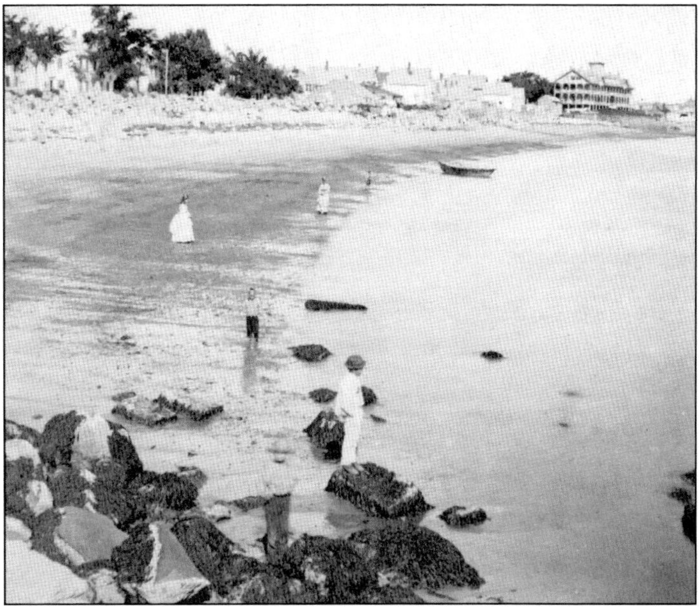

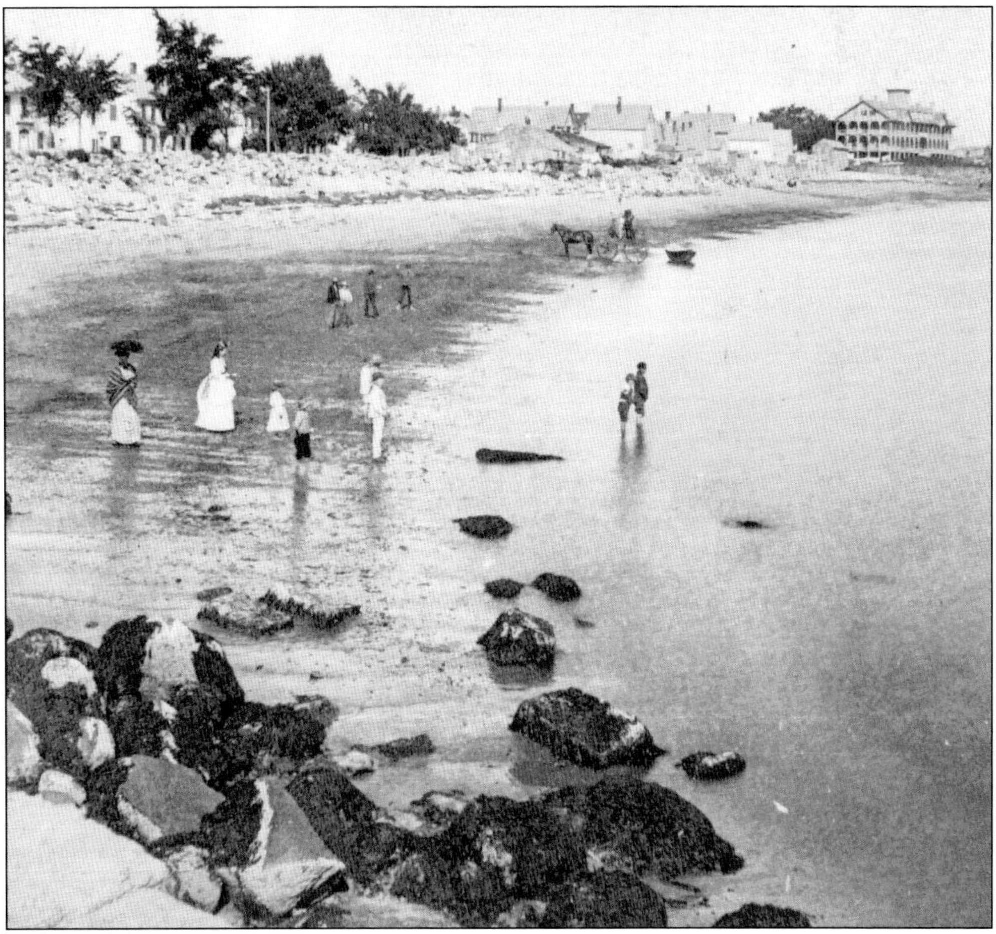

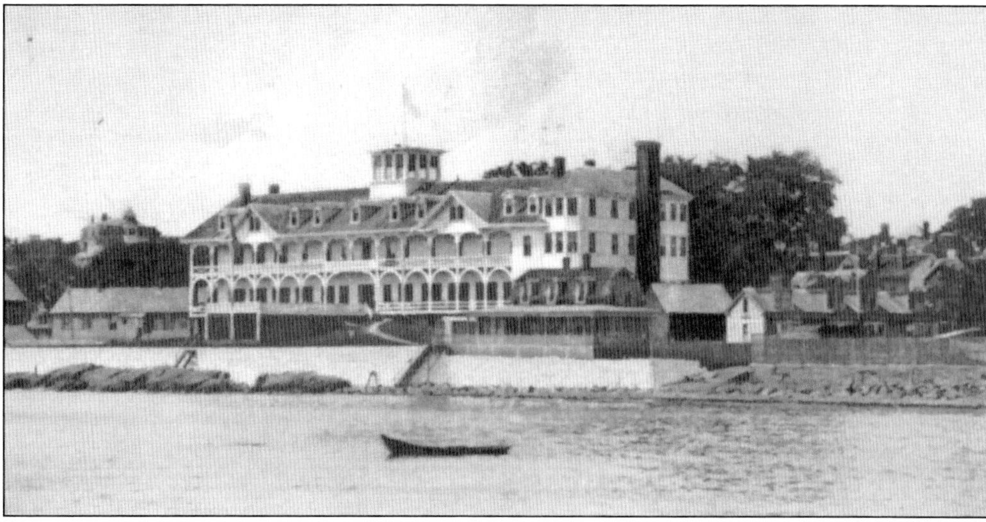

The Surfside. Two postcards show the evolution of the Pavilion into what became known as the Surfside. The postcard above (copyright 1905 by the Rotograph Company of New York) shows a seawall of sorts in place at oceanside. The real photo postcard below offers a closer look at the place. A verandah has been added at the left. On the verso, the card has a postmark of August 24, 1914; just 24 days later, on October 17, the Surfside went up in flames.

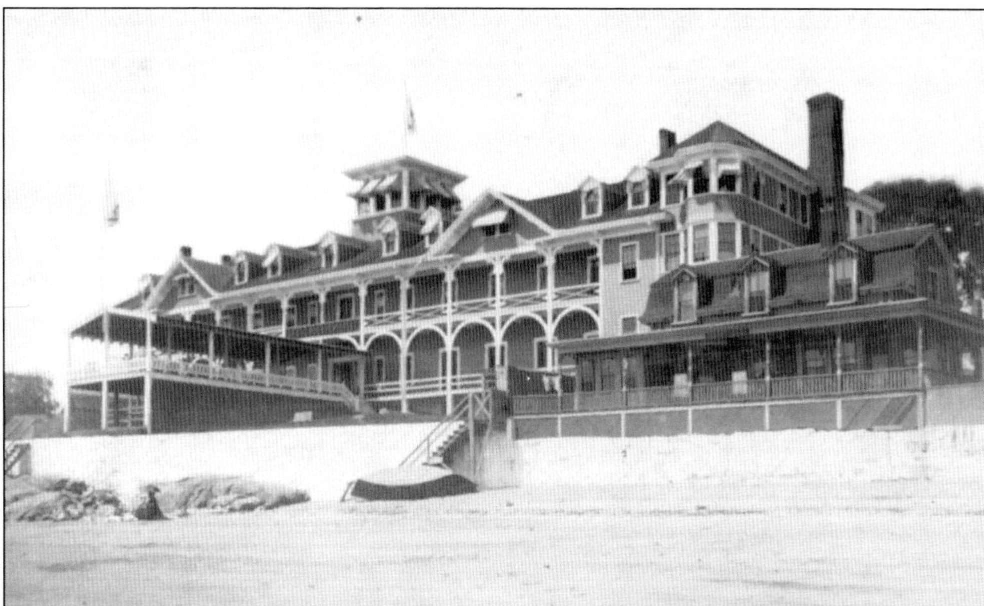

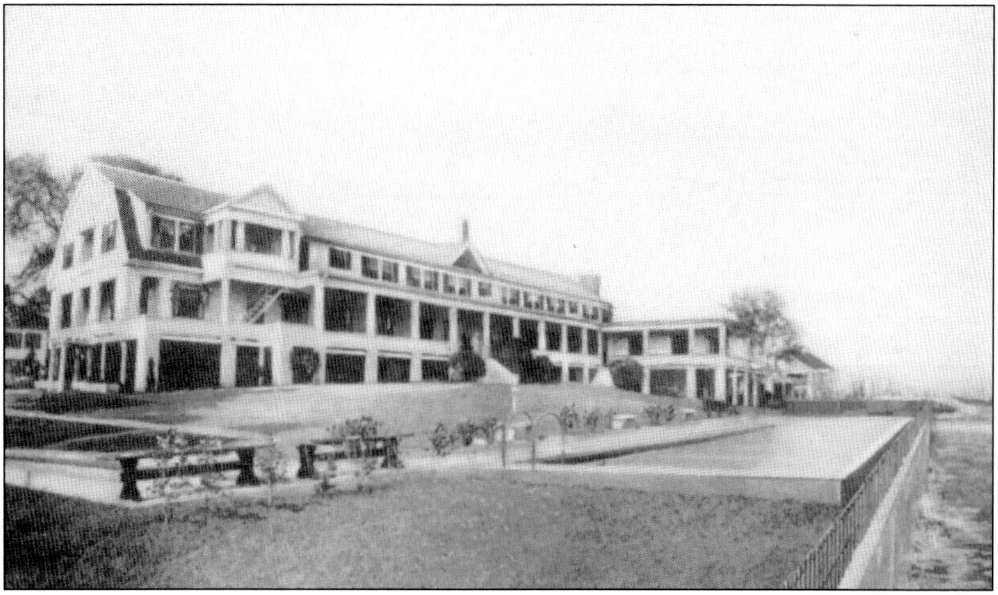

The Tavern. Much less imposing and nowhere near as beautiful than either of its predecessors (but a Gloucester landmark nonetheless), the Tavern was built in 1917, where the Surfside stood. The Tavern's design is credited to one Ezra Phillips. The oceanside view above comes from the American Art Post Card Company of Boston. The same publisher produced the postcard below at a later date, *c*. 1930s.

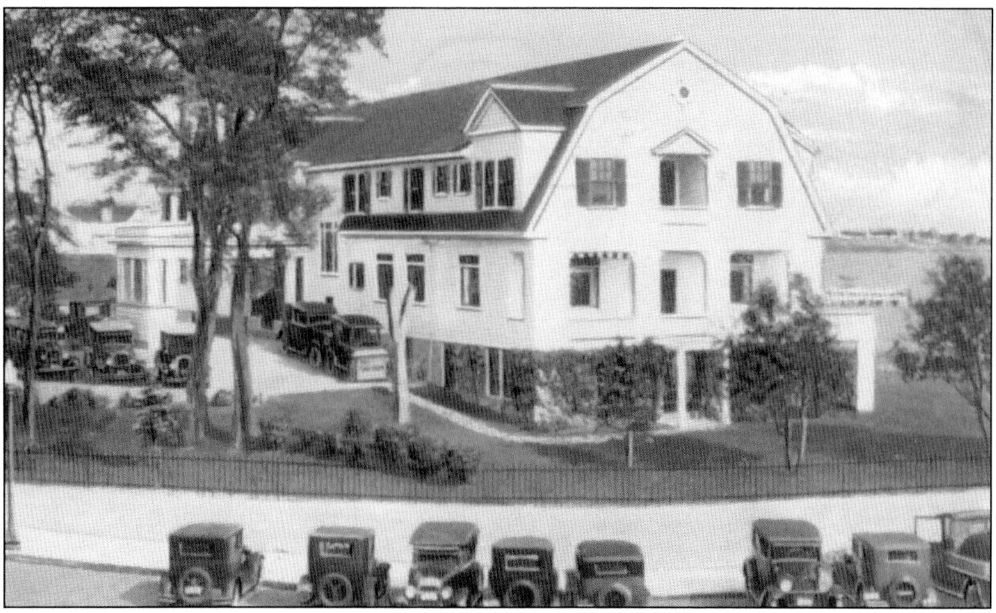

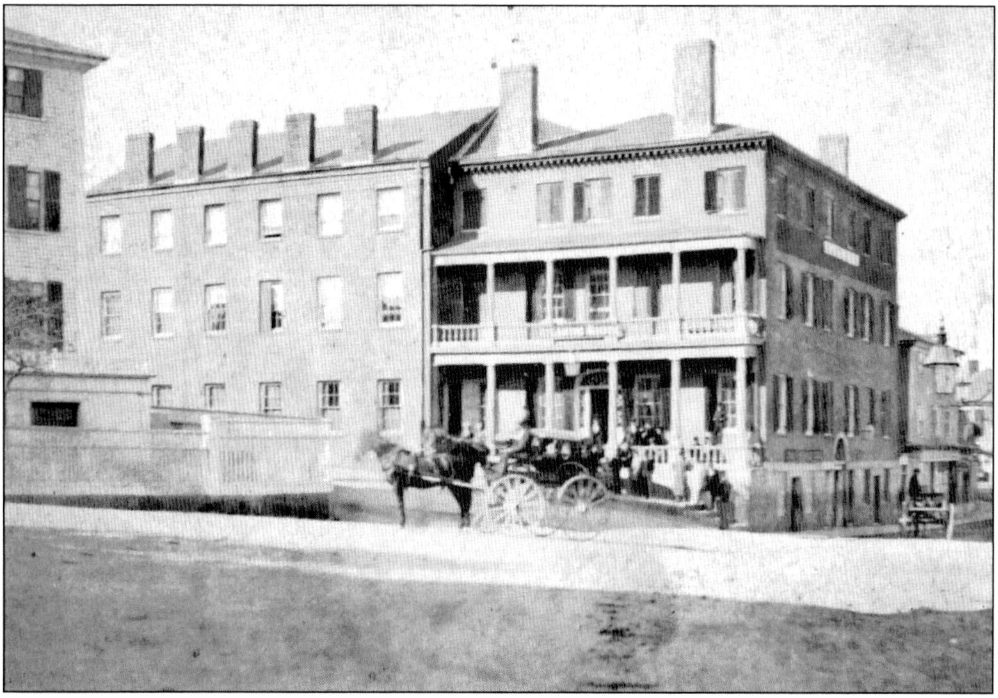

The Atlantic House. This early-1870s Proctor Brothers stereoview (above) shows the Atlantic House, located at the corner of Main and Washington Streets, Gloucester. Erected by Col. James Tappan in 1810, the old brick hotel had a variety of names and proprietors. A fellow by the name of Joseph C. Shepherd ran a small market about this time under the hotel. The early-1900s postcard (below) shows that the place's name has been changed to the Puritan House. The market is still there (but under new ownership) under the striped awning.

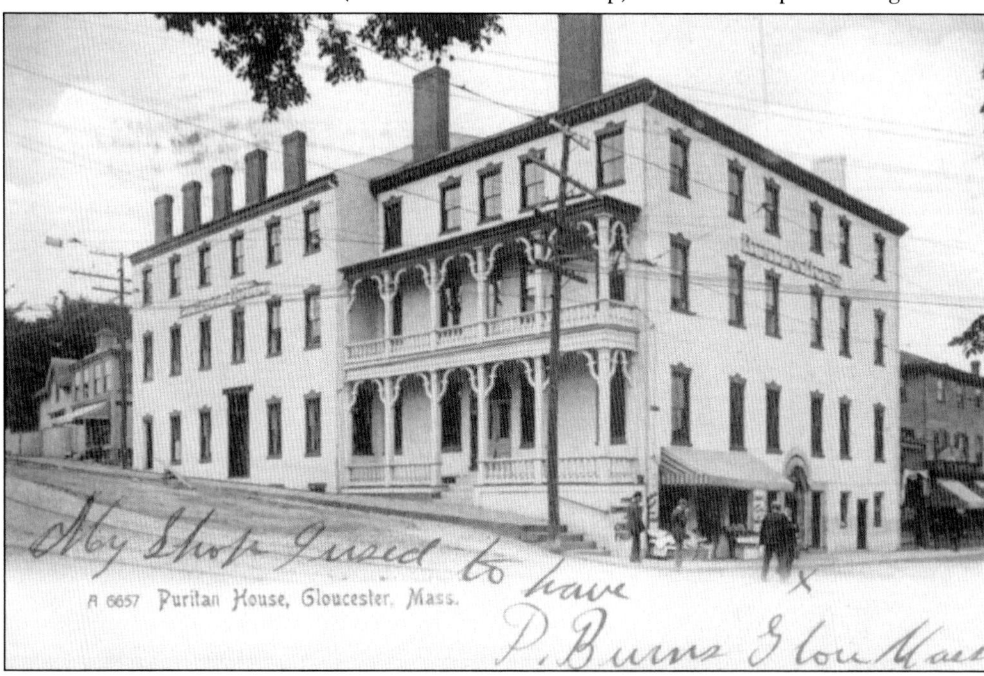

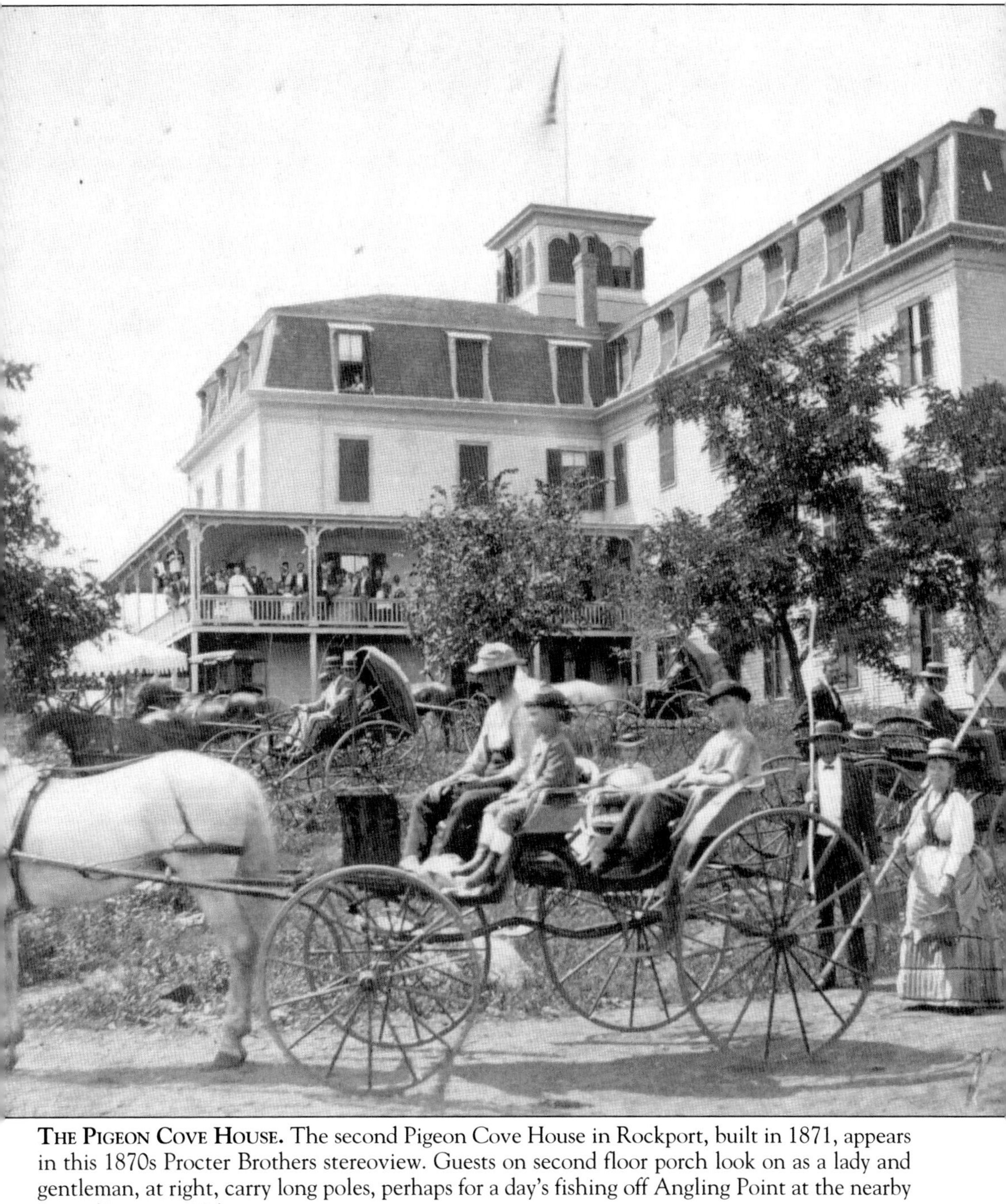

The Pigeon Cove House. The second Pigeon Cove House in Rockport, built in 1871, appears in this 1870s Procter Brothers stereoview. Guests on second floor porch look on as a lady and gentleman, at right, carry long poles, perhaps for a day's fishing off Angling Point at the nearby cove. (See page 22.)

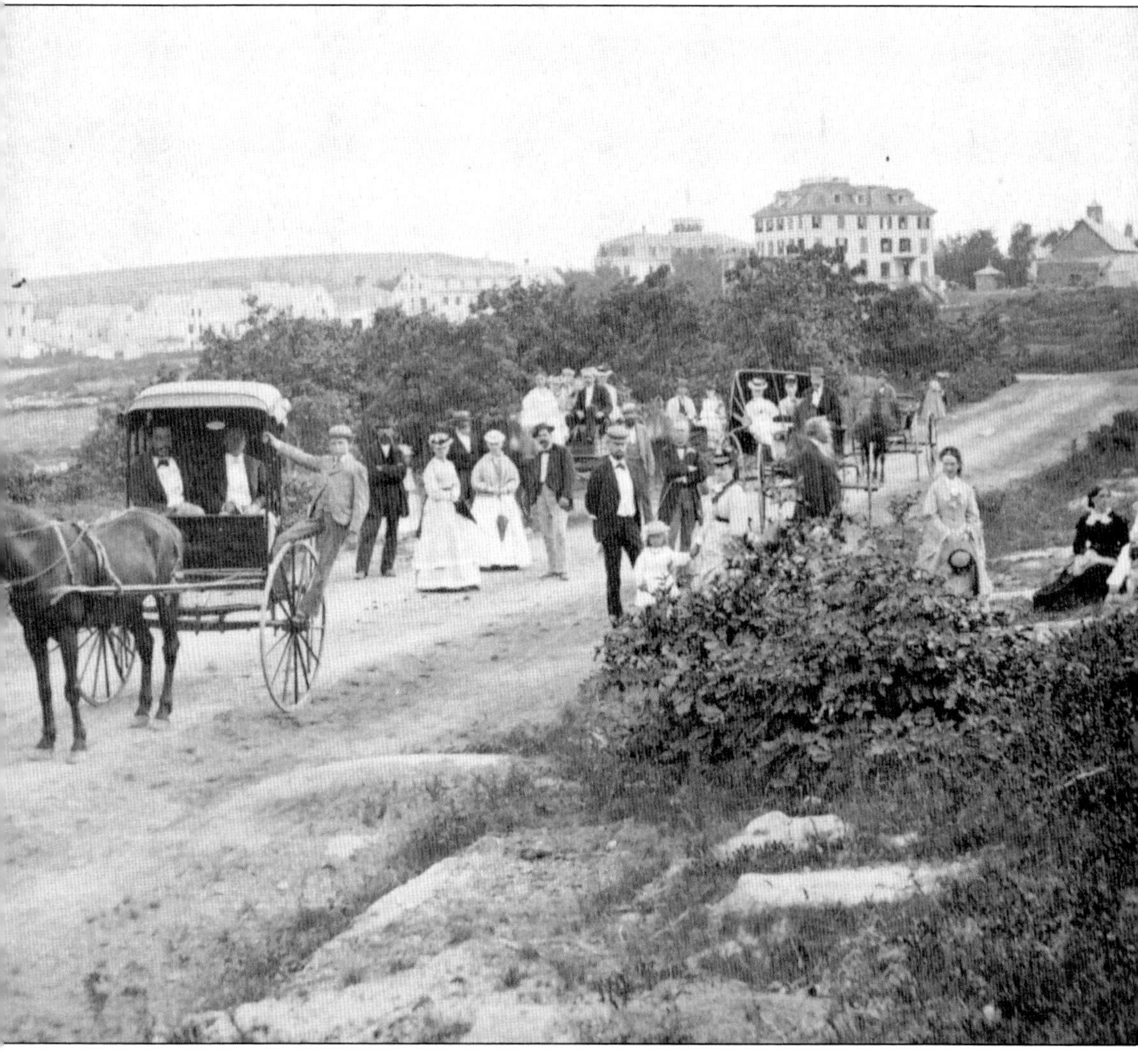

Out and About. With Pigeon Cove House in the background, hotel guests pause along Phillips Avenue, looking south in this 1873 Procter Brothers stereoview. Pigeon Cove House was one of several built in Rockport that attracted many well-known visitors for rest and relaxation, including essayist and poet Ralph Waldo Emerson.

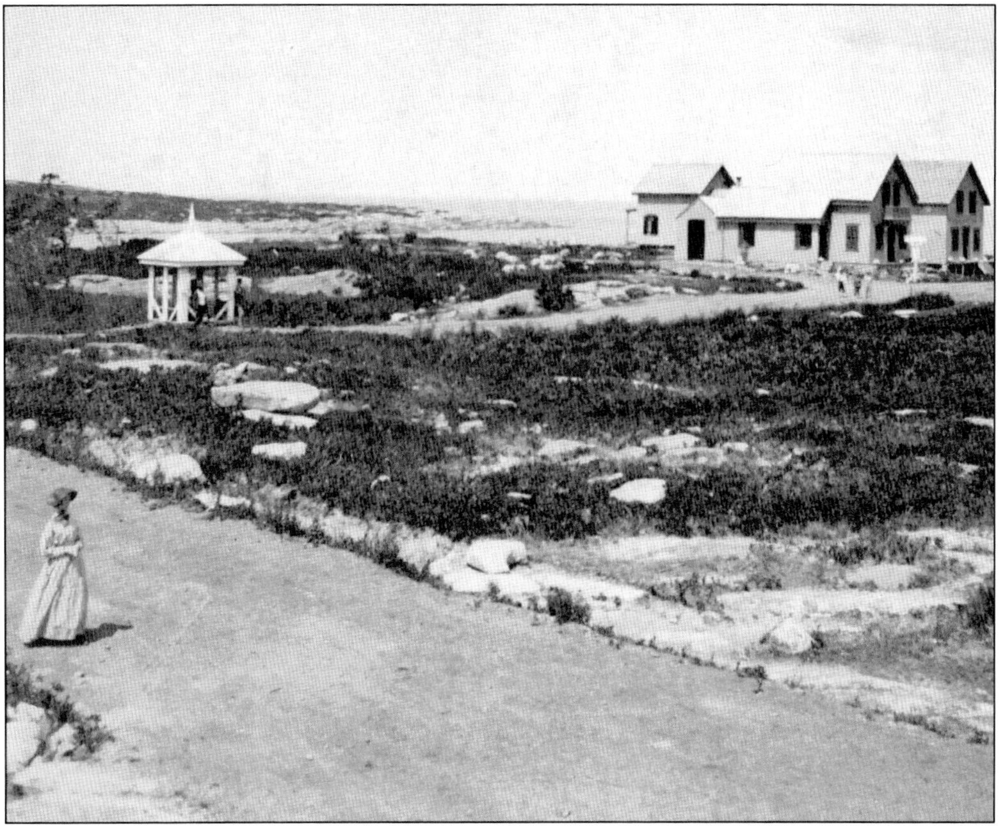

LOOKING TOWARD HALIBUT POINT. A pencil notation on the verso of the Procter Brothers stereoview above indicates this is Phillips Avenue at Pigeon Cove, looking north toward Halibut Point in the far distance. Halibut Point is Cape Ann's northernmost tip. Developer Eben Phillips linked his summer subdivisions north of Pigeon Cove with a mile-long road around the building lots he carefully mapped out. The *c.* 1905 postcard below shows a portion of Phillips Avenue and the development.

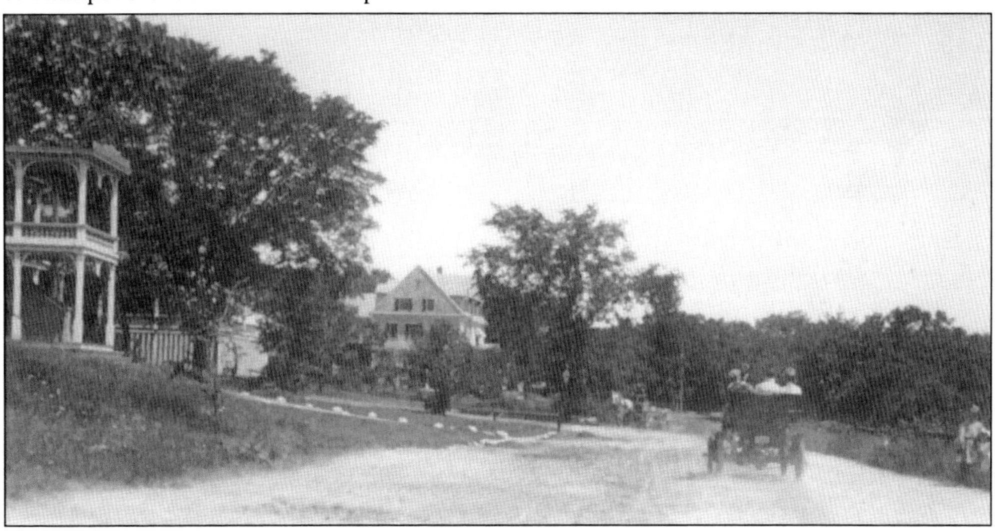

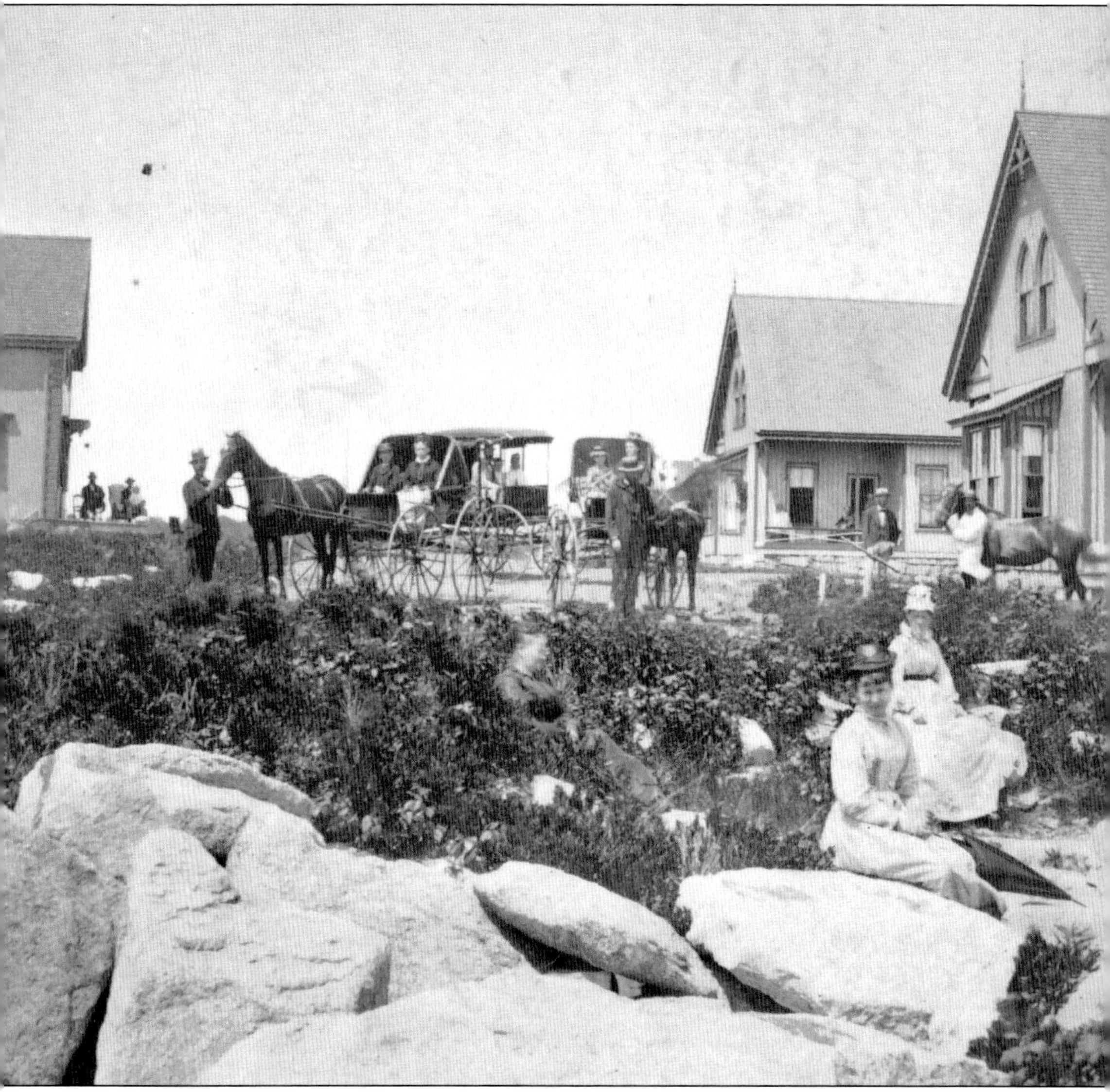

Long Branch Avenue. These cottages at Andrews Point, Long Branch Avenue, look toward Halibut Point in this scarce 1870s stereoview from J.W. and J.S. Moulton of Salem. Eben Phillips's overall plan for summer cottages there was called Ocean View. (See preceding page).

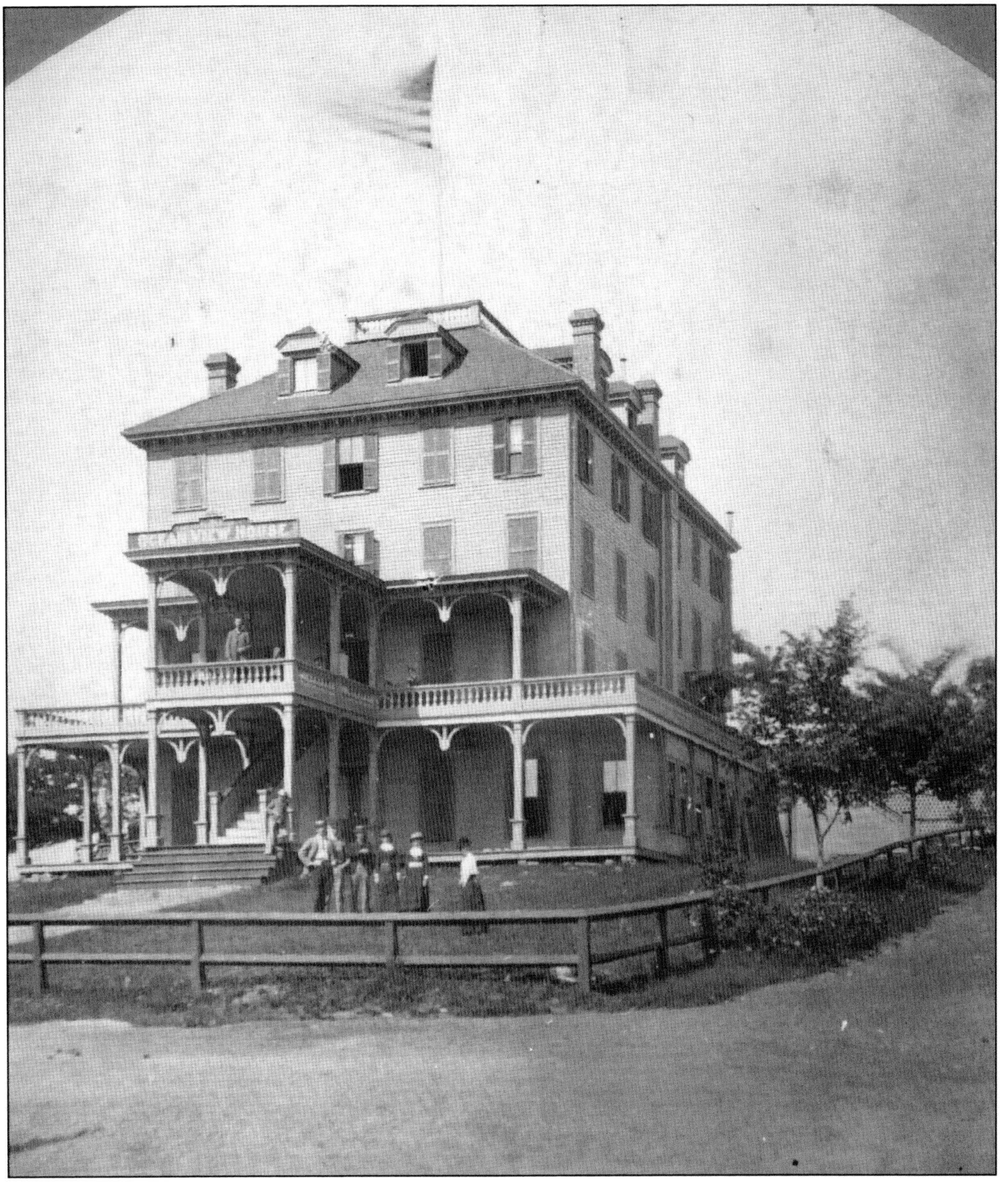

The Ocean View House. This 1882 stereoview, presumably by the Moulton Brothers, shows a few summer visitors on the front lawn and porches of the Ocean View House. Opened in 1871 by Phillips at the south entrance to his development, the hotel was in operation for more than 60 years. Unlike many of Cape Ann's grand summer places, the Ocean View House did not burn down. Instead, it was torn down sometime in the 1940s.

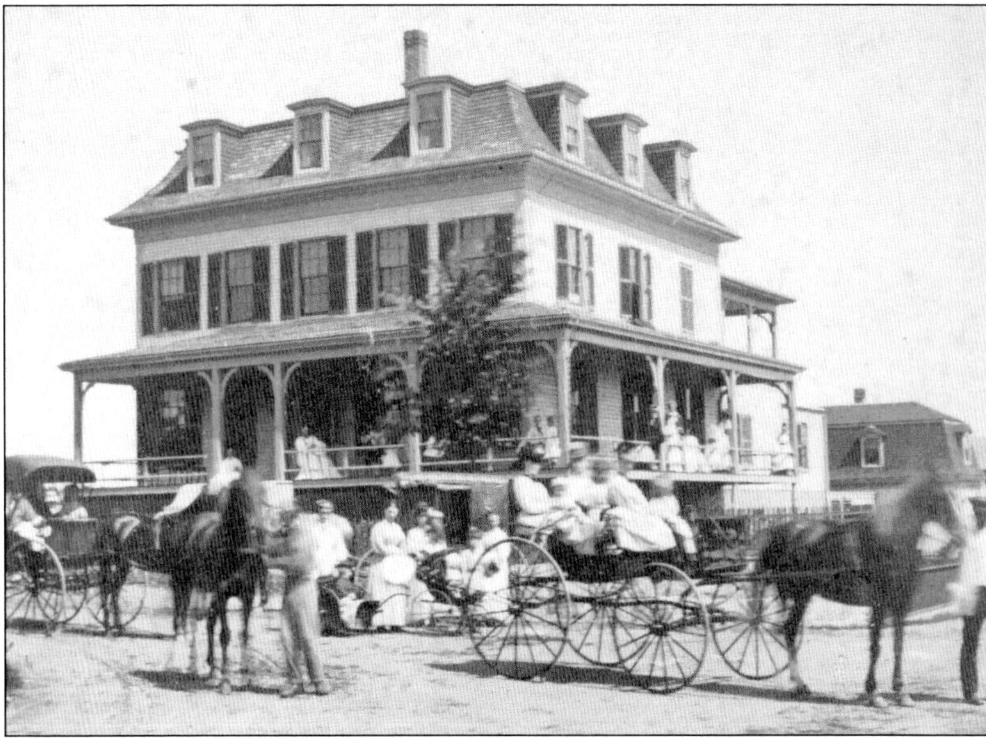

THE ROGERS HOUSE AND THE WHITING HOUSE. Colorful Gloucester merchant George H. Rogers bought up many acres of land in and around Bass Rocks (Back Shore) in Gloucester. Like Eben Phillips in Rockport, Rogers tried to reap a profit from his development efforts. This early Procter Brothers view (above) shows Rogers's summer home at Bass Rocks, which later became the Bass Rocks Inn. The Whiting House (below, also by the Procters) was a boardinghouse and sanatorium pieced together by Rogers from razed Boston mansions. This became the Bass Rocks Hotel, but was later consumed by fire.

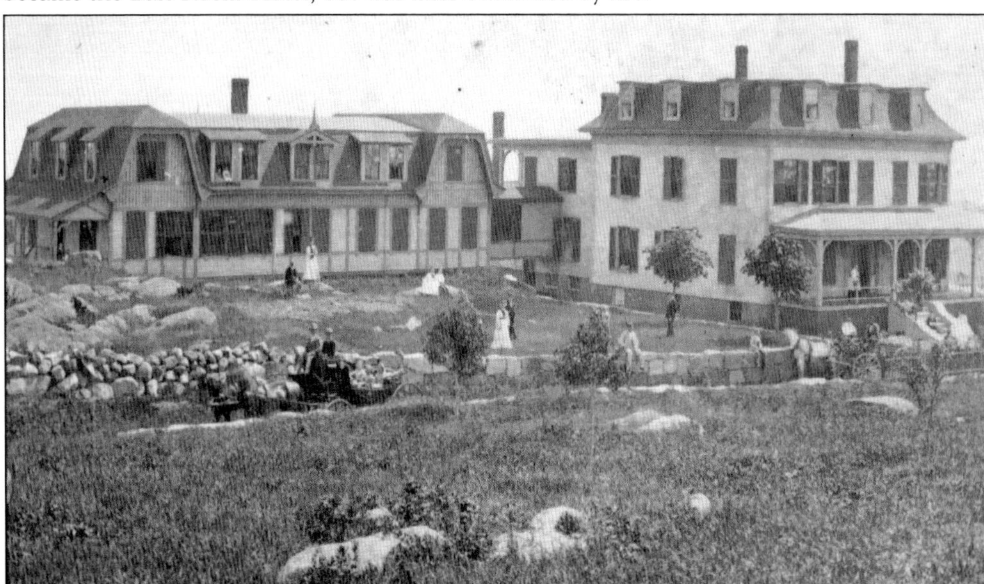

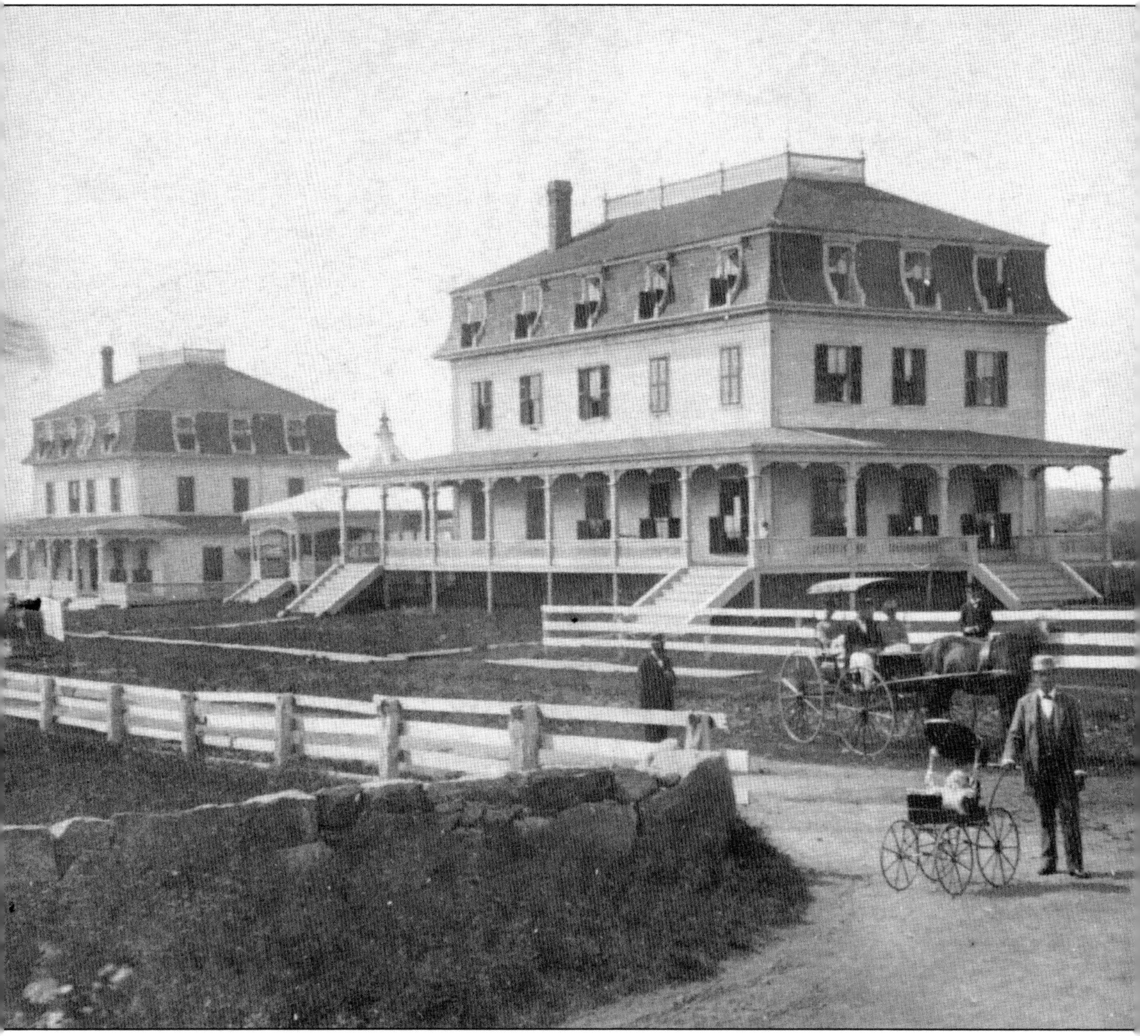

The Hesperus House, Magnolia. The Hesperus House, Magnolia's first fashionable hotel, appears in this 1880s stereoview from the Procter Brothers. It was built in 1877 by Daniel W. Fuller. An extension (left) was added in 1879 and joined to the main house by a pavilion in the center. This construction began a trend in Magnolia; as many as six summer hotels were filled with wealthy visitors during the 1880s.

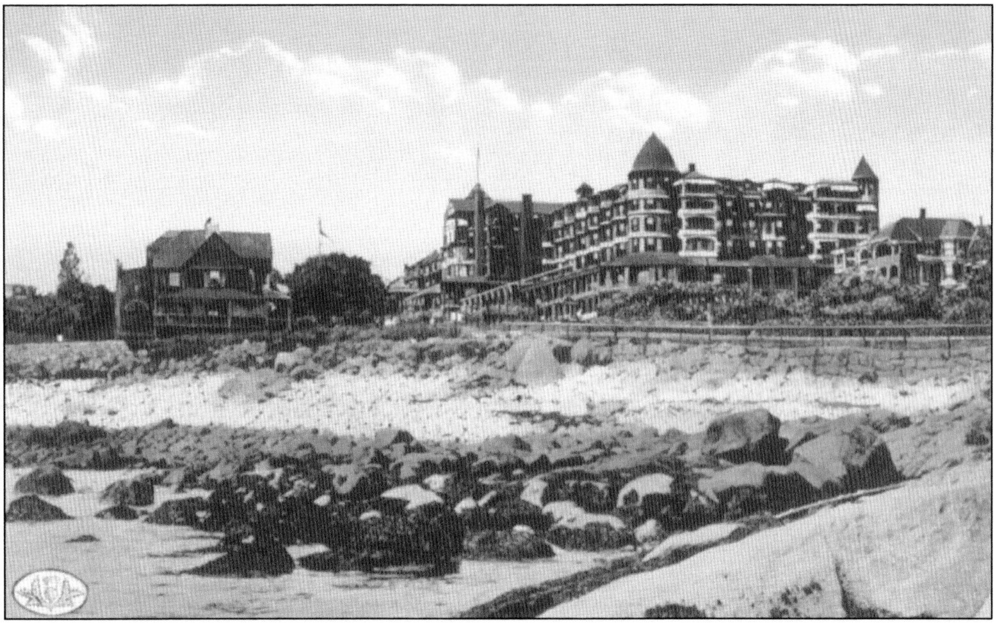

The Oceanside. These postcards, both from the early 1920s, show Magnolia's Oceanside in all its grand glory. It was at first (1878–1879) a rather modest two-story boardinghouse, but it grew into the biggest summer hotel in all of New England. When it burned in 1958, it had 750 rooms and 22 cottages.

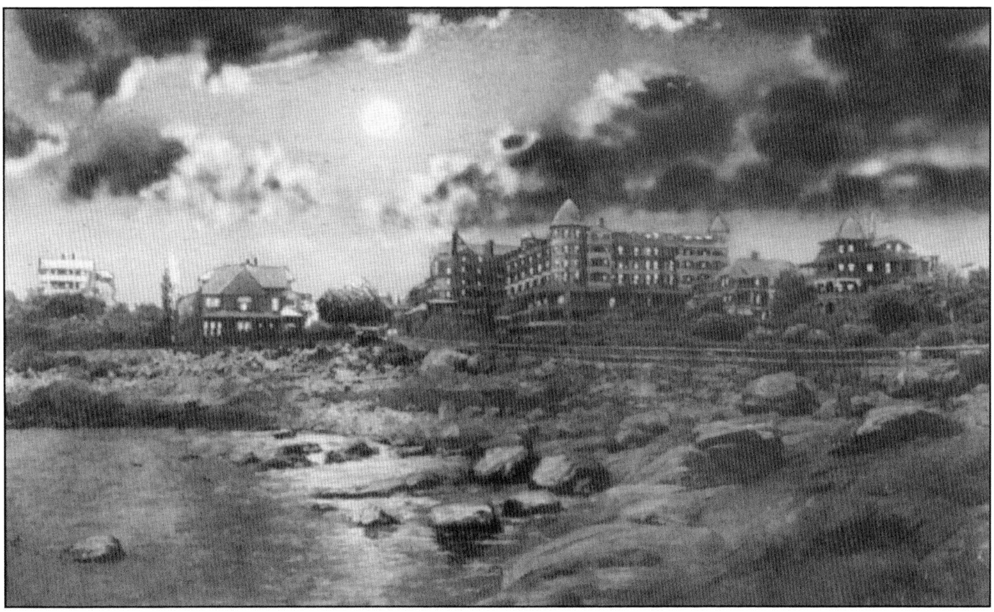

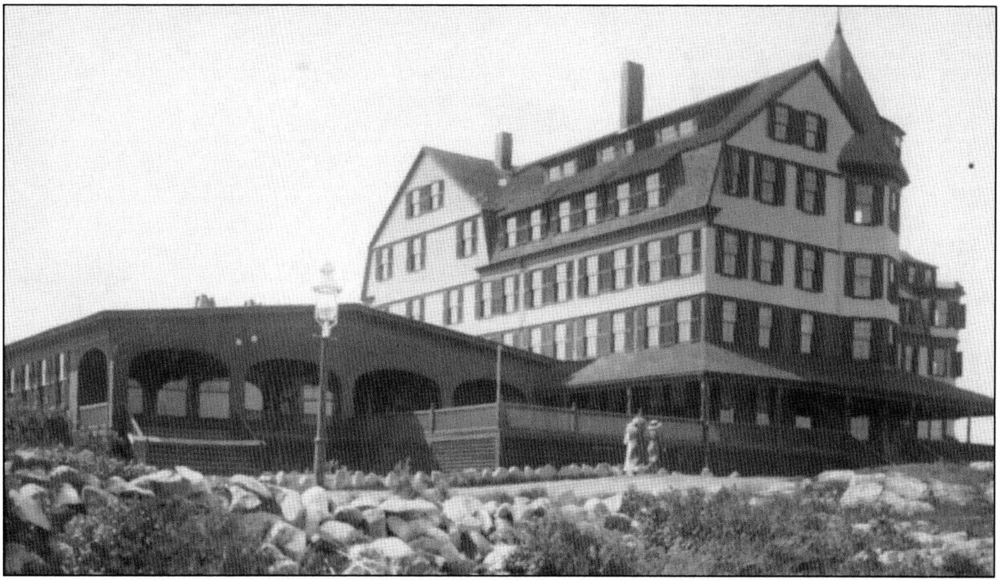

MOORLAND HOTEL, GLOUCESTER. These early-1900s real photo postcards feature the Moorland Hotel at Bass Rocks in Gloucester's Back Shore. Both the Moorland and the Thorwald (see next page) attracted a great many summer guests because of their wonderful Atlantic views and the surf at Bass Rocks. The 300-room Moorland was built after a smaller hotel on the site, the Pebbly Beach Hotel, burned in 1884. The Moorland succumbed to flames in 1958.

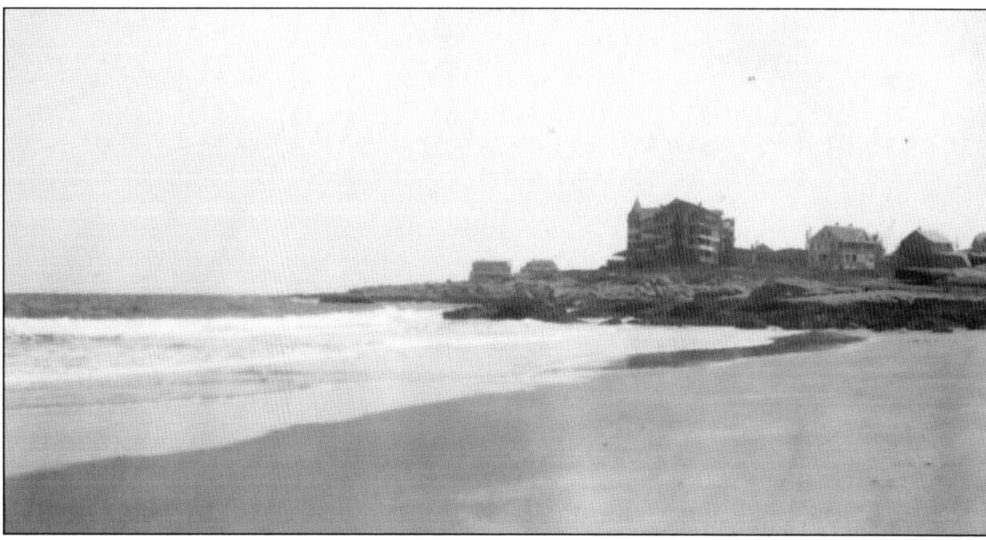

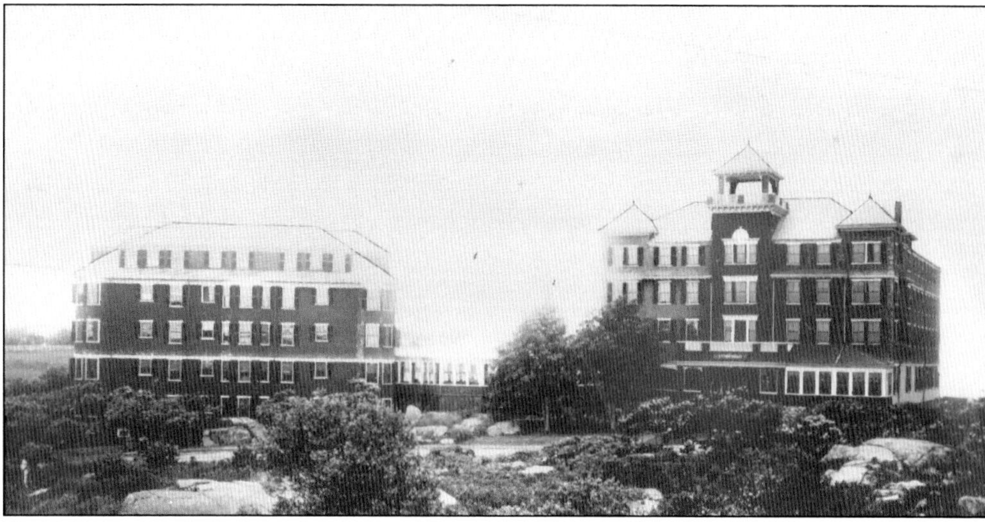

THE THORWALD AND THE COLONIAL ARMS. Two more of Gloucester's fine summer hotels included the Hotel Thorwald (above) at Bass Rocks, and the Colonial Arms (*c.* 1905, below) at Eastern Point. The Thorwald was built in 1899. The Colonial Arms opened in 1904. Situated on the water's edge at Eastern Point's Niles Beach, the massive Colonial Arms cost a reported $200,000, which was some serious money back then. A wind-whipped fire destroyed it on January 1, 1908.

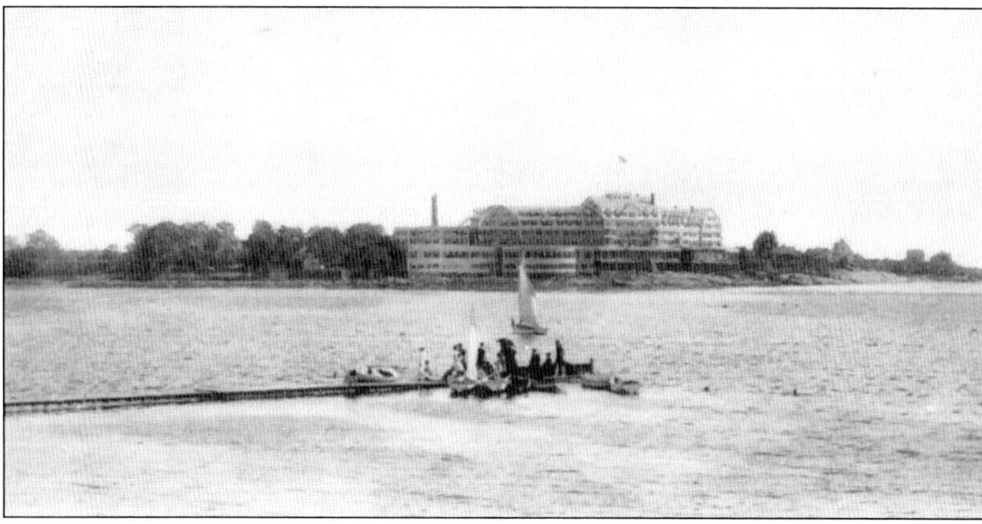

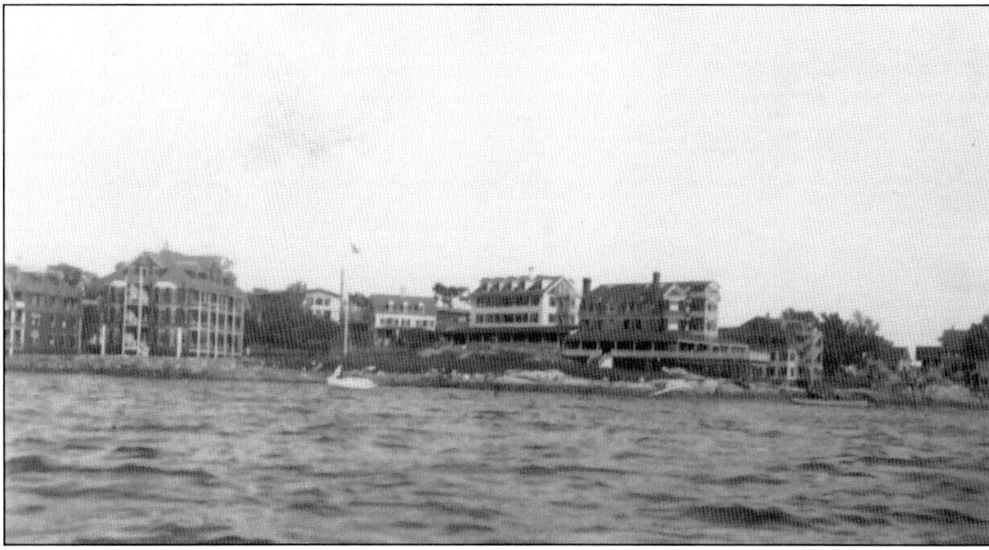

The Hawthorne Inn, East Gloucester. The Hawthorne Inn was started in 1891 on Wonson's Point by George Stacy, who also put up the Moorland and the short-lived Colonial Arms. The Hawthorne and its cottages had a capacity of 450 guests. It was very popular among notables of its day because of the pleasures provided by its casinos, boating, dancing, and much more. Both postcards were produced in the early 1900s.

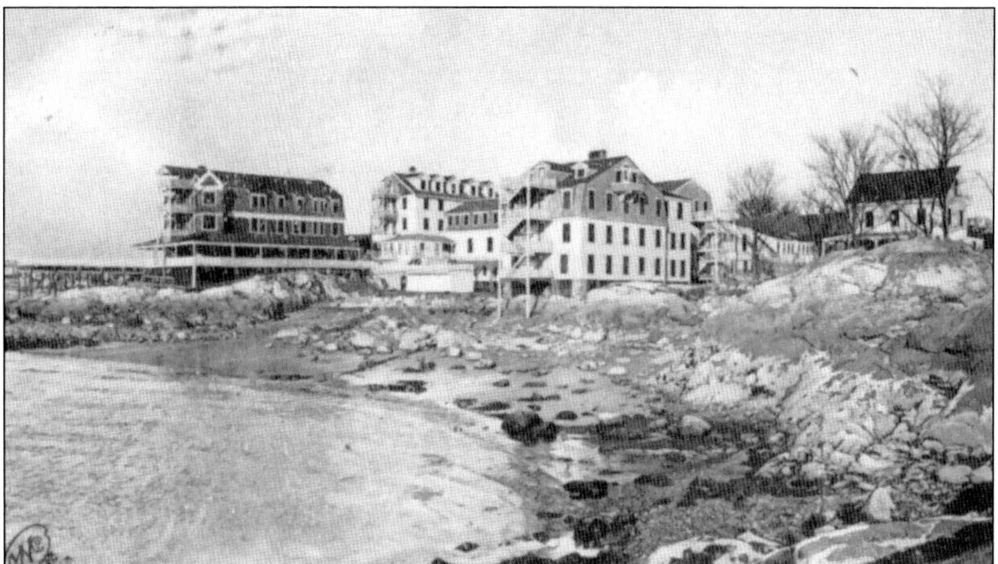

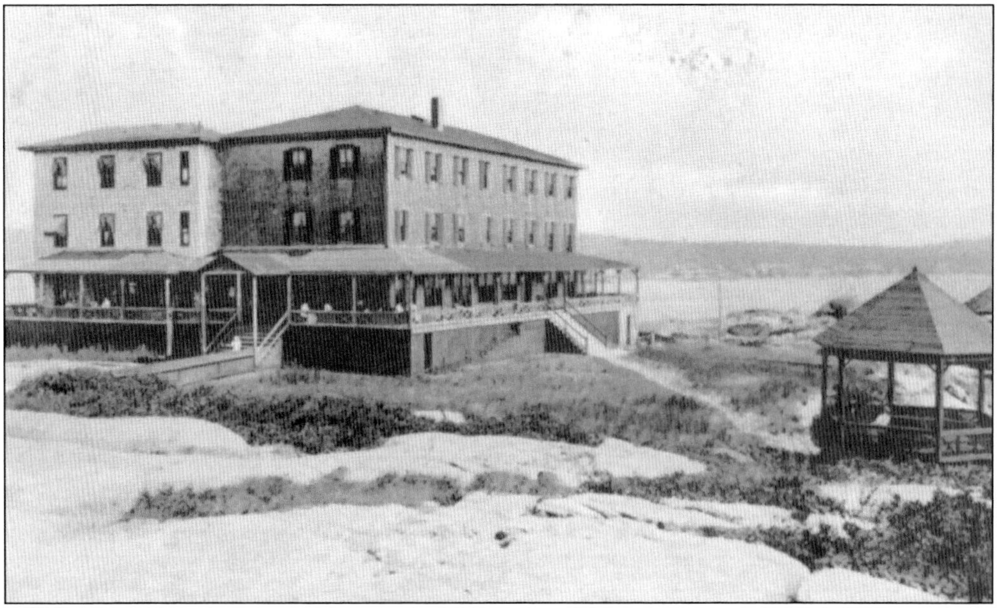

The Edgecliff and the Good Harbor Beach Inn. Nowhere near as pretentious as their exclusive-catering neighbors north and south, the Edgecliff at Long Beach (above) and the Good Harbor Beach Inn (below) still drew their fair share of summer visitors to Cape Ann. The Good Harbor Beach Inn on Salt Island Road in Gloucester is still operating today, but with a much different appearance than in this *c.* 1920s–1930s postcard.

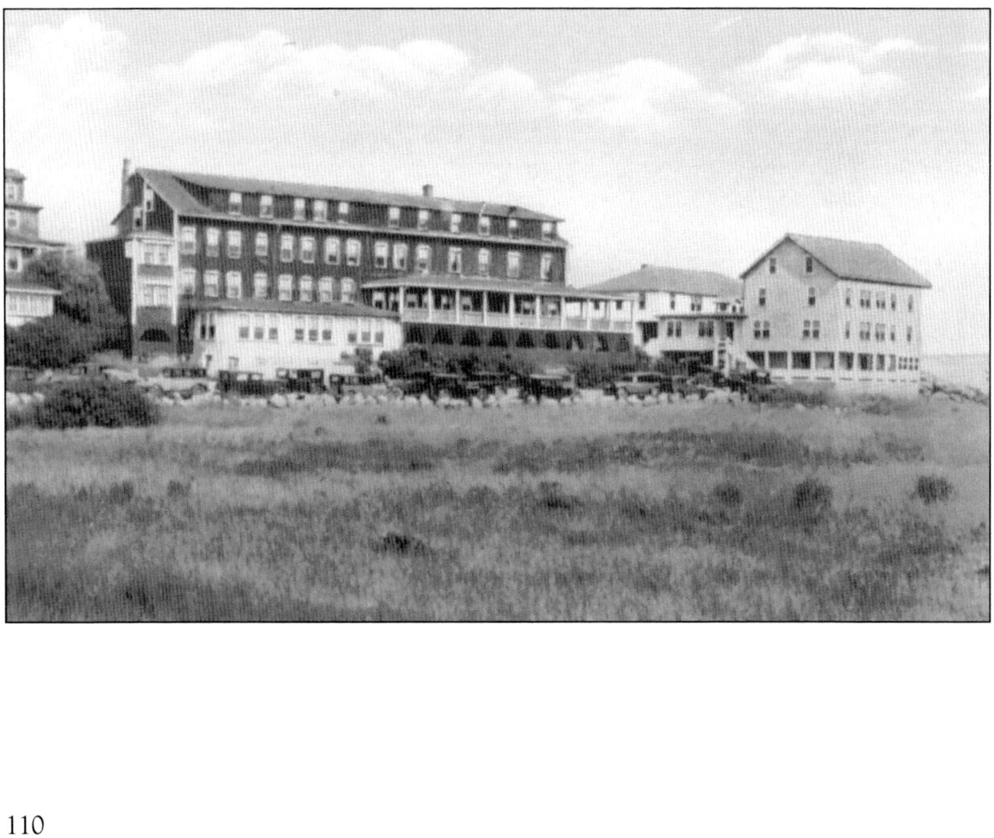

Seven

Churches

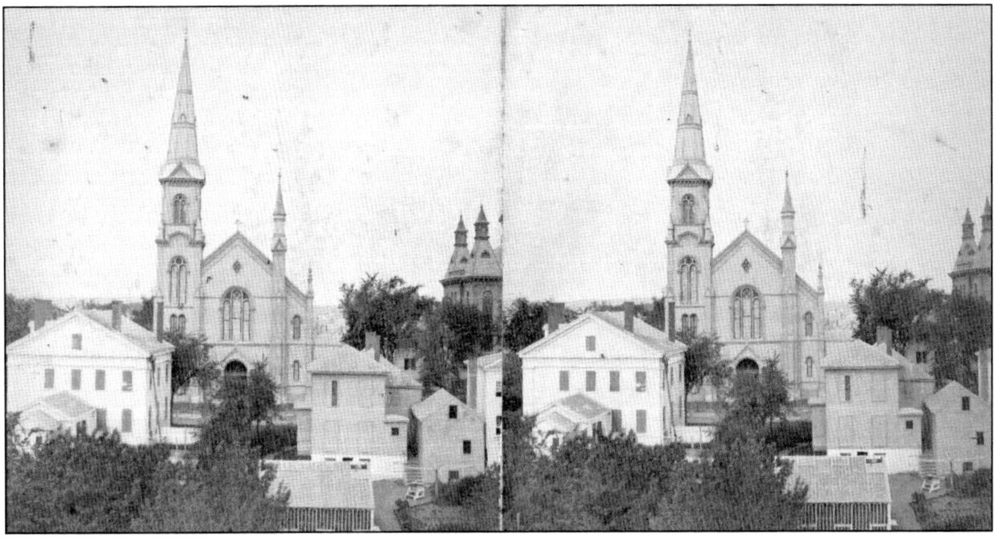

The First Baptist Church, Gloucester. This early-1870s stereoview by John S.E. Rogers shows a front view of the First Baptist church in Gloucester. The church was erected on Pleasant Street and was dedicated on May 4, 1871.

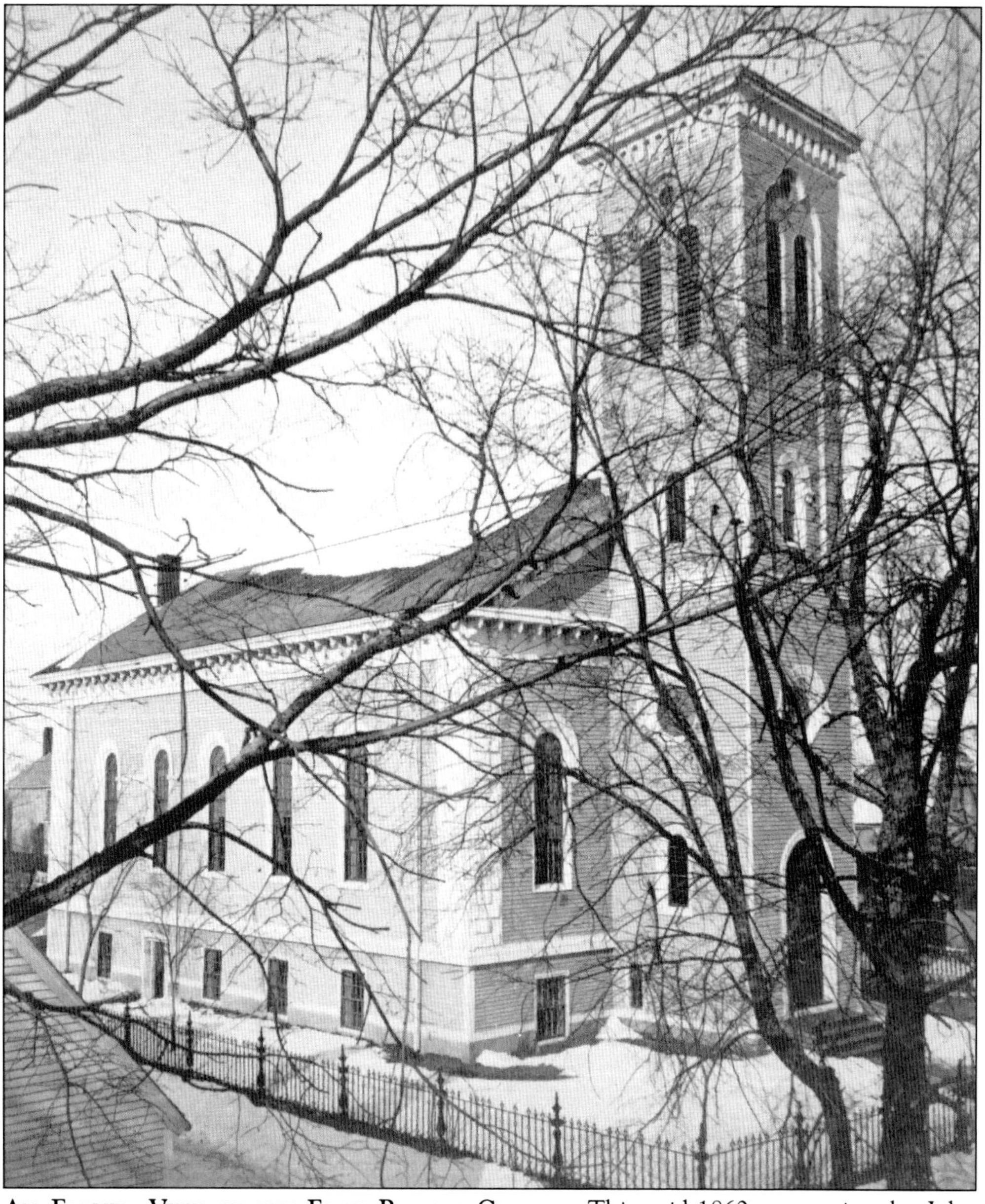

AN EARLIER VIEW OF THE FIRST BAPTIST CHURCH. This mid-1860s stereoview by John Heywood of Boston shows a much different structure than the one on the preceding page. The building at Middle and Pleasant Streets was dedicated in 1851 and was in the process of being remodeled in 1869 when it burned to the ground.

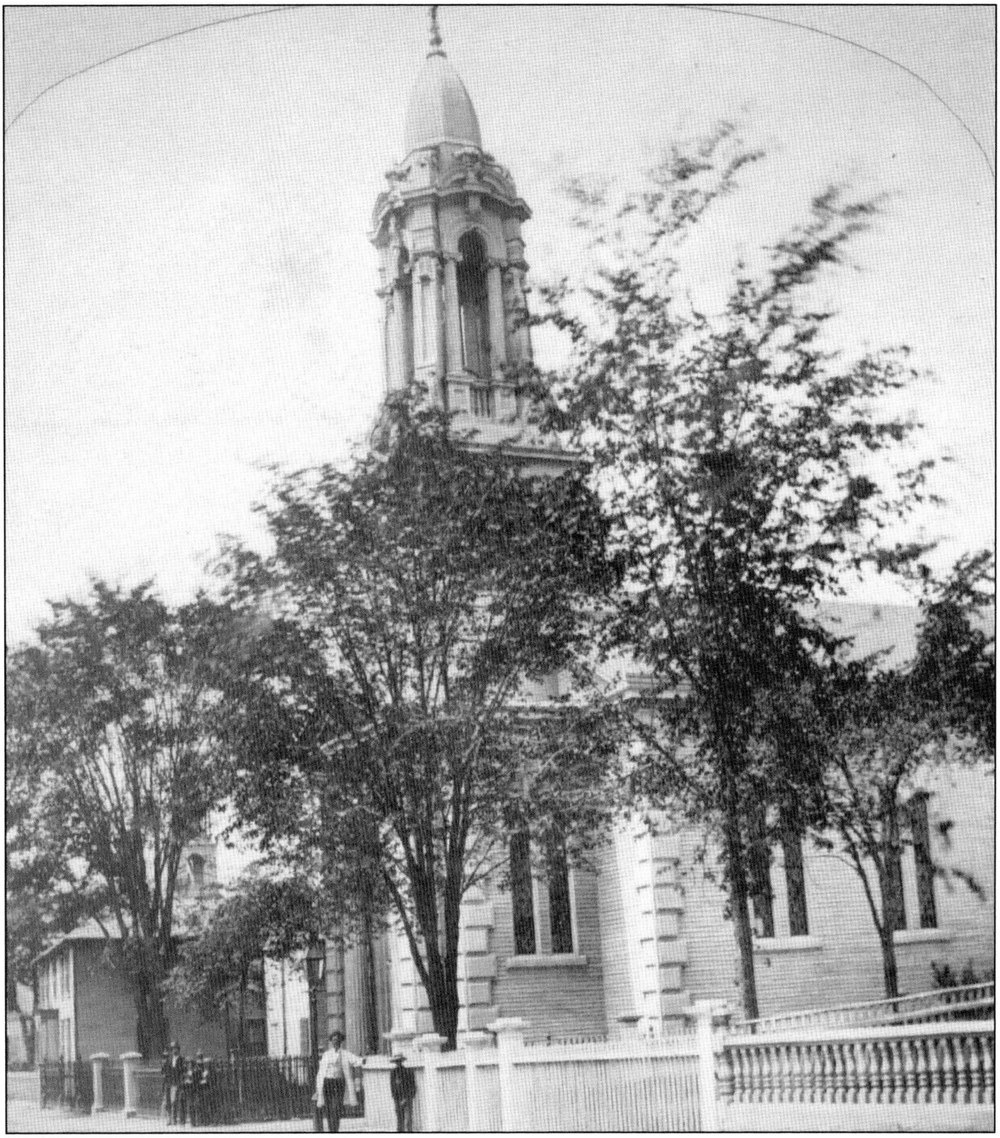

THE CONGREGATIONAL CHURCH. This stereoview, taken in August of 1875 and published by John S.E. Rogers, identifies the Orthodox Congregational church on the backlabel. This church, with its handsome spire, was erected in 1854 at School and Middle Streets in Gloucester. The spire was remodeled in 1865.

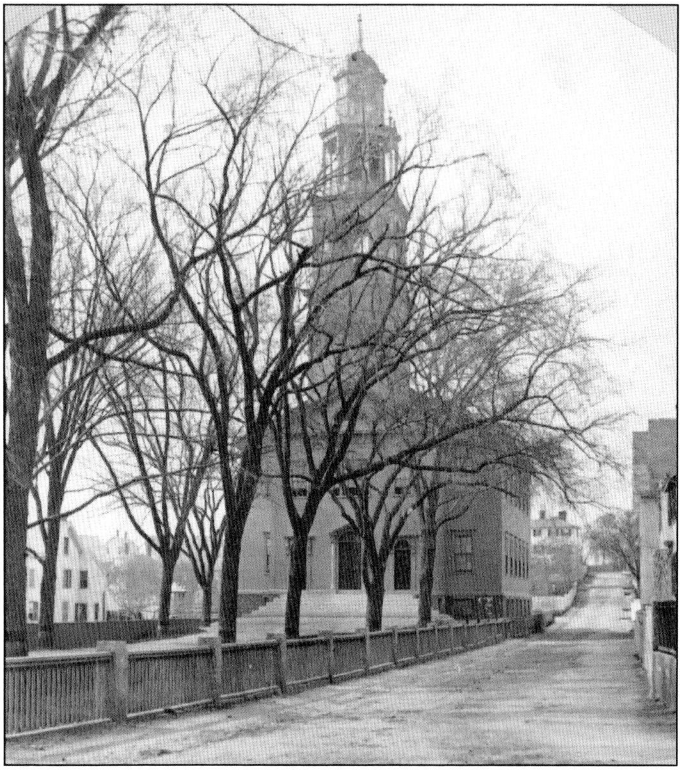

The Seat of Universalism. America's first Universalist Church was established in Gloucester, beginning in 1774, when Rev. John Murray made his first visit to town. This Hervey Friend stereoview (left) captures the church on Middle Street as it looked in 1880. The Cook & Friend view (below) was taken between September 20 and 23, 1870, at the Universalist Centenary Camp Ground in Gloucester. Church members celebrated the 100th anniversary of the preaching of Universalism during the four-day encampment. The large canvas tent at right could hold as many as 8,000 worshippers.

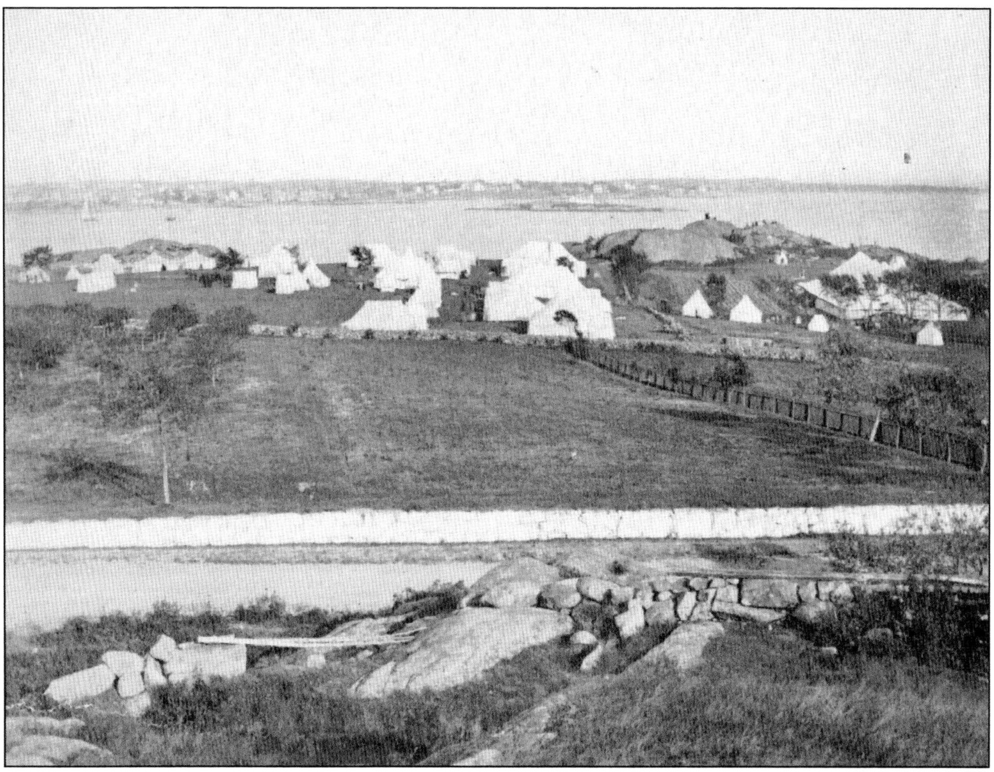

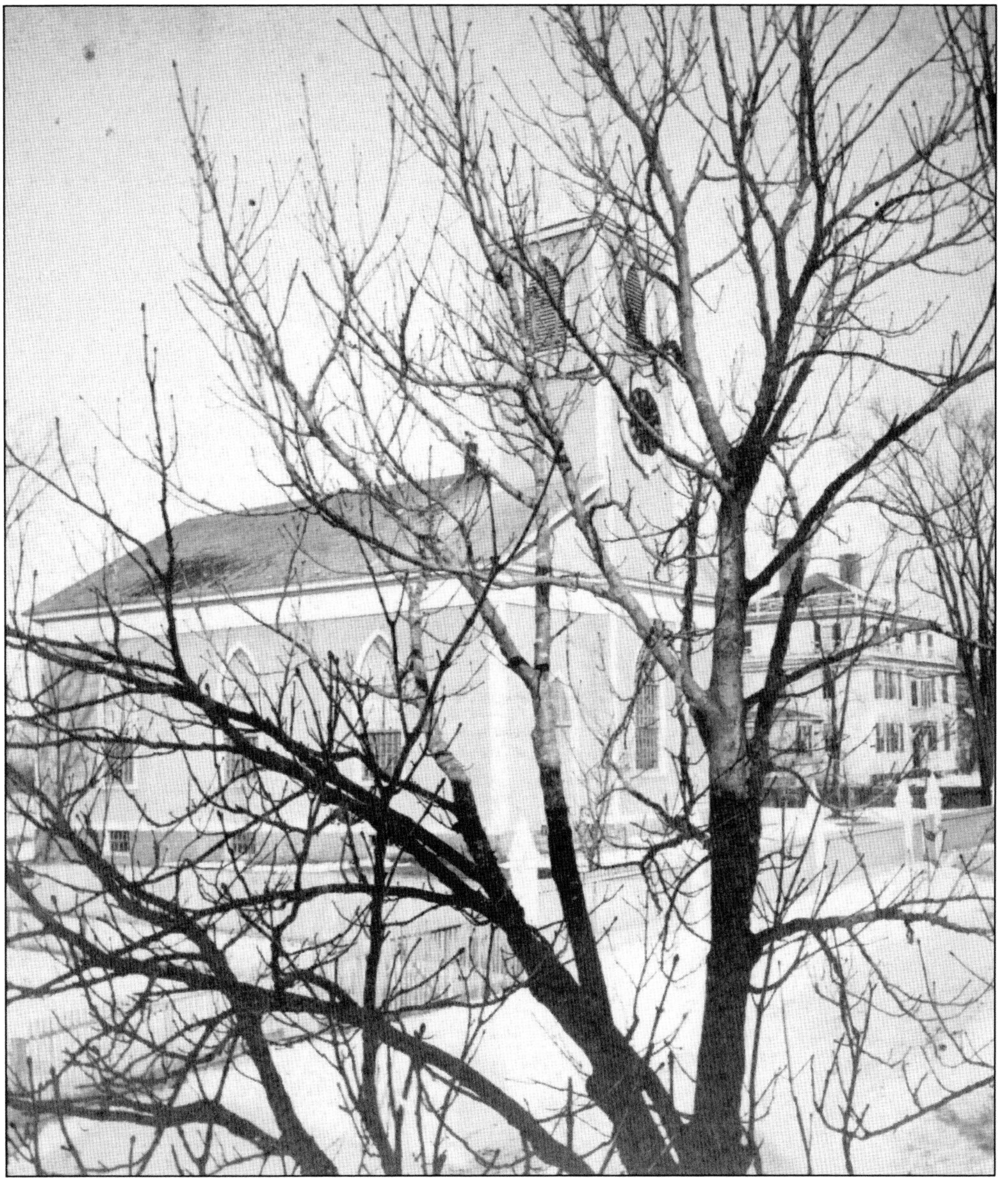

The Unitarian, or First Parish Church. This nicely composed 1860s John Heywood stereoview shows the Unitarian, or First Parish church on Middle Street in Gloucester. The church was erected in 1828 on the site of the First Parish meetinghouse, which had been there since 1738.

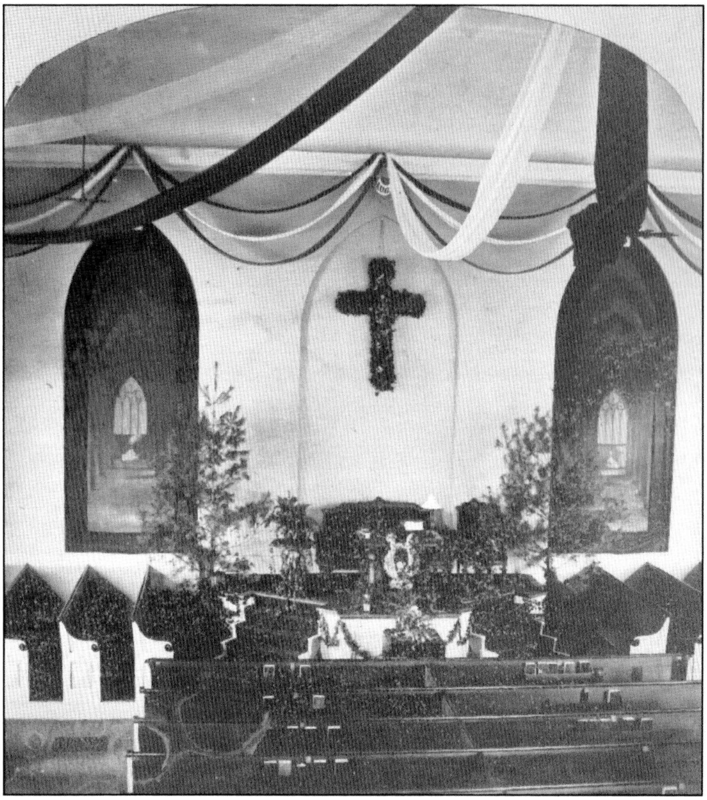

A CELEBRATION AND THE PORTUGUESE CHURCH. John S.E. Rogers took this interesting interior stereoview (above) on August 8, 1875, of the decorated Unitarian church. Services were held on that date to mark the 100th anniversary of the repulse by Gloucester citizens of a British warship that bombarded the town. One of the ship's cannonballs is embedded in a church timber. The postcard (right) shows the Our Lady of Good Voyage Church. The Portuguese community organized the parish at Prospect and Mount Vernon Streets. The stucco church, shown here, replaced the one that burned in 1914. A ten-foot statue of Our Lady holding a Gloucester schooner stands between the two towers.

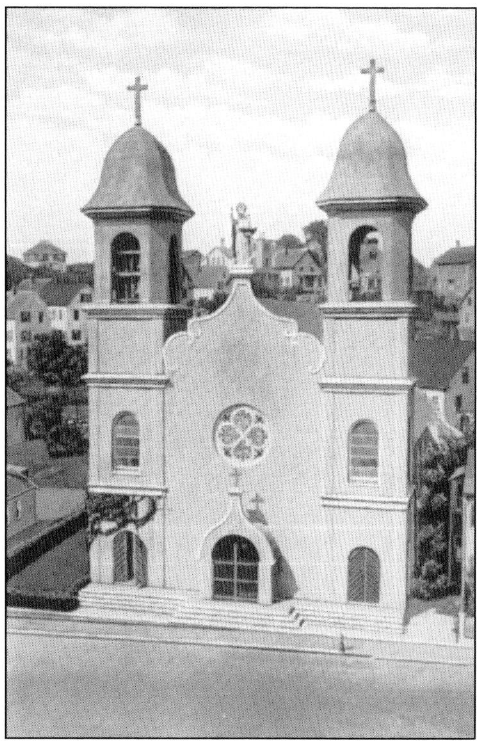

Eight

Around and About

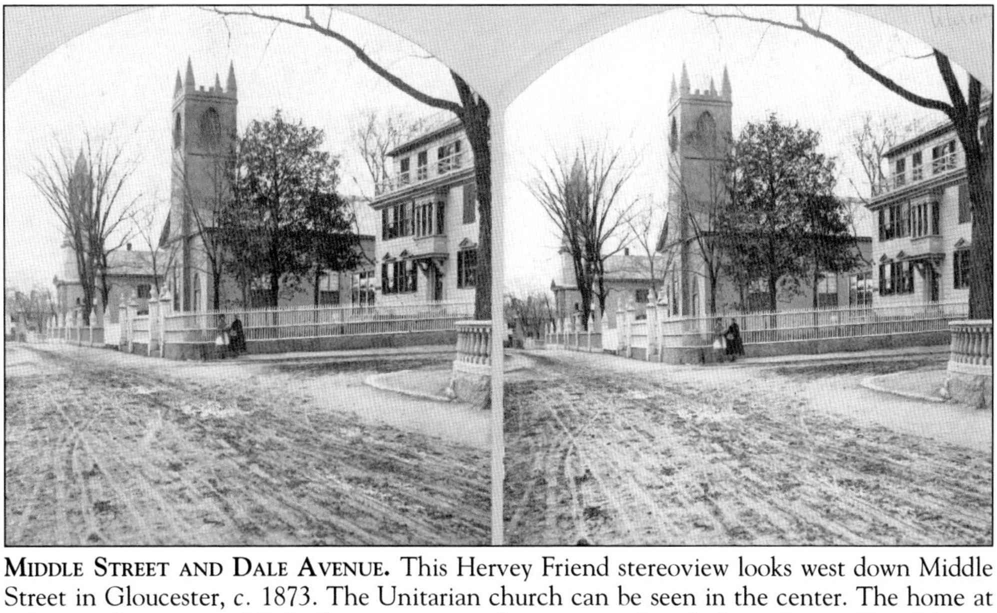

Middle Street and Dale Avenue. This Hervey Friend stereoview looks west down Middle Street in Gloucester, *c.* 1873. The Unitarian church can be seen in the center. The home at right, on the corner of Dale Avenue, is now the more modern-looking Sawyer Free Library. (See related image, page 59.)

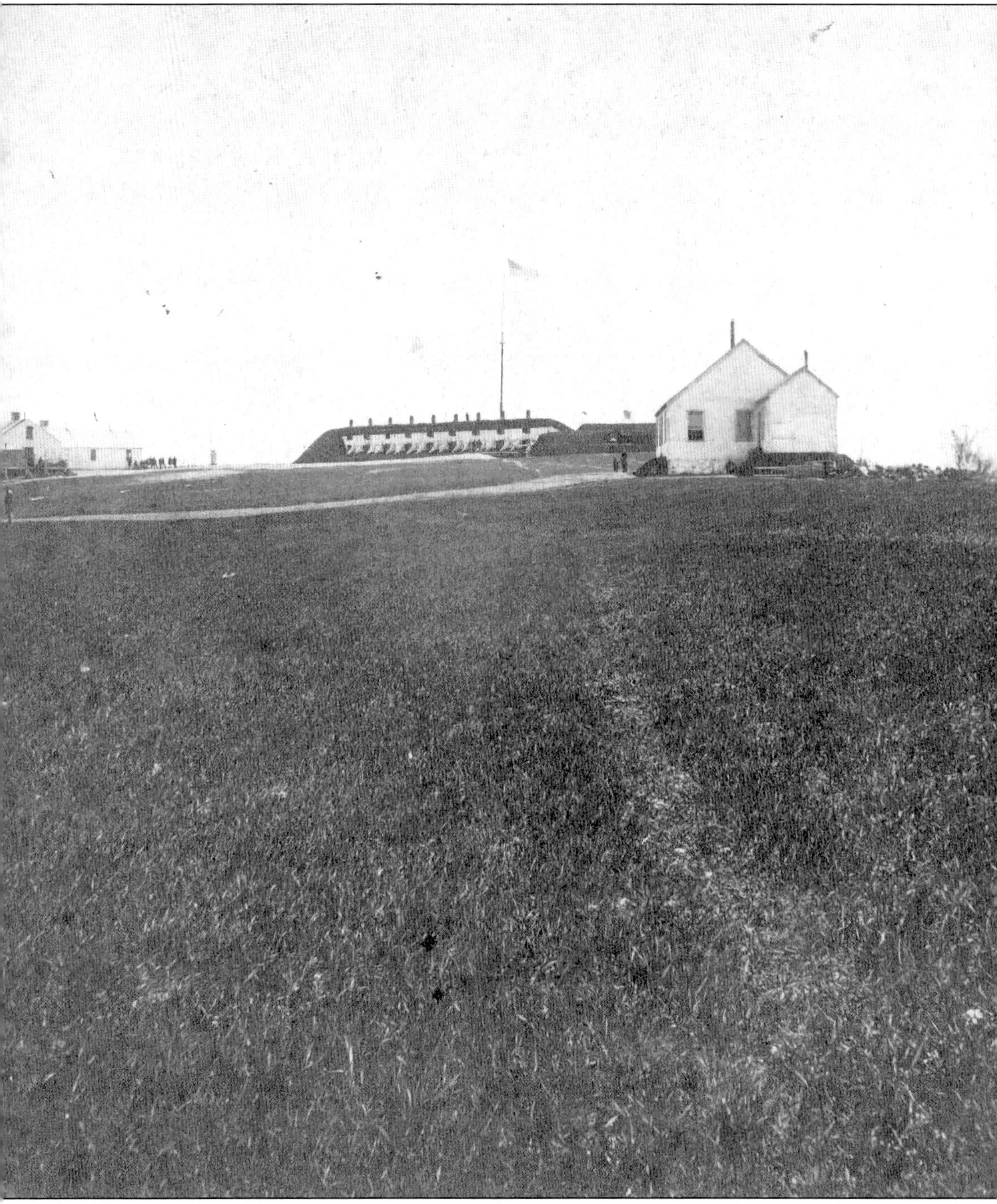

The Fort at Eastern Point. This *c.* 1864–1866 stereoview from Boston's John Heywood shows the Civil War fort at Gloucester's Eastern Point. A company of artillerymen manned the fortifications on the Niles Farm property to ward off attacks by Rebel raiders on the fishing fleet. In the War of 1812, it was known as Fort Defiance.

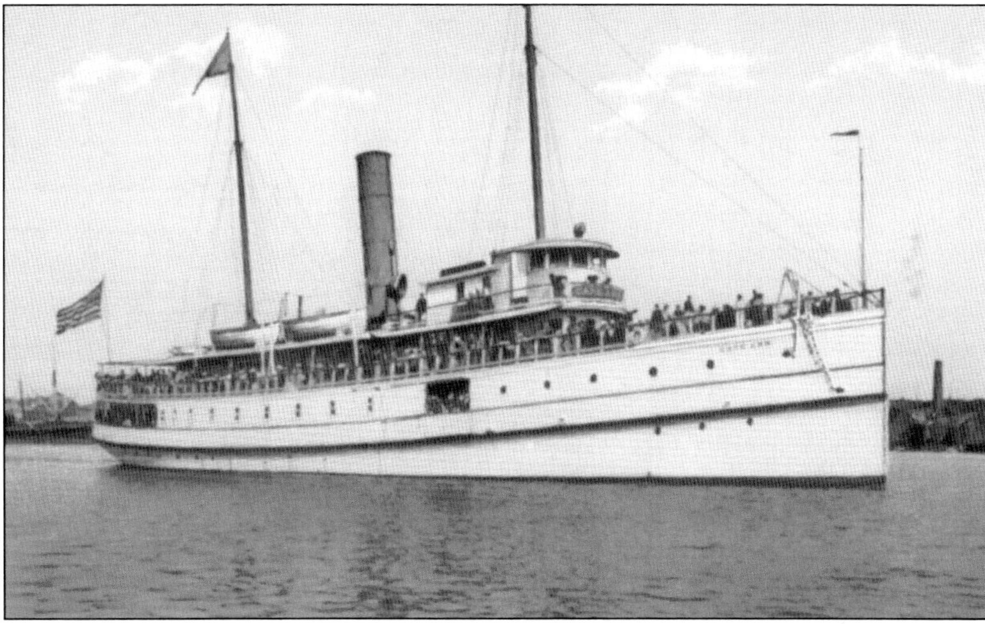

Cape Ann to Boston. This early postcard shows the all-white steamship *Cape Ann* leaving Gloucester harbor for its return run to Boston (above). Visitors from the Hub would enjoy a day in the city, perhaps hopping a trolley out to the Long Beach Pavilion (see the next page) or just meandering around town. Below, well-dressed ladies and gents leave the Boston and Gloucester Steamboat Company's Wharf, then located at Vincent's Cove. The round-trip fare aboard the *Cape Ann* cost 75¢.

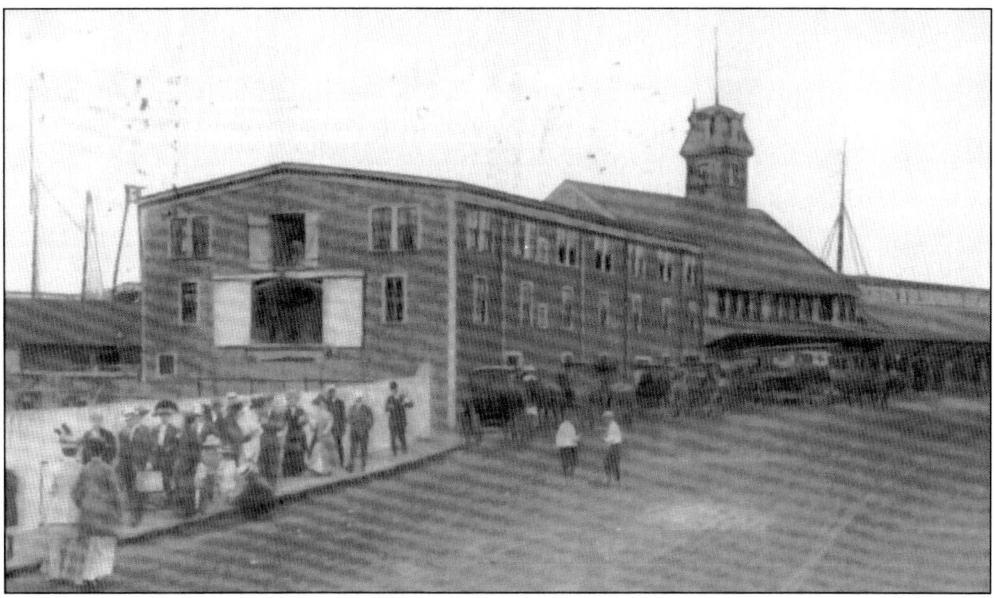

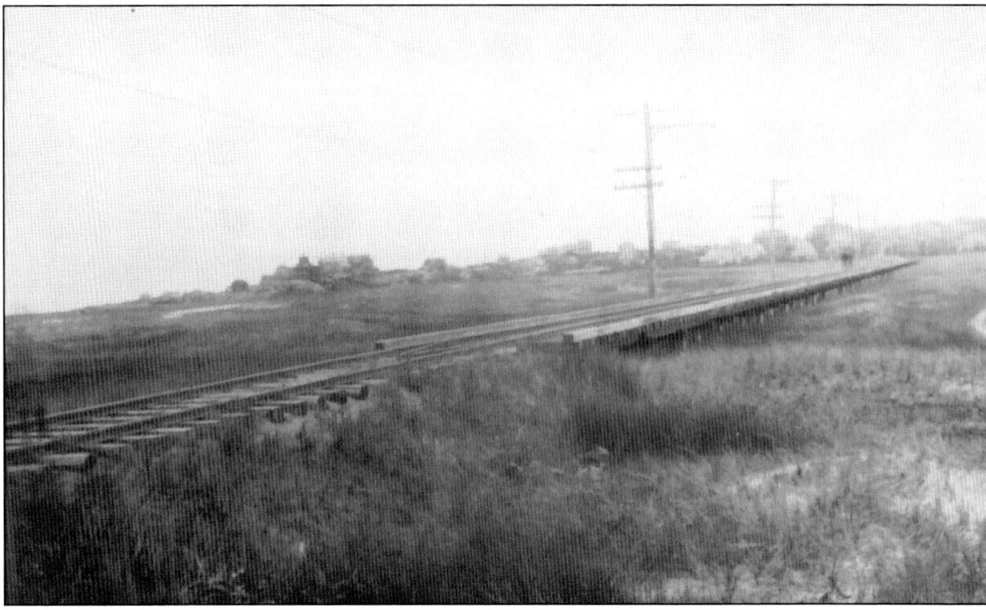

THE TRESTLE TO THE LONG BEACH PAVILION. This fine pair of early 1900s real photo postcards shows the trolley trestle (above) across the dunes to the rear of Little Good Harbor Beach and the Long Beach Pavilion (below) at the Gloucester-Rockport town line. The electrified line here opened in 1895. Trolleys dropped off their passengers at the Pavilion, which offered all kinds of fun, including dining, dancing, concerts, and amusements. The Cape Ann Motor Inn currently occupies the site.

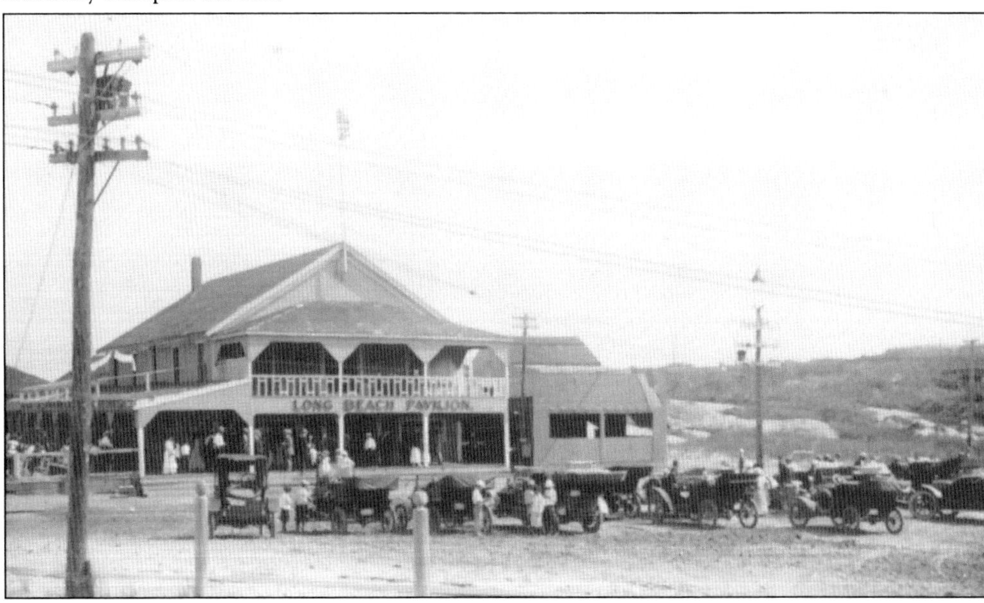

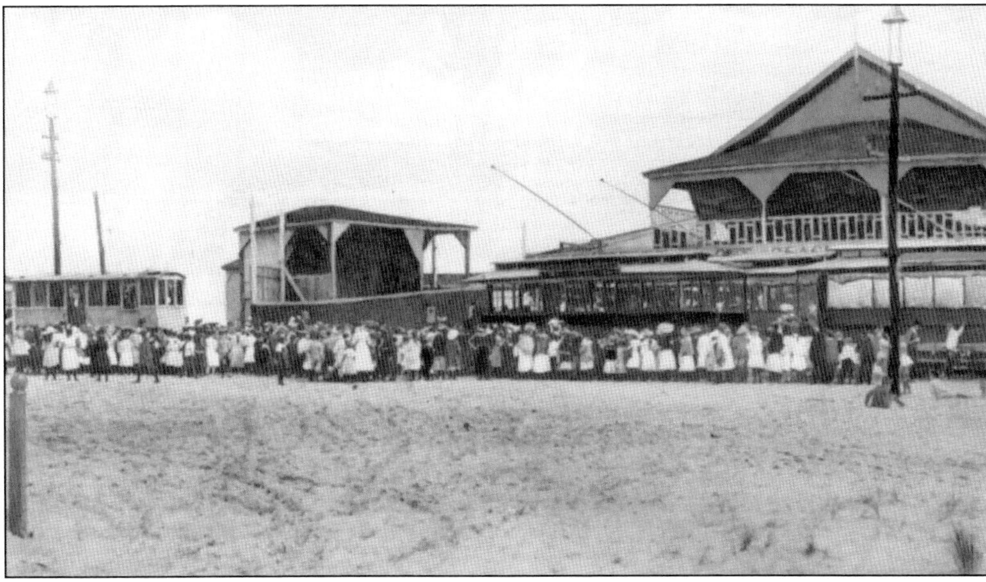

KIDS HAVING FUN. It is Children's Day at Long Beach in the postcard above, *c.* 1910. Scores of the youngsters disembark from the trolleys in front of the Pavilion. The building at left was an outdoor theater. Meanwhile, back in Gloucester, there are plenty of eager bathers on the beach in front of the Pavilion Hotel in the 1905 Rotograph Company postcard below.

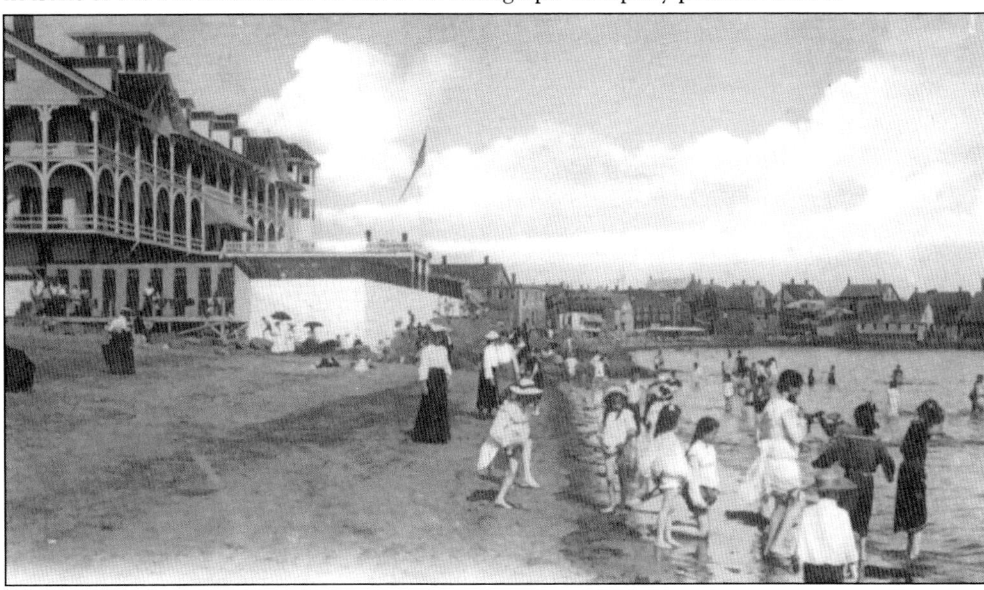

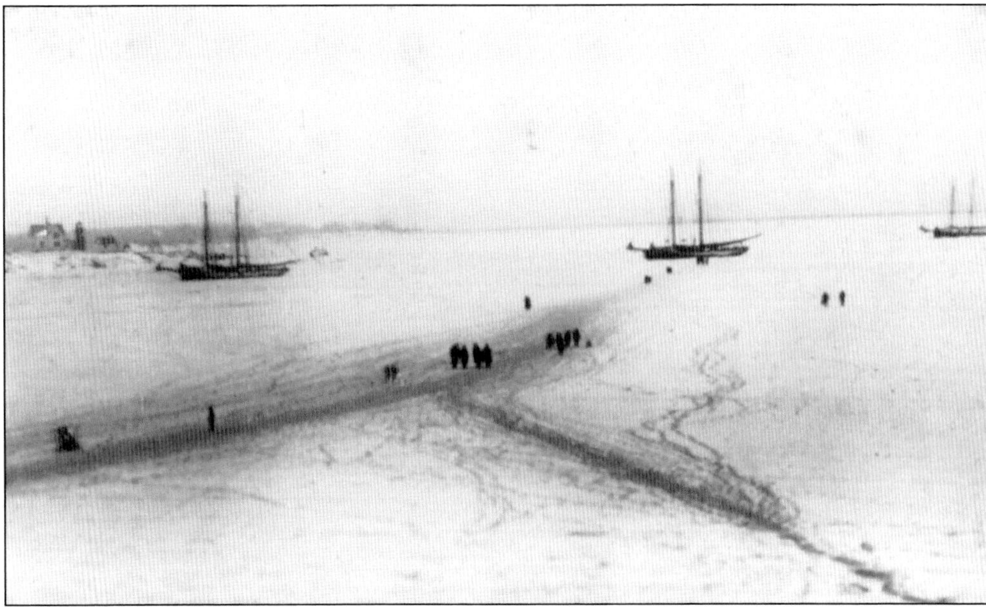

Tough Winters. Two early-1900s real photo postcards offer dramatic evidence of wintry hardships on Cape Ann. A pencil notation on the view above indicates a date of February 1918 and that Gloucester harbor was frozen solid all the way out to the breakwater at Eastern Point. Three schooners are trapped in the ice. According to writing on the back of photographic card below, the date is February 2, 1910, and the image shows the aftermath of a snow and ice storm that blew down the telephone poles all along this unidentified street.

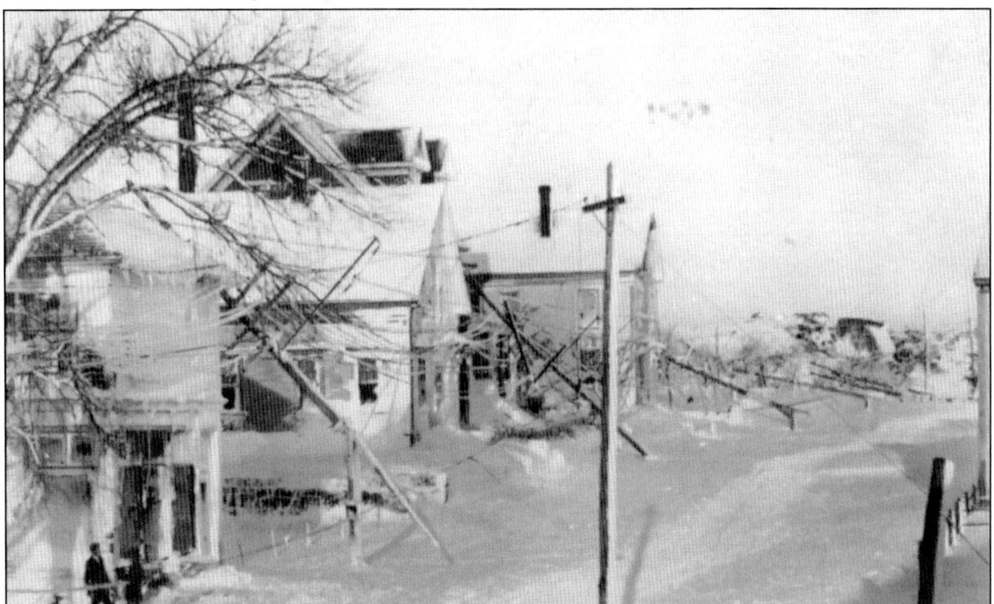

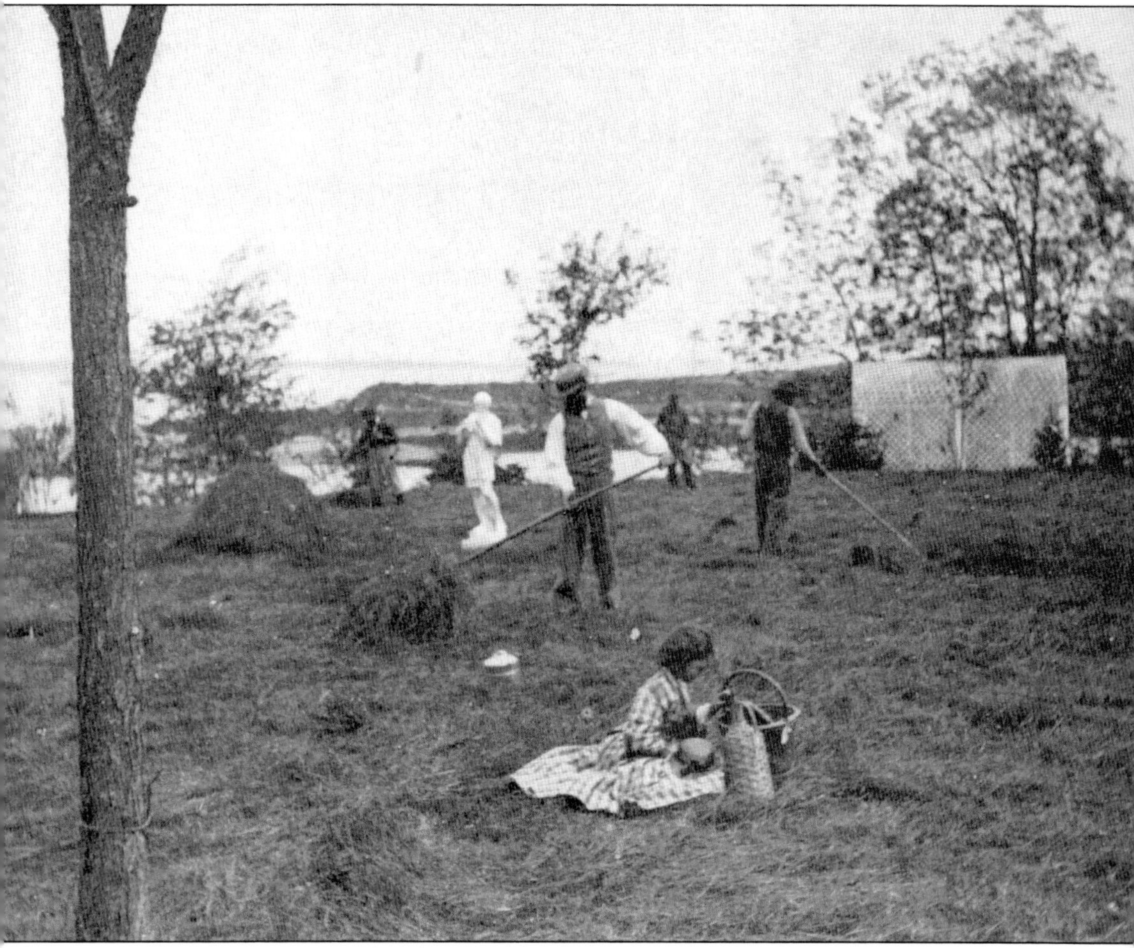

Haymaking at Brookbank. This charming mid-1860s stereoview by John Heywood captures a young lady in the foreground filling a basket, while men in the background rake the newly cut grass into small piles of hay. Brookbank, overlooking Gloucester's Freshwater Cove, was the Sawyer homestead. (Stereoview courtesy of Larry Gottheim.)

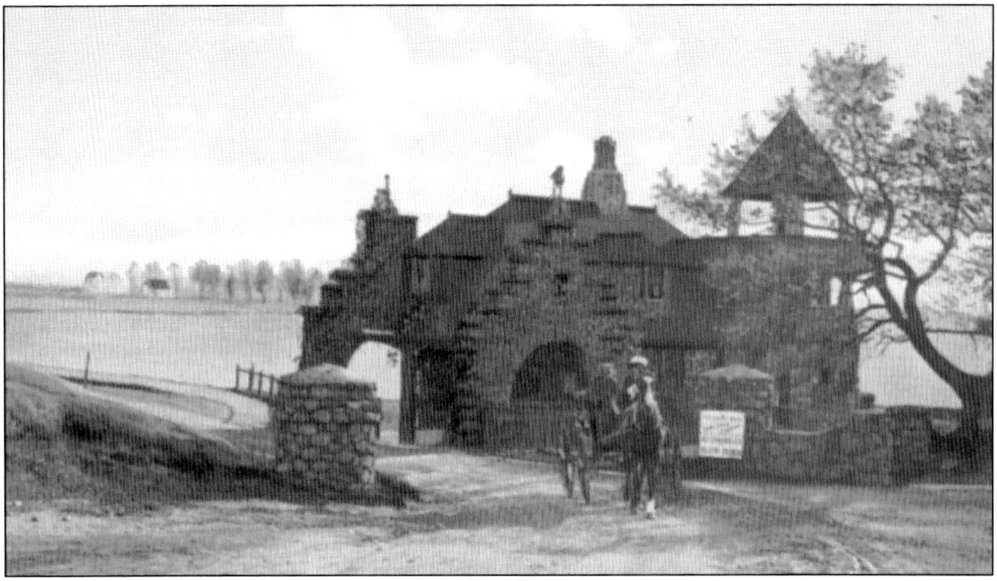

Gate Lodge and the Elliott Skating Rink. The postcard view above, published by Edwin C. McIntire of Gloucester, looks at the Gate Lodge at Eastern Point Boulevard in Gloucester. A sign on the stone pillar at right advises, "Private Way. Dangerous Passing. Automobiles Slow Down." Niles Beach, open to the public, is just beyond to the left. The delightful late-1880s trade card below advertises Smith & McKenna, proprietors of the Elliott Skating Rink in Gloucester. The message on the back promotes the week-long appearance at the rink of Carrie Gilmore of Worcester, the "Champion Lady Skater of New England."

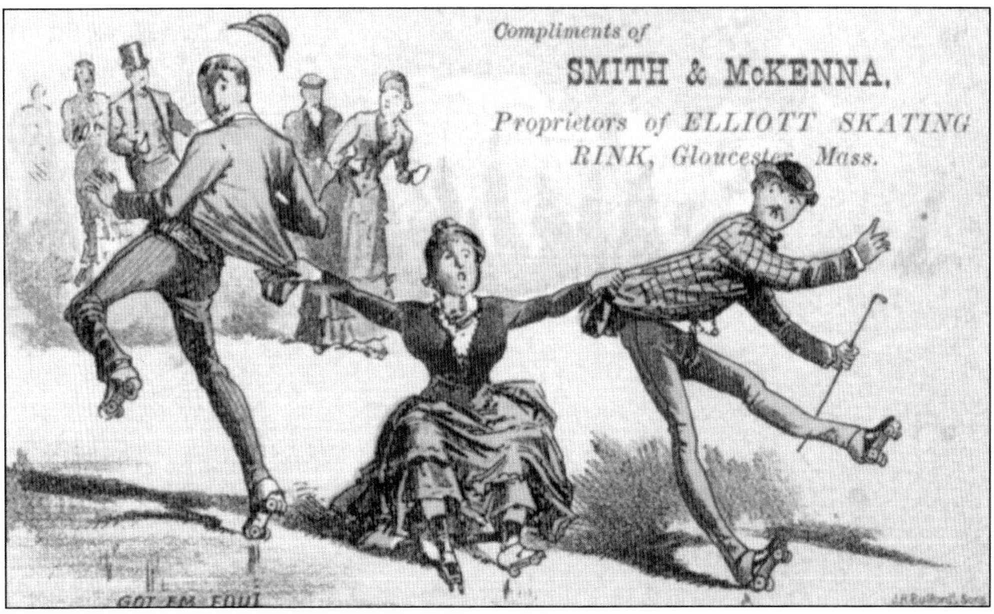

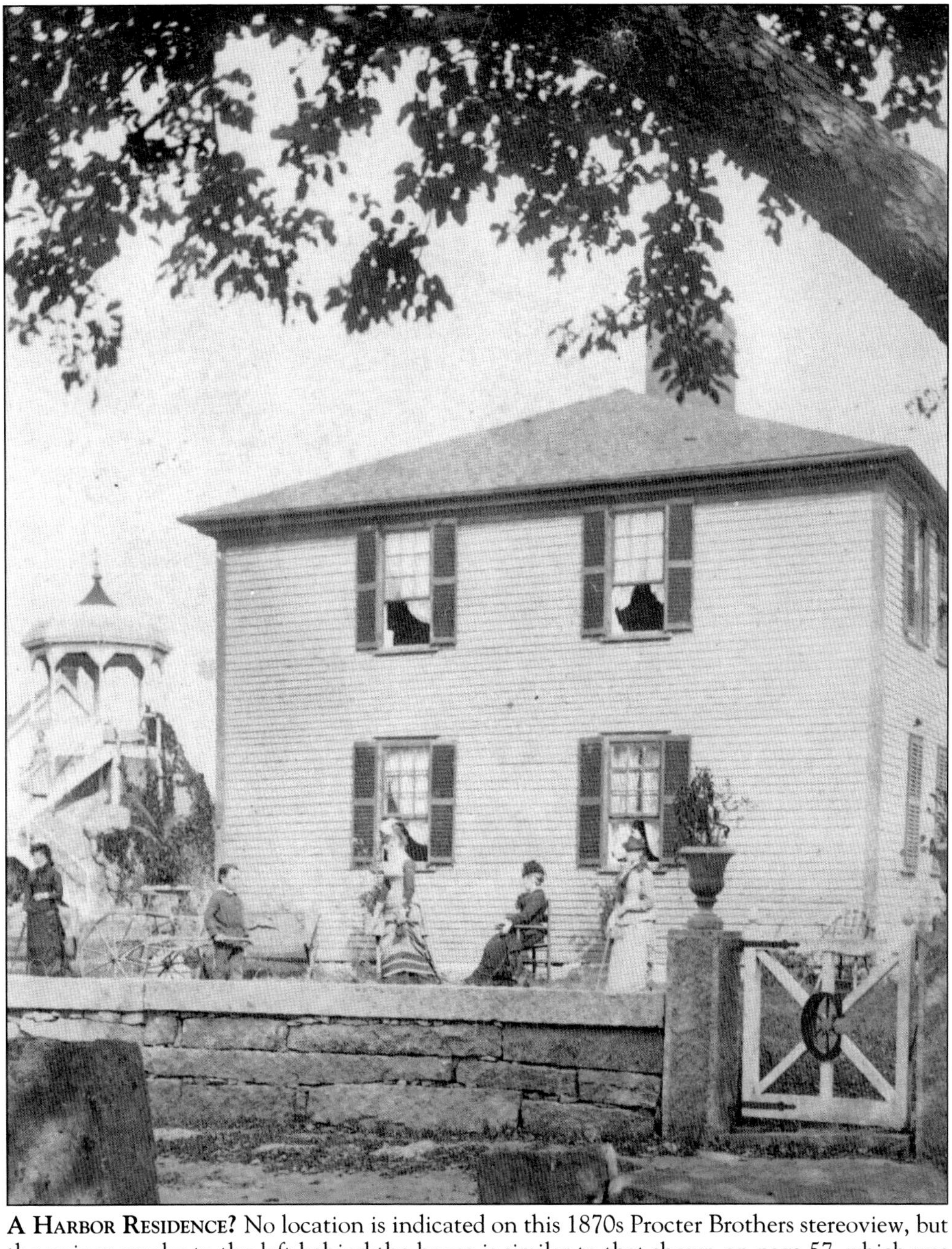

A Harbor Residence? No location is indicated on this 1870s Procter Brothers stereoview, but the unique gazebo to the left behind the house is similar to that shown on page 57, which was identified as coming from a home in Annisquam.

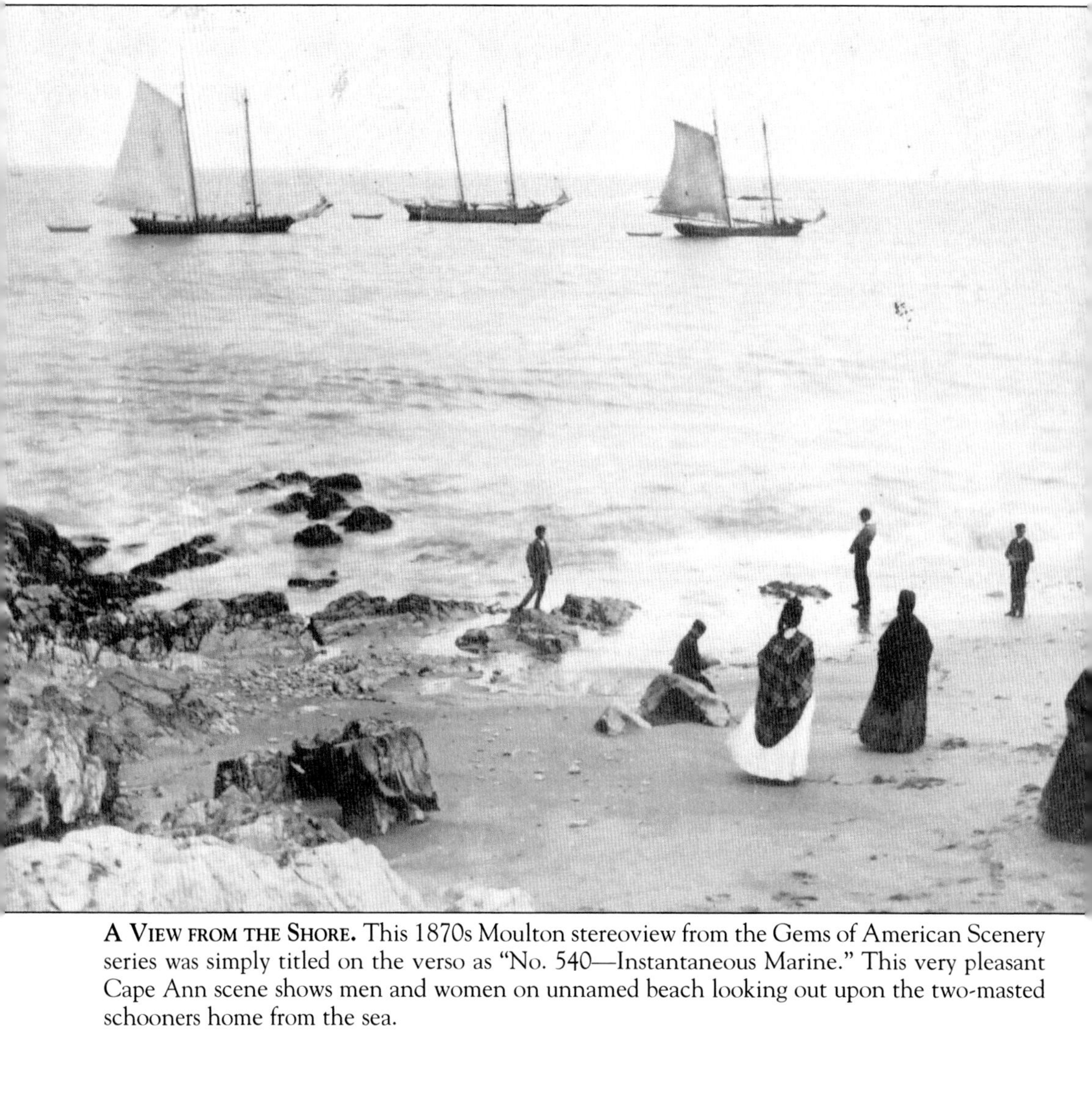

A View from the Shore. This 1870s Moulton stereoview from the Gems of American Scenery series was simply titled on the verso as "No. 540—Instantaneous Marine." This very pleasant Cape Ann scene shows men and women on unnamed beach looking out upon the two-masted schooners home from the sea.

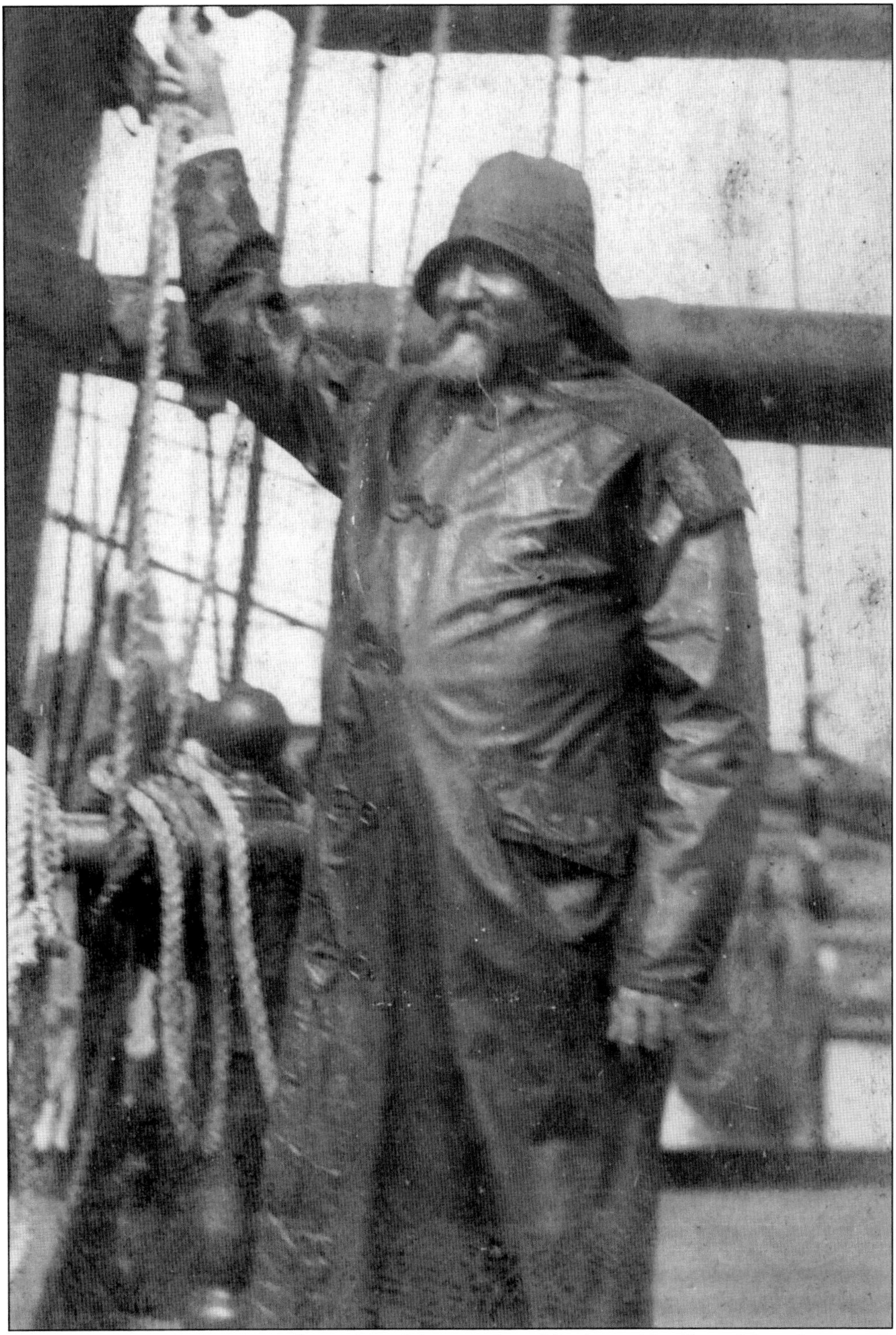

An Old Salt. Just imagine what tales of the sea this old salt could tell us. This photograph comes from a *carte de visite*, probably taken *c.* 1870. (Publisher unknown.)

Acknowledgments

Many thanks to Larry Gottheim for the generous loan of his John Heywood stereoview collection, some of which were used in the preparation of this work.

Sources

Babson, John J. *History of the Town of Gloucester, Cape Ann (Including the Town of Rockport)*. 350th Anniversary Edition. Gloucester, Mass.: Peter Smith Publisher, 1972.

Connolly, James B. *The Port of Gloucester*. New York: Doubleday, Doran and Company, 1940.

Copeland, Melvin T., and Elliott C. Rogers. *The Saga of Cape Ann*. Freeport, Maine: Peter Smith Publisher, 1983.

Darrah, William C. *The World of Stereographs*. Gettysburg, Pa.: W.C. Darrah Publisher, 1977.

Erkkila, Barbara H. *Hammers on Stone*. Gloucester, Mass.: Peter Smith Publisher, 1987.

———. *Village at Lane's Cove*. Gloucester, Mass.: Ten Pound Island Book Company, 1989.

Fifield, Charles Woodbury Jr. *Along the Gloucester Waterfront*. Gloucester, Mass.: Cape Ann Ticket & Label Co., 1955.

Fishermen's Own Book, The. Gloucester, Mass.: Procter Brothers Publishers, 1882.

Garland, Joseph E. *Down to the Sea: The Fishing Schooners of Gloucester*. Boston, Mass.: David R. Godine Publisher, 1983.

———. *Eastern Point Revisited*. Gloucester, Mass.: Association of Eastern Point Residents, 1989.

———. *Gloucester on the Wind*. Charleston, S.C.: Arcadia Publishing, 1995.

———. *The Gloucester Guide: A Retrospective Ramble*. Gloucester, Mass.: Gloucester 350th Anniversary Celebration, Inc., 1973.

———. *The Gloucester Guide: A Stroll through Place and Time*. Rockport, Mass.: Protean Press, 1990.

———. *The North Shore*. Beverly, Mass.: Commonwealth Editions, 1998.

Kenney, Herbert A. *Cape Ann: Cape America*. Philadelphia and New York: J.P. Lippincott Co., 1971.

Kenyon, Paul B. *People & Books: The Story of the Gloucester Lyceum and Sawyer Free Library*. Gloucester, Mass.: the Gloucester Lyceum and the Sawyer Free Library, 1980.

Martin, Roger. *A Rockport Album*. Gloucester, Mass.: the Curious Traveller Press, 1998.

Naismith, Helen. *Walking Cape Ann*. Gloucester, Mass.: Ten Pound Island Books, 1994.

O'Gorman, James F. *This Other Gloucester*. Gloucester, Mass.: Ten Pound Island Book Company, 1990.

Photo History of Gloucester. Vols. I–IV.

Pringle, James R. *History of the Town and City of Gloucester, Cape Ann, Massachusetts*. New Indexed Edition. Gloucester, Mass.: City of Gloucester Archives Committee and Ten Pound Island Book Company, 1997.

Rockport As It Was . . . A Book of Pictures. Rockport, Mass., 1975.

Steele, Chris, and Ronald Polito. *A Directory of Massachusetts Photographers 1839–1900*. Camden, Maine: Picton Press, 1993.

Story, Dana A. *The Shipbuilders of Essex*. Gloucester, Mass.: Ten Pound Island Book Company, 1995.

Waldsmith, John S. *Stereo Views: An Illustrated History and Price Guide*. Radnor, Pa.: Wallace-Homestead Book Co., 1991.

Webber, William S., Jr. *Waterfront: Around the Wharves of Gloucester in the Last Days of Sail*. Manchester, Mass.: the Cape Ann Savings Bank, 1973.